THE MOST UP-TO-DATE, AUTHO...
HANDBOOK OF STEREO EQUIPMENT
AVAILABLE

Stereo technology has exploded in the last few years, with developments from the compact disc to remarkably accurate speakers. This book guides you through the maze of stereo products, taking the static out of buying—and enjoying—high-fidelity sound. It tells you in plain English what to look and listen for to get the system you want at a price that's within your budget. In addition to the latest technology, this book also covers all the traditional stereo components— from tuners to tape decks—and the best accessories. Whether you're buying your first stereo, upgrading to something a little more sophisticated, or in the market for professional-quality sound, this is the only book you'll need to advise you.

THE NEW SOUND OF STEREO

IVAN BERGER is Technical Editor for *Audio* magazine, and a writer for numerous other publications. Along with Hans Fantel, he is the author of *The True Sound of Music*.

HANS FANTEL is the audio and video columnist for *The New York Times*, and the author of eight books.

T·H·E
NEW
SOUND
OF
STEREO

THE COMPLETE GUIDE TO BUYING AND USING THE LATEST HI-FI EQUIPMENT

IVAN BERGER AND HANS FANTEL

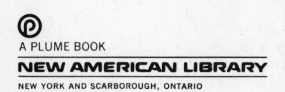

A PLUME BOOK

NEW AMERICAN LIBRARY

NEW YORK AND SCARBOROUGH, ONTARIO

Acknowledgments

The authors would like to thank Leynard Berger, Kay Blumenthal, Nora Edwards, Len Feldman, Stewart Hegeman, Katherine Lance, Cindy Morgan, Cyndi Rannels, Howard Roberson, Nan Schubel, Susan Schweers, Sheila Shiki y Michaels, Byrd Tetzlaff, and Roberta Thumim, for their various forms of advice, encouragement, and motivation.

NAL BOOKS ARE AVAILABLE AT QUANTITY DISCOUNTS WHEN USED TO PROMOTE PRODUCTS OR SERVICES. FOR INFORMATION PLEASE WRITE TO PREMIUM MARKETING DIVISION, NEW AMERICAN LIBRARY, 1633 BROADWAY, NEW YORK, NEW YORK 10019

Chapter 13 has appeared in slightly modified form in *Audio Compact Disc '86.*

 PLUME TRADEMARK REG. U.S. PAT OFF. AND FOREIGN COUNTRIES REGISTERED TRADEMARK—MARCA REGISTRADA HECHO EN FORGE VILLAGE, MASS., U.S.A.

SIGNET, SIGNET CLASSIC, MENTOR, PLUME, MERIDIAN and NAL BOOKS are published *in the United States* by New American Library, 1633 Broadway, New York, New York 10019, *in Canada* by The New American Library of Canada Limited, 81 Mack Avenue, Scarborough, Ontario M1L 1M8

Library of Congress Cataloging-in-Publication Data

Berger, Ivan, 1939–
  The new sound of stereo.

  Includes index.
  1. Stereophonic sound systems—Purchasing.
I. Fantel, Hans. II. Title.
TK7881.8.B46 1985   621.389′334   85-18813
ISBN 0-452-25747-6

First Printing, February, 1986

1 2 3 4 5 6 7 8 9

PRINTED IN THE UNITED STATES OF AMERICA

Contents

Preface

Art and technology are often considered opposites, but technology is at the center of all the arts, including music. Even the oldest musical instruments used the highest technology of their times.

High-fidelity stereo equipment uses today's highest technology—but only to make it seem as if there were *no* electronic gear between you and the music. The better you understand stereo equipment, the better your chance of winding up with both the best possible sound for your money and the convenience features that will please you best. The main thing to understand is that "high fidelity" is just another name for accuracy. The more accurately sound equipment and recordings reproduce musical sounds, the higher their fidelity to the original.

Today, high fidelity is getting better than ever by going through its biggest change since stereo arrived—the transition into a new digital era. Computer-based technology is beginning to replace the old method of sound recordings, which dates back to Thomas Edison's invention of the phonograph in 1877.

Digital recordings bring us closer to sonic truth than ever before—but still not to perfection (which has been claimed for every advance since Edison's day). Our job in writing this book is not to make such a claim, but to help you find the very best stereo gear—whether it's the latest Compact Disc player or a pair of extra speakers for the bedroom—and make the most of your shopping time and investment.

Today's hi-fi equipment not only is excellent in quality but gives high value per dollar spent. While the sonic quality of stereo equipment has risen, hi-fi prices have remained stable. Adjusted for inflation, real prices have actually gone down: for example, a two-hundred-dollar tape deck today is far superior to a two-hundred-dollar model of ten years ago. Although the price of the most expensive equipment has climbed to the stratosphere, new techniques and technologies quickly filter down to moderate price ranges, making affordable equipment a better bargain than ever before.

Much of the quality of stereo gear is summed up in the numbers found on specification sheets. We'll spell out what those mystifying numbers tell you—and what they do not tell. Many specs, which used to quickly tell low-fi from hi-fi, have become almost meaningless; the general level of audio excellence is now so good that high fidelity is the norm. Low-fi is gone, save from the cheapest price ranges. Still, some equipment is better than others, and we'll tell you how to pick the best. There is a lot more to compare than just the price.

Since specs have partly lost their meaning, educated ears remain the best guides to choosing sound equipment. All ears can be educated; it only takes a bit of listening, and learning what to listen for and why. We hope to impart this skill.

Along the way, we'll tell not only how to listen for the *right* sound (which is the main thing), but also how to understand the technical jargon used by salesmen and in sales literature. If the technical talk doesn't interest you, skip the chapters explaining it: you can still buy and enjoy good equipment without the deeper understanding the more technical sections are designed to give.

Brand names and models change with the speed of summer lightning. So we have skipped mention of specific models and have concentrated on specific principles, which last. As the proverb goes: "Give a man a fish, and you feed him for a day; teach him to fish, and you feed him for life."

—Ivan Berger
Hans Fantel

Analog, Digital, and High Fidelity

Since 1877, when Thomas Edison first barked "Mary had a little lamb" at a rotating cylinder of tinfoil, sound recording has gone through a tremendous development. Over a century there have been four major technical revolutions, spaced about thirty years apart: the shift from cylinder to disc recording (1890s); electrical recording (1920s); the long-playing record and stereo (both in the 1950s); and now the digital revolution.

The first revolution, the switch from cylinder to disc, involved no major feat of new technology, but did make it possible to stamp out records cheaply and in quantity, like precision cookies.

When Edison made his first recording, the sound of his voice powered a needle that engraved a wavering track in the tinfoil cylinder. In the second revolution, the needle was powered by amplified electricity from a microphone, which could pick up a greater range of sounds in finer detail. Records became more lifelike—the difference between the old acoustic and the later electrical recordings is dramatically apparent. Stereo made records more lifelike still. With stereo, sound could be picked up from two or more separate points, making it possible to reproduce the spatial feeling of a musical performance: the size of the hall and the musicians' relative positions on the stage. Where mono was like listening through a hole in a wall between your living room and the concert hall, stereo could give you the feeling that the whole wall had been knocked away, putting you in the concert hall with the music—at least if recording engineers had done their job properly.

All of these recording systems worked by the "analog" method. Sound is a physical vibration in the air, and the record groove, with its wriggles, represented a model—or analog—of those vibrations. High frequencies were represented by fast wriggles, low frequencies by slow ones; bigger wriggles meant louder sounds, smaller wriggles meant softer ones. Later, we learned how to replicate the sound wave as a varying magnetic field on recording tape.

Digital recording doesn't work this way at all. Instead of recording the sound itself, digital systems register the sound wave's strength at many different points along its path and assign a numerical value to each point. In playback, the numbers are decoded, to re-create the points on the original wave —like a follow-the-dots drawing. This is the system used in the new Compact Disc (digital sound is covered in chapters 13 and 14).

What are the advantages of such a roundabout—and expensive—way to store sound? For one thing, digital recordings have no audible hiss, hum, or surface noise and no wavery speed wobbles ("wow and flutter"). Digital recordings can reproduce all the musical frequencies without scanting the very high and low ends of the tonal spectrum. Moreover, digital recordings can be copied again and again without any degradation of the sound; this makes a digital recording played at home an exact duplicate of the master recording made in the studio. And digital recordings don't wear out. Barring abuse, they'll last forever.

To understand these advantages, you also have to understand traditional analog systems (tape, phonograph records, radio, TV, and videocassette). An understanding of analog systems is also necessary because they are likely to remain the backbone of home hi-fi systems for at least another decade.

Analog or digital, these systems deal with sound, the raw material of music. Sound waves are vibrations in the air with two basic properties: the first is frequency, from low (bass) to high (treble); the second is amplitude, from soft to loud. If you were to graph the simplest possible sound wave, it would look like figure 1-1.

The wave's amplitude is shown by its height; the further the curve swings above and below its center line, the louder the signal will be. Its frequency is shown by the number of times per second the wave goes through a complete "cycle"—for example, from one positive peak through zero to a negative peak and back to the positive peak it started from. The more cycles per second, the higher the wave's frequency. The average *young* human ear can hear frequencies from about twenty cycles per second (20 hertz, or 20 Hz), a very low bass tone, to about twenty-thousand times per second. The distance between peaks is the *wavelength*, which becomes shorter as the frequency rises.

Few real sounds are as simple as the one illustrated, which has only a single frequency. Most sounds mix their main frequency (called the "fundamental") with higher frequencies that are multiples of the fundamental one. These higher frequencies are called "overtones" or "harmonics." They are a major factor in determining the particular timbre, or tone color, of a sound. If you play the same note on two different instruments, or have two different people sing the same note, you can tell the two notes apart by their different harmonic patterns.

High fidelity involves reproducing all frequencies, from low bass fundamentals to high overtones, without adding or subtracting any or accidentally altering the balance between them. In stereo, it also means accurately reproducing where the different instruments were in the concert hall or studio and capturing the sonic ambience of the space surrounding them.

With these few basic facts in mind, you already have a good start toward understanding and evaluating sound equipment. We can therefore jump straight from theory to practice and take a look at the basic hardware and the specifications defining its performance.

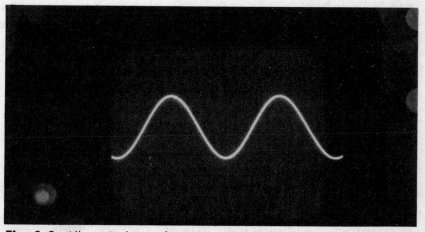

Fig. 1-1. *All musical waveforms are combinations of simple sine waves such as this.*

2 What's in a System?

What you really want from a stereo system is music. But what the stores are selling is equipment. So you have to understand the relationship between music and the pieces of equipment that bring it to you.

The best stereo systems comprise several items, called "components." They do basically the same thing a cheap radio-phonograph does, but they do it far better. Since you buy them separately, components also give you a wider choice, allowing you to pick the specific designs that will exactly suit your needs and even skip those components you have no use for. This chapter serves as an introduction to the different types, to help give you an idea of which components you might want (or not want) in your system. Each will be covered in more detail, later.

Stereo systems include two types of components. The first type consists of "signal sources," which provide the music: turntables, FM/AM tuners, tape decks, Compact Disc players, TV tuners, and players for videocassettes and videodiscs. Several of these sources are quite new, and their number is growing all the time.

The second type consists of the components that turn those signals into sound: the amplifier and speakers. (A receiver combines an amplifier and FM/AM tuner in one unit.) Sometimes accessory components are added, such as equalizers (essentially, multiple tone controls), to alter or enhance the sound.

As you can see from the diagram, the *amplifier* is the heart of the system. It performs two important functions: It strength-

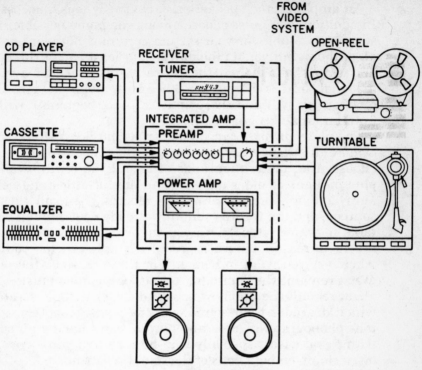

Fig. 2-1. *A component stereo system. Note that the preamplifier and power amplifier can be combined into an "integrated" amplifier, or combined with the tuner into a "receiver." Note, too, that the audio system can also carry sound from your video equipment. (Courtesy Imagination Technical Art)*

ens the weak signals coming from the signal sources until they're powerful enough to drive the speakers. It also serves as the system's control center, where you can select the sound source—tape, disc, or radio—you want to listen to and adjust the sound's volume and tone. Complex amplifier systems may have more than a dozen additional controls, most of which are rarely used once they have been properly adjusted.

The *speakers* turn the electrical signals they receive from the amplifier into sound waves. Of all the components in the system, they have the greatest effect on how the system sounds —not only because no other component actually produces sound (the rest just produce electrical signals), but also because speakers are the components that sound most different from each other. Buying the right speaker is a matter of selecting the one among the best models in your price range whose sound you'll find easiest to live with.

An amplifier and speakers are, obviously, basic necessities. In addition, you must choose among the many possible signal sources available for your system. You may not want or need all of them, but you'll probably pick at least two or three now, and perhaps add more in the future. More options are available in signal sources than in any other area, and in the rest of this chapter you will find these options listed, beginning with the familiar, analog signal sources.

The *phonograph*, or record player, is the oldest signal source —more than a century old—and is still going strong. You can choose from many thousands of records currently available, plus millions of older ones still lurking in attics and cellars. Many public libraries also lend records. With all these resources, and the records you may already own, having a turntable in your system gives you the widest possible choice of music, at reasonable prices, and lets you hear what you want whenever you want to hear it. For these reasons, the phonograph remains the dominant format for recorded music.

But records inevitably wear, get dirty, or become scratched, which degrades their sound over the years. Another catch is that phonograph records and players can't handle all sounds with equal ease, especially very high and very low ones, and often skimp on both ends of the sound spectrum.

Radio, the next oldest medium, offers two things the phonograph cannot: free music and surprise. You need only tune across the dial to find something more or less to your liking, and often something you've never heard before. This makes radio superb for musical exploration.

On the other hand, radio may not bring you exactly the music you want just when you want to hear it. Your choice of programs depends on where you live, too: you can hear rock anywhere (though not always the kind you like), but hearing classics, jazz, or country music can be a problem outside metropolitan areas.

All hi-fi tuners and receivers cover the FM radio band, and many cover the AM band as well. For hi-fi purposes, FM radio is all you really need, because it is the only broadcast medium capable of full-range sound. Yet AM could be on the verge of a small renaissance, thanks to changes described in chapter 18.

Tape has a unique advantage: you can record on it. The most common use is to copy records onto cassette for playback in the car or in Walkman-style personal portable tape players. You can also tape hard-to-find music off the air, to add to your music library. Or you can tape radio shows and listen to them later; there are even timers available to start and stop your tape recorder at preset times, when you're busy or away. Tape can also be used to record live events: your own music practice, to see how you're doing; your own and friends' musical recitals; parties; your children's voices; community musical and dramatic productions; and so on.

Most home taping is done on cassettes, because they're easy to use, inexpensive, and capable of very high fidelity. They also link your home sound system with the many other systems that use cassettes, such as car stereo systems and pocket-sized portable high-fidelity tape players.

There is, however, another form of tape, known as "reel-to-reel" or "open-reel." Open-reel decks are bigger and harder to load, which makes them less convenient, and they usually cost more than cassette decks do. But they make more accurate recordings than cassette decks do, and these recordings can be cut and spliced to edit their contents. Because open-reel tapes can be edited, open-reel recorders are the traditional favorite of people who make live recordings and have to remove musical clinkers from the tape. Open-reel decks can also play and record long events without as many breaks while you change tapes.

Today, *video equipment* is likely to be linked to audio systems. Videodisc players and the new Beta Hi-Fi and VHS Hi-Fi videocassette recorders produce sound so good that only a good playback system can bring out its full impact.

Digital signal sources are the latest and most far-reaching development. The most popular of these is the *Compact Disc* (*"CD"*) player (described more fully in chapter 13). Essentially, the CD player does the same job as a phonograph, but does it (say most critics) in a radically superior way. The discs are recorded and played digitally, a computerized process. Thanks to this, CDs handle high and low frequencies more accurately, add no noise or fuzziness to the signal, and have rock-steady speed. Compact Discs are scanned by a weightless light beam from a laser rather than by a phonograph needle, so there is none of the mechanical contact or friction with the disc that causes wear on phonograph recordings. Moreover, CDs are largely immune to dirt and scratches.

Digital players cost as much as the best phonograph turntables. The discs cost more than phonograph records, and far fewer of them are available. But with compact disc production increasing rapidly, the CD catalog is growing; still, it will probably be several years before the CD repertoire catches up with that of the LP phonograph record. Moreover, many older recordings now on LP will probably never appear in the CD format. For these reasons, it pays to have a phonograph turntable even if you buy a CD player.

It's also probable that you'll be able to record on CDs at home someday. In the meantime, you can already record digitally, using a PCM adaptor, which records signals digitally onto any ordinary home videocassette recorder. The latest 8 mm video recorders have digital soundtracks, though of only moderately high fidelity. And digital sound recorders using pocket-sized tape cassettes will be available in the late 1980s.

Current home digital recording systems compete with good open-reel decks in price and surpass them in recording quality. But while analog open-reel tapes can be edited down to the finest details (fractions of a note) with just a razor blade and an inexpensive splicing block, digital editing equipment is so expensive as to preclude home use.

3 Ways to Build Your System

The signal sources, amplifiers, and speakers that make up a sound system come in many forms. At the lowest extreme is the table radio, which combines just one signal source, the radio tuner, with a built-in amplifier and speaker. (Some high-quality table radios may also have an input for a second signal source, such as a tape deck.) At the other extreme lie complex and expensive systems in which every function is performed by a separate component, and even the amplifier is subdivided into a separate power amplifier and preamplifier (see chapters 11 and 12).

Most systems fall between these extremes, but all types have their purposes. The more elaborate, more expensive systems offer the best possible performance, especially because you can customize them by selecting the best component of each type for your needs. But simpler systems, aside from being cheaper, are often more convenient. That's why one listener we know has a ten-component system in his living room, a four-piece system in the den, and a high-quality table radio in a bedroom. Each is a reasonable choice for its particular use and setting.

The Component Approach

If your system is made up of separate components, you can choose exactly the features and performance factors you want in each. If you live in the country, for example, you'll need a more sensitive tuner than a city-dweller does. If you only record radio programs or records, you can be happy with a tape deck that has no place to plug in a microphone. If you play records for dancing, your turntable had better stay steady when the floor shakes, to prevent the needle from jumping in the record groove. In short, *you* set the requirements for each item in your system.

To get the right components to meet these requirements, you'll have to spend some time figuring out your needs, and listening to equipment in stores and asking questions about it. Personal attitudes toward shopping differ. You may enjoy the quest for a personal-best stereo system. Even if you simply follow a reliable dealer's recommendations, chances are that you'll get a fair match between your needs and your equipment, if perhaps not quite as good a one as you could have eventually made yourself. If, later, your needs change, or you realize better what they are, you can always change any part of the system for something more suitable.

This flexibility is one of the chief reasons to buy components. Another is the chance to get the latest and best, right at the technical frontier. When new advances in performance or features are developed, manufacturers put those refinements into their best components first.

A component system can (and often does) include components made by different manufacturers. Components of various makes are usually designed to work well together, so there's no need to restrict yourself to one manufacturer's offerings. Care is needed, though, to ensure a proper match between amplifier and speaker, and between a phonograph cartridge, turntable, and preamplifier. These matters of compatibility will be covered in chapters 8, 9, 11, 12, 16, and 17.

One-Brand Systems

On the other hand, there are reasons why it might pay to buy single-make systems instead. One is esthetic: if all the components come from the same manufacturer, they're likely to form a better visual match. They'll all be the same size, for easy stacking, and their colors, knob shapes, and other details will match. There are also conveniences to be gained from buying a single-brand system: you can usually get the whole system from a single dealer, in one trip, and the one-brand system may offer or include a single remote-control unit that operates every component.

Such remote controls are most often found in the "rack," or "one-brand," systems that have grown popular in the last few

Fig. 3-1. *A rack system, containing several stereo components from a single manufacturer (from top to bottom: turntable, FM/AM tuner, integrated amplifier, frequency equalizer and cassette deck). In use, the speakers would be spread apart about six feet and might even be across the room from the rest of the system. (Courtesy of Panasonic)*

years. The components of these systems are designed not only to look good together but to fit into a matching cabinet, or "rack," giving them a balanced and unified appearance. The equipment is stacked vertically in the cabinet, so that the system occupies a minimum of floor space. (You can also do without the cabinet and place the components side by side on furniture you already have, if you prefer.)

Rack systems often, though not always, give better value than the same manufacturer's separate components. Both manufacturer and dealer may be willing to shave the price a little more to make a single, large sale, which takes less of a salesperson's time than walking you through individual decisions about each separate component. The individual pieces may be less fancily finished, on the assumption that they'll all be hidden in a rack; the rack itself may be quite inexpensive, or even free. But you can't be sure about the value unless you compare what an equivalent component system would cost.

When you buy a complete system, whether assembled by a manufacturer, a dealer, or yourself, pay special attention to the loudspeakers. You can get some idea of the value of a tuner or amplifier by checking its features and appearance and reading its specifications (which will be covered in chapters 5, 6, and 11). But speakers may look similar while sounding very different, and there are few reliable specifications to guide you. As a result, both dealers and manufacturers sometimes cut corners on the speakers in their package systems. You should listen just as carefully to the speakers that come with a complete system as you would if you were buying speakers separately. Make sure these are speakers you can live with. If they aren't, find out what the system would cost with others which sound better to you and whose power requirements suit the system's amplifier (see chapter 8).

If the system seems a good value but its speakers are just so-so, it may still be worth buying. Find out whether the system's amplifier or receiver has a speaker-selector switch which lets you play two different sets of speakers, in different rooms. If so, you can start with the speakers that come with the system, eventually getting a new pair of superior speakers for your main listening room and relegating the original speakers to a room where you listen less critically.

One-brand systems come in several sizes. If you're interested in those built of smaller components, check them carefully to make sure their performance (judging both by their specifications and your ears) is comparable to that of full-sized units of equivalent cost. Check for heat buildup, too: cool-running components tend to be more reliable, and smaller units are harder to keep cool. And be sure the controls on the front panel are not uncomfortably cramped together or too small to grasp easily. (Check these features on any components, but especially on small ones.) The technology needed to make good equipment small costs money. But if your space is such that only small components fit, or if you simply like their looks, their sometimes slightly higher price may be worthwhile to you.

Combination Components

Whether you buy a one-brand component system or take your components à la carte, you have the choice of how to combine those components. In the fanciest systems, you'll find the amplifier function divided between two components: the preamplifier, which contains the controls, and the amp, which develops the electrical power to drive the speakers. This division allows more features to be contained in the preamp and more power in the amp (powerful amplifiers tend to be big). In less elaborate systems, the power amp and preamp are combined into an "integrated amplifier." This, in turn, can be combined with a radio to make a "receiver."

Integrating components in this way makes them collectively more compact and convenient, and usually lowers their collective price. On the other hand, these combinations usually limit available power, performance, and controls.

Integration is also a nuisance if service is ever needed. Single-function components (except for beefy power amps) tend to be lighter and easier to carry to the shop. And meanwhile you can, in some cases, listen to the components left behind when one of them is in for service. For example, if the preamp's out, your tuner can drive your amp directly, if either has a volume control. Or if the tuner's out, you can still use the amp and preamp to listen to your other signal sources, while if the amp is out, you may still be able to hear everything through headphones.

A more noticeable advantage comes at trade-in time. When you're ready to update or upgrade your equipment (generally it's most worthwhile to do this every five to ten years), you can replace just the piece whose performance least satisfies your current needs, or the one which has become most outdated or is starting to show signs of age.

One-Piece Systems

As you may have already gathered, the more components a system is divided into, the higher its cost, even if nothing is gained in performance. A tuner, amp, and preamp cost more separately than when combined into a receiver, because cabinets and some circuits need to be duplicated for each unit. So the lower-priced the system, the fewer separate pieces it will include (though its front panel may be marked to look like an assembly of components).

In the lowest price ranges are systems all in one piece, such as table-model phonographs, portables of many kinds, and many car-stereo systems. Such one-piece units *can* be made very well, but they're usually built cheaply, to sell at low prices. Nevertheless, at those prices, you're better off with one-piece units, because multicomponent systems have to sacrifice performance to cover the cost of the extra packaging.

One-piece systems have several intrinsic limitations. Powerful amplifiers won't fit into their small cabinets, nor would such systems' limited prices allow big amps. One-piece systems' speakers are often small and therefore can't produce low (bass) tones. (Small speakers can be made to deliver good bass, but only if they require a lot of power—which small systems don't have.) And if their speakers can't be removed and repositioned, they can't be set up for the best sound in a room—nor can they even deliver good stereo, except to nearby listeners. Yet within these limitations, many one-piece and portable systems sound tolerably good, especially if you don't turn them up loud enough to overload them (which makes them sound harsh and distorted).

Whatever is good about complex, expensive systems can also be found, to a lesser degree, in simple, inexpensive ones. The main thing is learning how to recognize what's good—which is the subject of our next chapter.

4 How to Tell Hi-Fi from Low-Fi, by Ear

By the classic definition, a high-fidelity system is one that reproduces the original sound as naturally and realistically as possible. But today, this definition is no longer completely true. The sounds on many records—rock, electronic music, and so on—are themselves *un*natural, deliberately so. For such music, the most accurate system is not the one that makes the music sound most natural but the one that makes it sound most like what the musicians and recording engineers meant you to hear. Good systems also let you adjust the sound, to make highly gimmicked recordings sound less gimmicky, if you find that appropriate, or jazzier, if that's what you want.

But accuracy is still the basic goal. A good sound system neither adds nor subtracts anything from the signals it reproduces, unless it is commanded to. Over the years, ways have been found to measure most of the ways sound systems inadvertently add to or subtract from the sound. Manufacturers of good equipment usually list the results of these measurements in specification ("spec") sheets available from dealers, and in the owner's manuals supplied with the equipment.

A typical specification sheet may read like this:

Frequency Response: 20–20,000 Hz, +0.3 dB
Distortion: THD, 0.02%;
          IM, 0.03%
S/N: 96 dB

To a novice, it looks like a code message. In a sense, it is. But the code is easy to learn. And each item corresponds to something you can hear.

The *frequency response* specification shows two things: First, it shows how wide a frequency range the system can handle—in this case, from 20 Hz (the lowest bass tone you can hear) to 20,000 Hz (considered the highest frequency for human hearing). Then, it tells you that (in this case) the frequencies will all be reproduced with so little variation (no rise or fall greater than 0.3 decibels) that you'd have great difficulty noticing which frequencies were being faintly over- or under-emphasized.

The *distortion* figure tells how clean the sound is, how free of fuzziness or grittiness. ("THD" and "IM" are two specific types of distortion.) The last entry, S/N, is an abbreviation for "signal-to-noise ratio"; it tells how much extraneous noise you'll hear.

These three specifications (see the next two chapters for more information) won't completely tell you how a system sounds. But they do measure three fundamental aspects of system performance.

Two of these specifications, and others we'll encounter later, use a unit called the "decibel" (dB), which indicates not loudness per se but *differences* in loudness. A sound-level change of 3 dB is about the smallest readily apparent difference of loudness in music, though sharp-eared listeners may discern differences as small as 1 dB. It takes an increase of about *10 dB* to make a sound seem *twice* as loud. (One reason symphony orchestras are so large is that it takes ten violins to sound twice as loud as one. Another, and probably better reason, is that ten violins together sound more complex and richer than one violin does.)

Hi-fi specifications matter because they help indicate how the equipment will sound. The ear is a surprisingly sensitive, yet adaptable tool of sound measurement—sensitive enough to hear slight imperfections of an amplifier even through the far greater imperfections of the speaker, yet adaptable enough to ignore all those variables.

This adaptability makes it difficult, at times, to judge a system's sound by ear. When we're evaluating audio equipment, it's necessary to suppress that adaptability, to listen critically, in order to hear and analyze quickly those defects and virtues that we'll become aware of—sometimes painfully—after prolonged listening at home. Learning to listen critically can be work, fun, or both, depending on your tastes. But it's worth doing, because shopping knowledgeably gets you the best quality and the best values, whether in hi-fi, cars, clothing, or bananas.

The beginning hi-fi buyer often shrugs off these matters by saying, "Oh, I don't have trained ears." This may be so . . . for the time being. But your ears are trained by what you listen to, which means you will eventually learn to recognize and regret any sonic defects you failed to notice in the store. It makes more sense to train your ears beforehand.

Learning by Listening

One way to do that is to listen to the best—live music (if it's available) and the best available sound systems. The value of casual listening to live music can be overrated, as our memories of sound blur easily. But if you listen analytically, you will remember better. It helps to characterize the sound in words—they are easier to remember than the sound itself is.

Listen both to the quality of sound and (at concerts of unamplified, "acoustic" instruments) to how clearly you can locate the instruments on stage with your eyes closed. Pay attention to the way the instrumental textures blend together and how readily you can still hear them as individual strands within that blend. (You needn't be able to name the instruments to do this, as long as you can recognize the differences among their sounds.) What you hear at home or in the showroom never will quite match what you hear in the concert hall because the listening conditions are so different; but a good system can give you a surprisingly close match.

Before you hit the showrooms, listen to your friends' systems, good and bad, and ask those friends to point out what they like and dislike about their sound. Friends with good ears will be able to alert you to sound qualities which are not apparent on first hearing, but which are apparent to those who have lived with them. You'll also get to hear these qualities in rooms somewhat similar to your own.

Even friends who speak knowledgeably about hi-fi may not be totally reliable as guides. They may be emotionally attached to their existing choices, or to the dream equipment that they did not or could not buy. They (and you) may also misattribute faults in the system, blaming the speakers, for example, when only the speakers' placement is at fault, or blaming the phono cartridge for a problem in the preamp.

In the showroom, the best (but not the only) thing to listen to is music. Listen to the kinds of music you are most familiar with, and will listen to most when you get your system home; your familiarity with it will help you pinpoint what's wrong and right about the sound. (Most systems tend to sound better on some kinds of music than on others; select yours to suit your listening.)

When you go shopping for a system, bring a fresh, clean copy of a record you often listen to, so you can compare how components in different stores sound when playing the same, familiar material. The fact that you like the music will also keep you from getting tired of it after a few listening sessions. This record should cover a fairly wide tonal range, from low to high, and as wide a range of musical effects as possible.

If necessary, bring two or three records with you, to get as wide a musical range as you need. Listen to as many records as you like—but do keep at least one as a benchmark. Also feel free to listen to the records the dealer has on hand; if you find one that particularly reveals sonic differences, you might even want to buy a copy of your own and add it to your demonstration arsenal.

If a dealer is unwilling to let you listen at length to your choice of music, listen elsewhere. Don't be intimidated. But be fair to the dealer, too: don't expect to have the run of the showroom on a busy Saturday afternoon.

Beware of special "demonstration" records, sonic spectaculars—even those involving the same kinds of music you normally listen to. They're designed to make almost anything sound brilliant. A few demo discs, however, have been made with easy, natural sound in mind.

When you listen, close your eyes part of the time, so your eyes won't fool your ears. With your eyes open, you're likely to conclude that the big speaker sounds better than the small one (not always true) or that the sound image you hear in a concert is precise enough to tell you just where each instrument is (not usually true, either). What you're buying is sound—so ignore everything but that, except for such practical matters as features, price, component size, and looks.

One advantage of visiting a showroom over listening in your friends' houses is the chance it gives you to compare different components, one right after the other. To avoid confusing yourself, compare only two at a time—if you want to compare three products, let the third be compared to the winner of the first face-off. Be sure that both systems in each trial are playing at *exactly* the same volume level (don't go by volume-control settings—judge carefully by ear). Otherwise, the slightly louder one will seem better—even if it's actually a little worse.

In most stores, you can switch instantly between any two components of your choice, either by pushing a switch yourself or by having the salesperson do it. Most people switch at breaks or turning points in the music, just where its sound character changes. Don't. Instead, switch in the middle of a phrase, so you can hear how two different systems or models handle the same material.

The two speakers you're comparing will sit in different spots in the room and may project their sound into the room at different angles. Since this can mask other differences in how the speakers sound, make additional comparisons by turning down the volume before switching and turning it up again immediately afterward. This, says one famous speaker designer, "keeps you from shocking your ears."

When shopping for a specific component, try to make that the only variable. Audition speakers, for example, through systems whose other components are as much like yours as possible. Some combinations of speakers and amplifiers, or cartridges and preamps, sound far better together than their components do in other systems. For example, a phono cartridge that underemphasizes high tones may mask a speaker's overemphasis of them—which is fine, until you play signal sources with normal highs (such as the tape deck or radio tuner) through that speaker.

As you listen your way down from the finest sound systems your local dealers carry, to the ones you can afford, try to consciously analyze the differences you hear. Once you've gotten an ear for such differences, it's time to begin using that knowledge to evaluate systems in your price range.

The more kinds of music you like, the more you can learn about the components and systems that you hear, for each reveals different things about performance. Following are specific tips on what to listen for. Though they vary with the type of music, the general principles behind them are the same. Even if you only listen to one kind of music, the tips on the other kinds should give you some guidance.

Classical Music Tests

Symphonic music is a good test for tone quality, because it features a full range of frequencies and a wide variety of sound textures. The violins should have a silky sheen, without harshness; but you should still be able to tell that many individual violins are playing, not just a single, enormous one, and in solos you should be able to hear the "bite" of bow on string. Cymbals and triangles should sound clear and silvery. These, and the bite of sharply played brass, are good high-frequency tests.

Both the strings and brass should also have full-bodied middle tones, a test of tonal balance. The cello, contrabass, and kettledrum should project firmly and solidly.

You should be able to distinguish different musical tones, even at a speaker's lowest frequencies: When there is no bass in the music, you should hear none.

Drums and plucked strings are good tests of transient response (the ability to follow fast changes in the music). The note should rise and fall sharply, not glide up to full level and down again. All transients test the high-frequency portions of the system, but bass drums or kettledrums also test the bass transient response. Pay special attention, as this is the frequency range where sogginess is most apt to set in. turning the drum note into a dull thud.

When the whole orchestra plays, the sound should remain clear, a sign of low distortion. When the sound is quiet, it should still remain clear and natural. The ear tends to make music sound thinner when it's quieter (see chapter 12), and some speakers augment this tendency by faltering at low volume levels, a trait to be avoided.

With stereo, we're concerned not only with tone but also with a feeling of the space in which the music was recorded and the placement of the instruments within that space (see chapter 7). Good as they are for checking tone, symphonic recordings are not always good sources for judging this quality of stereo "imaging." A few record companies, chiefly the smaller, audiophile-oriented ones such as Telarc, record symphonies with few microphones and a natural sense of perspective. But many, especially the major record labels, use microphones by the dozen, which muddies the perspective.

Chamber music is generally recorded more naturally, perhaps because the engineers feel silly using more microphones than there are musicians. Here, too, there is a fairly wide range of tones and frequencies to listen for—the bite of solo violin bows, if not the sheen of massed strings, clear pizzicato string-plucks, and bass whose location is easier to spot because only one instrument is producing it.

Not everyone has heard live symphony orchestras, but most everyone has heard live piano. This, and the fact that the piano has wider sonic range than most other instruments, makes piano music an excellent test for fidelity. Percussive notes should bang out sharply; the bass should have power and the treble a clear ring. The more you feel that a piano is actually in the room, the more accurately that piano is being reproduced. Bear in mind, though, that the concert grand pianos used in most recordings tend to have a crisper, cleaner tone and more bass power than do typical home upright and spinet models (and also the less well-cared-for grand pianos found on the stages of high-school auditoriums).

Choral music is one of the best tests for midrange clarity. You should be able to make out individual voices in the blend. Choruses are hard to record, so check your demonstration record on a few good systems to make sure it's not the record that's homogenizing all the singers into one sonic mush.

Organ music makes a stirring demonstration, but it's often a misleading test. A piece like Bach's Passacaglia and Fugue in C makes an excellent test for low bass response; but unless you know the music very well, you may not be aware of when the speakers are making one organ stop masquerade as another.

Rock Tests

Classical listeners can use the natural sound of instruments as a comparison. Listeners to rock music have less of a chance to do this because most of the instruments have no "natural" sound—what you hear, even at live concerts, is a function of the speakers that you hear it through.

The piano is a prime exception. While some groups use electric pianos, quite a few still use acoustic ones; and since most of us have heard pianos live, it's comparatively easy to judge how realistically this instrument is being reproduced, using the same criteria outlined for classical music. Cymbals are another acoustic instrument still used by rock groups—their "whiish" is a good test of accurate high-frequency response. As with classical cymbals, they should be clean and silvery.

In the bass, systems need to deliver more power than they do for classical music but don't need to go down as deep into the lowest frequencies. (The best systems, of course, can handle both requirements.) Because rock emphasizes the upper bass frequency, getting sufficient power isn't too difficult. But accuracy is: listen for a sharp kick on the drums, an "oomph" that has a snap to it, that does not sound like a hand slap on a large vat of solidified Jello. As with classical music, the different bass notes should be clearly defined, not all merging into one, repetitive frequency, and there should be no bass but what is in the music.

Clarity is harder to find in rock, since much of the music is so enriched with harmonics and processing in the recording studio that the net (and desired) effect is a tangled mass of sound, like jungle underbrush. Still, nearly every band has some cuts which let individual voices speak for themselves. Find those cuts, and use them to compare speaker clarity.

Few rock records allow you to judge stereo perspective, because of the way they are recorded. Natural stereo depends on each microphone picking up a bit of music from both the left and right sides of the group being recorded. In most rock and pop recordings, each microphone picks up only one or two instruments; eventually, these sounds are mixed together into a version which has left and right signals but is not really stereo. It may simulate stereo by electronically stringing out instruments between the speakers and by adding reverberation to give some sense of space. With such recordings, listen to discover whether the equipment you're auditioning lets the position of these images be clearly heard and doesn't let them wander, except when the mix on the record has been changed to make them move.

Voices and Other Test Material

The human voice is another instrument we've all heard live, which makes it an excellent test of sonic accuracy. Listen to recordings, both of song and of speech (which is easier to find on radio than on records), and try to determine how lifelike they sound. Male voices (such as announcers on FM) should sound warm but not overrich; avoid loudspeakers which make men sound as if they were in barrels. Female voices should be clear, not shrill or steely. (Choose your singers with care, though—some men *do* sound a little barrel-y and some women *are* steely and shrill.) Check for overemphasized sibilance on *s* sounds; they should hiss a bit but not spit or jump out at you.

Your own ears must be the final judge; but if they disagree with what friends, salespeople, hi-fi magazines, and other authorities say, stop to find out just why you like what others don't. Discuss it with someone whose ears you trust. What makes that component stand out to you at first may prove a flashy overemphasis of one aspect of sound, which will become annoyingly obtrusive in the long run. The more dramatic the difference, the more you should be suspicious of it; it's difficult for a component to be dramatically better than similarly priced components, but it's easy for one to be melodramatically worse.

By following these hints, you'll soon develop the knack of critical listening—the prerequisite of valid judgment.

5 "From 20 to 20 Thousand..."

Probably the most often quoted specification in hi-fi is "20 to 20,000." The question, is 20 to 20,000 what?

To answer that, we need to step away from high-fidelity equipment and take a look at sound. Sound is a periodic vibration of the air. The speed of that vibration gives sounds their pitch—the more frequent the vibration, the higher the tone.

Frequencies are measured in "cycles per second." So that we don't have a different phrase for that in every language, all countries measure frequencies in *hertz* (or *Hz,* for short). A sound wave whose frequency is 440 Hz vibrates 440 times per second. (The unit has nothing to do with car rental but with the nineteenth-century German scientist Heinrich Hertz, who discovered radio waves, decided they were a lab curiosity of no practical value, and died too soon to find out differently.)

The nominal range of human hearing extends from 20 Hz at the very low end to 20,000 Hz (also called 20 kilohertz—20 kHz, for short) at the very high. Young people with normal hearing can hear that full range or more; as we age, our hearing deteriorates, especially for higher frequencies. (This is largely due to the noise that civilization bathes us in.) And our bodies can sometimes feel frequencies that are too low to hear with our ears.

The range of musical notes falls well between these frequencies. The eighty-eight notes of a piano, perhaps the widest-ranging instrument, run only from 27.5 Hz to 4,186 Hz, and the extreme ends of the keyboard are seldom played. But the rest of the 20-to-20,000 Hz range still has musical importance.

You may occasionally hear (or at least feel) low organ notes at 20 Hz or below. And every time you listen to music, you hear *overtones*, or *harmonics*, above the top note on the piano.

Overtones exist because the objects whose vibrations stir the air into sound vibrate at several frequencies simultaneously. Watch a slowly vibrating string or rubber band, and you'll see this. The lowest of these several frequencies, called the *fundamental*, gives the note its pitch. The fundamental tells us, in other words, what note we're hearing: 440 Hz for the A that orchestras tune to, 392 Hz for the G just below it, and so on.

The rest of these simultaneous frequencies, which are all multiples of the fundamental, give the note its individual tonal quality. These overtones are one of our major clues in telling which instrument is playing the note: a trumpet, for example, will have more of some harmonics and less of others than a clarinet playing the same note.

To hear how much difference harmonics make, have someone play you music over the telephone, whose frequency response ends somewhere below 5,000 Hz. High-fidelity systems, by contrast, are designed to reproduce the full frequency range that we can hear. This allows us to enjoy the individual character of each instrument and voice, to hear music in full color.

In practice, few systems really reproduce the entire range from 20 to 20,000. Speakers which can reproduce bass all the way down to 20 Hz are quite expensive, so most systems use moderately priced speakers, which become rapidly less effective below a point in the 50–100 Hz range. Not all speakers reproduce well all the way to 20,000 Hz either, so the output from many systems tends to drop off somewhere, usually well above 15 or 18 kHz. Most signal sources, except the digital ones and the new Beta Hi-Fi and VHS Hi-Fi videocassette decks, also tend to have trouble with the frequency extremes. But the speakers are the biggest bottlenecks. (Amplifiers can usually handle all the frequencies that can be heard by humans—or bats, for that matter.)

Losing the extreme frequencies is a definite fault, but not the worst of faults. Much music contains no really low frequencies, and much of the music that does has only a few, sporadic low-bass notes. Even then, our minds can partially re-create the missing tones from other clues. But there are limits to how much we can do without and still enjoy the music. Limited frequency range is the main reason telephones sound like telephones, not like reality.

The difference between a system that goes down to 20 Hz with all its power intact and one that starts to lose impact below 50 or 75 Hz, is sometimes less heard than felt. But that feeling of low bass is pleasant, worth pursuing, and, for some, addictive. A lack of low bass is, nonetheless, one of the compromises most people are willing to make when more important issues are at stake. Nor is it the worst of faults to lose some of the very highest frequencies, even though they definitely affect tonal quality.

The ability to reproduce the frequency extremes is one of the glories of a good sound system. But the more extreme the frequency, the less important it is to the enjoyment of most music. So if costs or other aspects of the equipment force you to compromise a bit on the frequency extremes, well . . . that's life.

That is also, most hi-fi fans will tell you, heresy. The ideal is and remains flat frequency response to the very ends of hearing—and we totally agree with that. Yet we recognize that few people can afford the very best of everything, at least to start.

Far more annoying than frequency response limitations are response irregularities. All systems and components have their frequency limits; what's most important is that the system respond with equal ability and accuracy to all frequencies between those points. If the system does, it's said to have "flat" response, because a graph of it looks like figure 5-1:

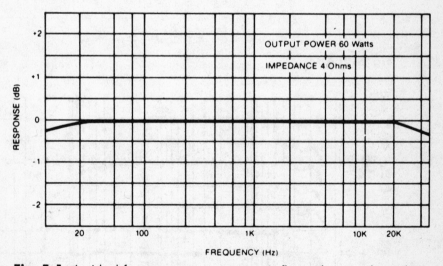

Fig. 5-1. An ideal frequency-response curve is flat, with no peaks or dips. The response curves of amplifiers, such as this one, meet that ideal, though they do drop off at the very highest and lowest frequencies. (Courtesy of Precision Power)

Frequency response charts like this show how a component's output varies (or, ideally, doesn't) when it's fed a signal whose strength remains constant while its frequency changes. In this curve (from a fairly typical amplifier), the response drops off below 20 Hz and above 20 kHz but is perfectly flat within those limits. Not all components have such flat response, as shown by the sample frequency response curves (all from fairly good products of their kind) in figure 5-2 B, C, and D.

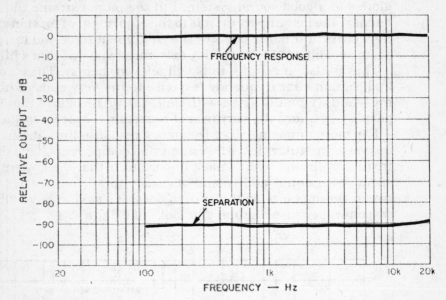

Fig. 5-2: A.

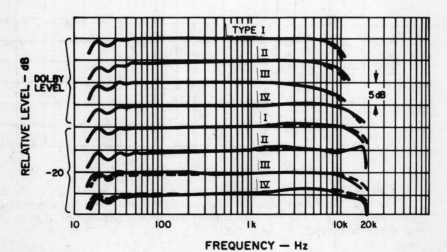

Fig. 5-2: B.

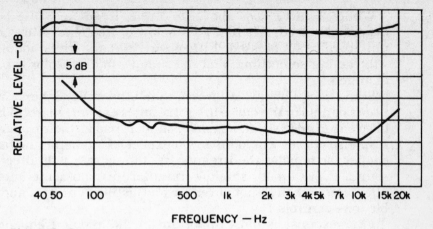

Fig. 5-2: C.

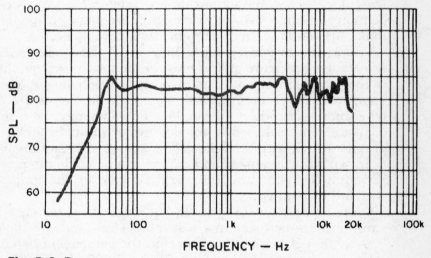

Fig. 5-2: D.

Fig. 5-2: A, B, C, D. *The frequency-response curves of Compact Disc players (A) are flat. But the curves for other components are less flat, as shown by a typical cassette deck (B), phono cartridge (C), and speaker (D) —and the speaker shown here is flatter than most. (Courtesy of Audio)*

The several curves for the cassette deck show its response with two differ-ent tape types and at two different recording levels (high-frequency re-sponse is limited at high signal levels).

Where a curve goes above its 0 line, frequencies are being overemphasized; where it goes below 0, frequencies are being unnaturally suppressed. Either way, the system is adding or subtracting something, and the sound's natural color is being changed.

Some irregularities are worse than others. Very short, sharp peaks or dips in the curve are sometimes easy to ignore. (That's one reason good speakers don't sound as bad as their frequency response curves would have you expect.) In general, the taller, deeper, or broader the irregularity, the more it will affect the sound. (Very broad, shallow irregularities can sometimes be alleviated—though not cured—by adjusting your bass and treble tone controls.)

Flat response is most important in the middle frequencies, where our ears are most sensitive and where most of the music is. As you move out toward the frequency extremes, response irregularities become somewhat less intolerable—with one exception: a rising, or sharply rising high-frequency response can make the sound seem overbright, shrill, even piercing.

Frequency response charts like those above are found in some sales literature and in most of the test reports published in hi-fi magazines. They can give you a rough idea of how the components they describe will sound. Some curves are more revealing than others, depending on how they were made. (Certain test techniques smooth away sharp irregularities: graphs drawn with thick lines look smoother than they would if drawn with thin ones, and curves can be made more or less revealing by changing the vertical scale of the graphs on which they're drawn.)

Often there is no curve at all, but just some numbers which summarize a component's response. Thus, the specification "20–20,000 Hz, ±3 dB" states that the component listed can cover all the frequencies from 20 to 20,000 Hz, and that its response neither increases nor decreases by more than 3 decibels at any point between those extremes. If the specification read "20–20,000 Hz, +0, −3 dB," it would indicate that the response of the model described never rose above the 0 line; presumably, it would also have no significant dips below 0, but would just "roll off" at the ends like a curve in figure 5-1A.

The smaller the variation in frequency response, the better. So a component rated "20–20,000 Hz, ±1 dB" would be flatter than one rated "±3 dB." Note, however, that a given curve can be summarized by more than one set of figures. For example, curve (c) in figure 5-2 could be summarized as either "50–12,000 Hz, ±4 dB" or "30–15,000 Hz, ±6 dB," depending on whether the person rating it was more interested in emphasizing flatness of response or a wide frequency range. (The curve could also be summarized, with a bit more justice, as "30–15,000 Hz, +3, −6 dB." Splitting the difference and calling the 30–15,000 Hz response "±4.5 dB" would be less just; it's common to use the response level at 1,000 Hz as the 0–dB reference point.) The main thing to remember is this: *be suspicious of specifications which show just a frequency range, without stating how much or how little the response varies with that range; such specifications are almost meaningless.*

Listening to Frequency Response

Your ears must be the ultimate judges of frequency response, as of all high-fidelity performance factors. Some frequency response problems are easy to spot, but others are only easy to hear when you compare two components or systems directly, alternating between each.

A lack of bass, for instance, may not be obvious at first, both because the brain tends to supply an impression of bass when the ear gets clues that there should be bass tones in the music, and because not all music has low bass. Listening to a record with good bass while alternately switching between speakers will show up such differences clearly. Remember that more bass is not necessarily better bass; a natural sound is easier to live with than a flashy, ever-present thump.

The same holds true for treble. A very slight treble overemphasis can sound pleasantly airy, but a strong treble boost or sharp peak in the treble response can cause screechiness, or make record-scratch and tape-hiss unduly prominent. Underemphasized treble is easier to live with, but it can make music too soft, too smooth, without the bite that gives some music its impact.

In the midrange, peaks and dips in the frequency response are even more annoying. Too little midrange makes details hard to hear and words difficult to understand; too much gives a honky, nasal quality to the sound. (For an illustration, listen to your voice when your hands surround your mouth like a megaphone.)

While you're learning to recognize these effects, try listening to a system that includes an equalizer (a multiple tone control) like the one shown in figure 5–3. Slowly move its controls, one at a time, up, down, and back to the center position, listening to how these artificially induced peaks and dips affect the

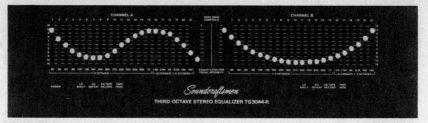

Fig. 5-3. *A typical "graphic" equalizer, so-called because its sliding controls graph the frequency corrections it is set for. (Courtesy Soundcraftsmen)*

sound. Do this with music and again with a noise signal which includes all frequencies at once; many equalizers have "pink-noise" generators to provide such signals; if not, you can use the noise picked up by an FM tuner when tuned between stations. The noise should sound characterless; if you can discern any individual tones, the system is overemphasizing them.

The public's perception that 20 to 20,000 Hz is synonymous with high fidelity is almost right. Now that other problems (discussed in the next chapter) have been brought down to manageable levels, frequency response does account for most of the differences we hear between components. But remember: it's not just the frequency range that counts—it's also the system's behavior within that range. Better a flat but narrow frequency response than one which covers the whole range but looks like a profile of the Rocky Mountains.

6 Clean and Dirty Sound

While frequency response may be the best-known hi-fi specification, it is not the most important one. Hearing all the tones and overtones in music adds a great deal to your listening pleasure. But even sound with a more restricted tonal range can be enjoyable . . . if that sound is clean.

When the sound is clean and pure, you hear only the tones that were in the original music. When it's not, it contains extraneous noises (such as hum and hiss) or becomes fuzzy and distorted. Even if you aren't conscious of their presence, such noise and distortion cut your musical enjoyment, making you tire of listening far sooner than you would if they weren't there —a phenomenon called "listener fatigue." So the cleaner your system sounds, the more you'll listen to it and the more it will give you your money's worth.

If you don't know how to recognize them, noise and distortion can make you uncomfortable without your realizing why. Once you've learned to recognize them, you'll quickly be able to tell clean sound from dirty—a useful skill when selecting sound equipment.

To hear *distortion* in raw, recognizable form, take any piece of sound equipment you have, from a portable radio to a component hi-fi system, start playing music, and then slowly turn the volume up as far as you can stand. As the volume rises, the sound changes—first strained, then fuzzy, then harsh and grating. The better the system, the louder it can get before those changes become noticeable. On the best systems, the changes never become audible unless the sound is turned up to ear-shattering levels.

To hear *noise* clearly, you also need to turn up your volume —but without music. You can do this at home, if you have some stereo equipment already, or in the store. Play a blank tape, or tune to a space between stations on an FM radio, and you'll hear it clearly. On the best systems, noise is rarely audible during normal listening—and any noise which can be heard usually comes from the recordings or broadcasts you're listening to, not from the system itself.

Noise is most often heard when the music is too soft to drown it out; distortion is most audible when the music is loud enough to push the system to its limits.

Between them, noise and distortion define the limits of a system's *dynamic range*, the range of loud and soft sounds it can reproduce cleanly and clearly. A system's dynamic range is usually defined on its specification sheet by its *signal-to-noise* ratio ("S/N," for short) in decibels (dB). This ratio measures the difference in level between the system's own noise and the highest signal level the system can handle with reasonably low distortion.

The higher the S/N, the better: an S/N between 60 and 70 dB is fairly decent, one between 70 and 80 dB is rather good, and anything over 90 dB is excellent. The dynamic range you should expect depends a good deal on the kind of component you're considering: 75 dB, for example, is pretty good for a cassette deck but shamefully low for an amplifier.

Since the ear is more sensitive to noise at some frequencies than at others, some manufacturers give S/N figures which have been "weighted" to take greater account of the most annoying frequencies and less account of the least bothersome ones. Weighted averages are usually higher than unweighted ones, because much system noise occurs at frequencies the ear is not particularly bothered by. You can't compare a weighted S/N given for one component with an unweighted S/N given for another; if both weighted and unweighted figures are available, use the weighted ones for your comparisons—they correspond better to what you'll actually hear.

While a single S/N number can define a system's noise level, several may be given to define its level of distortion. This is because there are several types of distortion: harmonic, intermodulation, and transient intermodulation. All are specified as percentages, which should be as low as possible—definitely under 1 percent and preferably below 0.1 percent. (Some components achieve distortion levels under 0.001 percent; almost no one believes the differences between this and 0.1 percent are audible, but some experts feel that such low distortion indicates audible improvements in other areas.)

Harmonic distortion occurs when a component generates a whole series of spurious frequencies which are multiples of the frequencies in the signal. (Since all of these harmonics are measured together, the specification usually reads "total harmonic distortion," or "THD.") Modest levels of harmonic distortion may be difficult to notice because they can mimic the genuine harmonics produced by musical instruments; but even mild THD can become audible on the pure, single-frequency notes sometimes produced by flutes or organs.

Intermodulation distortion (IM) is produced when two or more tones in the signal "beat" together to form spurious tones whose frequencies are equal to the sum or difference of the original ones. Since these frequencies are not harmonically related to those in the signal, high IM levels are more annoying than corresponding amounts of THD.

Transient intermodulation distortion (TIM) is a newly defined phenomenon, a form of IM which chiefly occurs during a note's onset, or "attack." It occurs when the signal is changing too fast for the component to handle. Tests for TIM are not standardized, so few component spec sheets list it, and one cannot necessarily compare TIM figures given in spec sheets from different manufacturers.

Another form of distortion is heard sometimes from record players and tape decks, which have rotating parts. When some of those parts rotate at uneven speed, the signal frequencies fluctuate, rising when the parts speed up, lowering when the parts slow down. Slow-speed variations are known as *wow*, because they make a steady sound go "wowowowow" (not all technical terms have technical origins). Fast variations create *flutter*, which gives sound a gargly, underwater quality. The two are usually lumped together into one "wow and flutter" number. This should be as low as possible, by no means more than 0.1 percent and preferably under 0.003 percent.

Since the ear is more sensitive to some flutter frequencies than others, wow and flutter specifications are often weighted, just as S/N specs are, to indicate how audible there speed variations will be. The figures given above are unweighted.

Frequency response, S/N, and distortion are specifications which apply to just about all audio components; wow and flutter applies to most of those with moving parts (digital players, as we'll see, avoid this problem). Other specifications apply only to specific types of components; the chapters devoted to those components will cover those specs.

All these specifications cover imperfections in the system. Some of those occur at all times, others only when the system is under stress (playing very loud signals, for example).

7 Sound in Dimension: Stereo (and More)

A high-fidelity system is like a window on the concert hall—the higher the fidelity, the more transparent the window. Stereo, if it's done right, eliminates the window altogether, and plunks your listening room down in the middle of the concert hall. To create this illusion, stereo requires two sound pathways, or *channels*, extending from the microphones at the recording all the way to your two loudspeakers.

Stereo tape, FM, and phonograph records have been with us for decades. In the past few years, however, even those sound sources which used to be strictly monophonic—AM radio, TV, and videotape—are now available in stereo as well. We can hear stereo wherever we go, too, through those personal headphone portables you see everywhere. More and more, equipment is designed with stereo in mind and judged by how well it produces the stereo illusion.

And illusion it surely is. For, although there are only two sound channels, your ears and brain can process the sounds heard, to re-create the positions of several instruments—from side to side and even from front to back. This is called *imaging*.

By a similar process, most people can sense the sounds which reach the microphones by reflection from the walls, floor, and ceiling of the room in which the music was recorded. From this comes a feeling for the room's size and acoustics, or its sonic *ambience*.

If you close your eyes, imaging can give you the feeling that the musicians are right there in front of you; ambience can give you the feeling that you're sitting in the concert hall. These feelings are not identical, as concertgoers can attest.

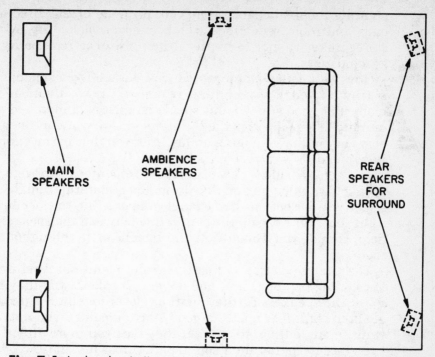

Fig. 7-1. In the classic "stereo triangle" room arrangement, the speakers are about six to eight feet apart and the listeners about that distance from the plane of the speakers, on the center line between them. The speakers shown by dashed lines are optional for extra ambience or surround sound. (Courtesy Imagimation Technical Art)

Most listeners in the concert hall hear ambience, but very little imaging—unless they're sitting in the front half of the concert hall, in which case they're likely to hear imaging, but less ambience. The strong imaging heard from many recordings on good systems can be considered a step away from realism; but many people enjoy it, because it makes up for the absence of the visual clues by which we locate the instruments at live performances. How much imaging and ambience you get depends on your system, your room, and the recordings you play.

Recordings made with comparatively few microphones will usually have better imaging than those made with dozens of mikes. Recordings made in large, reverberant rooms (such as concert halls) will usually have more ambience than those made in studios designed to absorb instead of reflect sound. Rock records, in which the instruments may be recorded separately (even in separate places) rarely have good imaging, though they frequently have artificially added ambience. Such recordings are sometimes referred to by engineers as "multichannel mono" because they contain none of the directional cues and room reflections which must be picked up by both stereo mikes at once to create a true sense of stereo solidity and spaciousness.

How well your system reproduces these effects depends primarily on your speakers and where you place them in your room. For good stereo, your speakers must be a matched pair; unmatched speakers make the stereo image wander. Speakers also vary in their imaging ability (more on that in the chapters just ahead).

The general rule for good stereo placement is to arrange your speakers so that you and they form an equilateral triangle. The effect will be best at the triangle's apex. But you needn't sit right there, or even on the center line between the speakers, to hear stereo; you should get the benefit of it throughout the room.

The triangle set up is just a starting point, not a rigid rule. Depending on your room and on your speakers, you may have to set the speakers further apart or closer together (a distance of six to eight feet makes a good starting point). You may also want to angle them in, so that they face you more directly (or even face in so that their sound paths cross just in front of you) or angle them out a little. You'll find that some speakers sound best when mounted flat against the wall, others when pulled a few feet out from it.

Ideally, check and adjust for good stereo with a recording made with as few microphones as possible. Such records usually come from small labels, such as Telarc, rather than from big recording companies; if you have no such records, ask your hi-fi or record dealer for recommendations.

With such a record, check first to make sure the sound spreads evenly from speaker to speaker when you're seated at the peak of the triangle. If all the instruments on the record seem to be concentrated in a narrow space in front of you, the speakers may be too close together or angled in too far. If the sounds all group by the speakers, with a "hole in the middle," then the speakers may be placed or angled too far apart, or may be wired incorrectly (see chapter 23). Listen for this while walking across the room near the speakers. Since it takes a while to learn to recognize too-narrow stereo perspective, it may be easiest to start by deliberately spreading the speakers till you get a hole in the middle, then move or aim them inward just past the point where the "hole" fills up with sound.

These simple guidelines will get you close to the best stereo effect your system is capable of. As you become more familiar

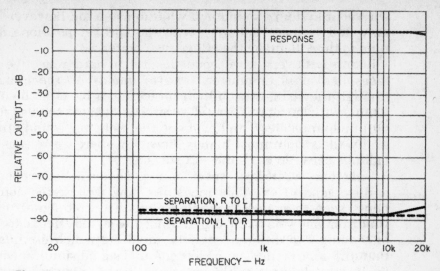

Fig. 7-2: A.

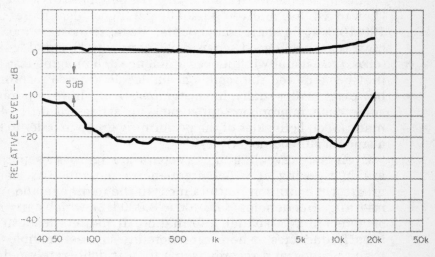

Fig. 7-2: B.

Fig. 7-2: A, B. *Separation curves show frequency response (upper line) and the amount each frequency leaks into the opposite channel (lower line). The greater the separation, the farther apart the two lines will be. In a CD player (A), there is more separation (and smoother response) than in a phono cartridge (B). (Courtesy of Audio)*

with your system's sound and what to listen for, however, you may find yourself tinkering with the speaker positions from time to time, to make the effect even better.

Rooms with very "live" acoustics, full of hard, reflective surfaces like glass or plaster, tend to muddy up the imaging (though they can, especially if large, add a bit to ambience). Rooms with lots of soft, sound-absorbing surfaces such as rugs, curtains, upholstery, and acoustic tile make the sound unnaturally "dead." In most homes, however, there's a reasonable balance between hard and soft surfaces.

Only one numerical specification relates to stereophonic ability: *separation*. This measures how well stereo components keep their two channels isolated, so that signals don't leak from one side to the other. Since the stereo effect depends on having two different signals, anything which diminishes that difference (such as the left channel signal simultaneously leaking softly through the right channel) diminishes that effect.

The higher the separation figure, the better (25 dB is the very least to ask for, and you'll usually get a good deal more, up to 100 dB or so for some components). Because most components have reasonably good separation, interchannel signal leakage (*crosstalk*) usually influences ambience and imaging less than the speakers and the room's acoustics do. (Stereo recordings, however, will usually have comparatively little separation, since each microphone must pick up at least a little of the material on both sides of the performing group in order to form a smooth stereo image.)

Even more revealing than a separation figure is a separation graph, showing at which frequencies separation is least or greatest. Separation matters most in the midrange and upper midrange frequencies (say, 400 to 8,000 Hz), which carry most of a recording's spatial information. It matters least at low bass frequencies, where directionality is least audible. (On many phonograph records, separation is deliberately reduced at low frequencies, to make the record easier for the turntable to play.)

While separation always refers to the two stereo channels, crosstalk is sometimes also used to mean leakage from one signal input to another—causing you to hear the tuner signal softly while you're listening to the turntable, for instance. This is more troublesome than diminished stereo separation but has a simple cure: turn off the unused signal source (the tuner, in this example).

Routes to Extra Realism: Binaural, Quadraphonic, and Delay

Stereo recordings are intended to be heard through loud-speakers, through which each of the listener's ears hears both channels. When we listen to stereo through headphones, with each ear hearing only one channel, ambience is exaggerated, and the imaging becomes peculiar, with instruments seeming to play in our heads, or even behind us.

Some recordings, however, are made for headphone listening. Such *binaural* recordings are usually made with microphones spaced on both sides of a dummy head, like electronic ears. The results can be startlingly realistic—but only if heard, as intended, through headphones. Through loudspeakers, binaural recordings tend to sound a bit thin and flat—like seeing bas-reliefs where you expected solid sculptures.

Two other, and related, routes to extra stereophonic realism use speakers—four of them:

The better known is four-channel *(quadraphonic)* sound, which had a modest boom about ten years ago but never quite caught on.

What killed quadraphonic sound was a combination of cost and confusion: the equipment cost more than stereo and, worse yet, the manufacturers could not agree on a single system for making quadraphonic records. There was even disagreement over what four-channel sound should do: reproduce realistic ambience (best done with two speakers in front and one on each side of a room) or give the listener the dramatic feeling of being right inside the orchestra (for which speakers in the room's four corners were best).

The quadraphonic principle, however, is still valid: since sound in real concert halls reaches you from all directions, home sound will also seem more realistic if it reaches you from all sides. And four-channel is coming back for video.

The Compact Disc system includes provisions for four-channel recording (though current players are not designed for this). Older four-channel techniques have already returned as offshoots of the video boom. Many movies, in the past few years, have been made with multichannel sound, to add spaciousness, impact, and a sense of being in the middle of the action. The video discs and stereo videocassettes of these movies have multichannel sound encoded into them; a suitable decoder, feeding extra speakers, can separate those channels out again, bringing theatrical impact to home viewing and listening.

Some quadraphonic decoders also simulate the ambience that reflections of sound from different directions add to listening in the concert hall. (Here, too, extra speakers are needed.) Depending on the recording, the effect of such ambience simulation can range from negligible through realistic to overstated; most decoders have controls which let you choose the degree of ambience you want.

Delay systems also add ambience from multiple directions; this, too, requires extra speakers. Such systems—and a cheap way of simulating one—will be discussed more fully in chapter 24.

8 Listening to Loudspeakers

Choosing loudspeakers is the most important hi-fi decision you can make, for the speakers have the greatest effect upon the sound you hear.

Choosing the right speakers isn't all that easy. For one thing, there is more variety among speakers than among components of any other type. Speakers range in size from shoeboxes to pony stalls, in price from the cost of a good lunch to the cost of a fine automobile, and in shape from flat to chunky. So it's not surprising that they vary so much in sound as well.

If speakers were perfect, they'd all sound alike—they'd have no character of their own but would simply reproduce the signal fed to them, thus re-creating in your living room the exact sound the microphones picked up at the original performance or recording session.

The difference in sound you can hear from different speakers is evidence that speakers are farther from perfection than the other components in the system. Yet even the imperfect can be excellent, and today's speakers are astonishingly good—especially when you consider that speakers do the most difficult and least understood job in the system. The speaker must transform an electrical signal into a totally different kind of energy—sound—and feed that energy into an environment—your listening room—that the speaker's designer can't possibly predict. Designers of speakers are still learning what a speaker must do to sound right, and are learning new ways of making speakers do it. This is another reason for the incredible diversity of designs.

Fig. 8-1. *Speakers vary in size, even more than shown here. In general, the bigger the speaker the deeper its bass—but only as long as the speakers being compared are of the same type. These speakers are "two-way" types, with large woofers for low frequencies and small tweeters (here, the common dome type) for the highs. (Courtesy of Celestion)*

You'll hear a lot about this when you shop for speakers; salespeople need superiorities to talk about, and specific design features they can point to. Some of these superiorities are real, and some of these features are significant. But a speaker that's excellent in one area may lack something important in another. Regrettably, specifications tell you less about speakers than they do about the other components. What counts—even more in speakers than in anything else—is what you hear.

Practical Considerations

Practical aspects, such as size, cost, appearance, and compatibility with the rest of your system, also count, of course. Consider them your allies, because they cut the list of candidates from hundreds to a few dozen or so.

You can also trim your search still further by starting out with speakers you have already heard of. Bear in mind, however, that a name familiar from other fields may not mean much here. Many of the best speakers are made by specialized companies which make nothing else. By asking around among your knowledgeable friends, and by reading reviews in hi-fi magazines, you'll come up with a list of speakers worth auditioning.

Dealers are likely to recommend others, some of which are equally good, but which your friends and the magazines have not auditioned yet. (Some dealers, though, may recommend models whose major merit is a high profit margin. While all dealers would rather sell you something good than something bad, some would rather sell you whatever they happen to have than sell you nothing.)

Invest as much as you can in your speakers (about one-fourth to one-third of the total cost of your system is reasonable) and as much time as possible in shopping for them. Don't choose them hastily just because you have "uneducated ears." As we've already mentioned, your ears will become educated soon enough, and it's cheaper to educate them before choosing speakers than it is to educate them by making a bad choice too fast and growing disappointed later. (If your initial choice was not the best, all is not lost. You can always add better speakers to your system, and move your original choices to another room, for casual listening.)

Your home and your lifestyle may impose special requirements on your choice of speaker: If you have cats who use your speakers for scratching posts, then look for speakers with high-mounted or metal grilles. If you give a lot of parties, look for speakers whose tops are made of alcohol-resistant materials or are too small, too steeply angled, or too high for people to set their drinks on. If the traffic pattern of your home requires it, get speakers designed to sound their best when placed against a wall rather than a few feet out in the room.

Consider, too, compatibility with the rest of your system. The main thing to watch here is amplifier power: your system should produce at least as much power per channel (check your amplifier's spec sheet) as the speaker's recommended minimum (check the speaker specs). Surprisingly, big speakers often work well with small, low-powered amplifiers, since such speakers often need less power than small ones of similar quality.

A speaker's maximum power rating is less significant. This usually refers to the maximum power the speaker can take continuously. But most music requires high amplifier power only for short, loud "peaks." Long before you reach power levels that could damage the speakers, you'll hear the speaker begin to distort. When you do, turn down the volume, fast. If you have a high-powered amp, though, use it cautiously: leave the volume turned down low before selecting a signal source, so that you don't switch to a signal loud enough to blast your speakers out; never plug and unplug cables while the system's on; put fuses in line with the speakers to protect them; and don't use equalizers (see chapter 24) to boost bass frequencies excessively. When auditioning speakers at a store, use an amplifier of approximately the same power as the one you'll use at home.

With some amplifiers, a speaker's impedance (roughly, its opposition to the passage of alternate current, such as audio signals) may also be significant. Most speakers have impedance ratings of 4, 6, 8, or 16 ohms. Many amplifiers deliver more power into lower impedances (a factor to consider when matching speaker and amplifier power ratings). With some amplifiers you'll also have problems dealing with very low-impedance loads—occasionally when driving one pair of 4-ohm speakers and often when driving two or more pair at once. The amplifier's instructions will usually tell you what kinds of speaker loads, if any, the amplifier shouldn't drive.

Your speakers should also match your other equipment in quality. Using a superb speaker with a mediocre system won't hurt anything, but it's wasteful. The rest of the system won't take full advantage of that speaker's quality. At the extreme, a very good speaker can make a poor system sound even worse by revealing sonic defects (such as high-frequency distortion) which cheaper speakers would mask.

A few speakers and amplifiers interact so as to sound better —or worse—together than they would with different mates. The differences are usually subtle, but they sometimes do exist. If possible, audition speakers with the same model amplifier you'll be using, or one of similar design. And ask your dealer if he knows how your intended amp and speakers will work together.

Listening to Loudspeakers

Once you've eliminated those speakers which aren't practical for you, you're left with a double mission: first, to find the speakers which add the least coloration to the sound you hear, then (since even the best speakers add some trace of color) to select those whose colorations sound most pleasing to you.

And that involves listening. In fact, it is more necessary to listen to loudspeakers before buying them than any other parts of the system. You can buy amplifiers, tape decks, and the like based on their reputation and specs alone, and do reasonably well for yourself; but you should never buy speakers that you haven't heard, unless your circumstances prevent it.

The pointers in chapter 4 apply here, as they do to all other parts of your stereo system. But there are additional listening hints which apply to speakers alone.

The main difference is that speakers are heard in space. So it's not enough for the speaker to have good treble response when you stand in one spot; the treble should disperse evenly throughout the room. You should be able to walk from side to side of the demonstration room, and stand or sit, without hearing any sharp changes in the character of the sound. (With even the best speakers, though, the treble will gradually drop off as you walk from in front of the speakers to one side.) Bass response may also change with your position, but that's attributable to the room, not the speaker.

The easiest way to test a speaker's treble response is to listen to a random noise signal rather than to music. That's because the treble content of such signals doesn't vary rapidly, as music's treble does. Your dealer may have a "pink-noise" generator available (many equalizers have them built in); if not, the noise between stations on the FM dial makes a good speaker test. (You may have heard of "white noise," a random signal with all frequencies equally loud; pink noise is a similar, random signal, but with a frequency balance more like that of music.)

Noise signals also make good tests of frequency balance, since they contain almost all the audio frequencies at once, evenly distributed across the spectrum. Pink noise should sound like a smooth hiss, whose pitch you can't determine; FM noise will sound less hissy, more of a roar. If the sound becomes nasal, hisses sharply, or gives you a definite sense of pitch at any frequency, then the speaker has poor sonic balance.

Listen for consistent stereo imaging, too. If an instrument seems to be coming from one spot in the room (or from behind the rear wall), its image should stay rooted in that spot as you move around, at least until you get much closer to one speaker than the other.

Bear in mind that your listening room will have different acoustics than the showroom, so the speaker you buy will sound slightly different when you get it home. This doesn't mean that speakers which sound good in the store will sound

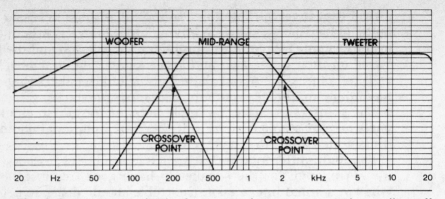

Fig. 8-2. *A crossover divides frequencies between two speakers, rolling off one speaker's output above the crossover point and the other speaker's output below.* (Courtesy Design Acoustics)

bad at home (or vice versa), but it does mean that a speaker which sounds only marginally better than another in the showroom might sound marginally worse at home.

Some of these differences are predictable: if your room has more soft, padded surfaces than the dealer's, all speakers will sound a bit softer in the treble when you get them home; if your room has more hard, unpadded surfaces, speakers will sound brighter.

To minimize acoustic differences between home and store, some dealers demonstrate only one pair of speakers in a room. This is to prevent other speakers from absorbing sound and changing the apparent frequency response of the room and speaker (especially in the bass).

Many speakers have controls that compensate for differences in room acoustics by varying the upper frequency levels. On most speakers, these controls are out of sight, behind the speaker or behind a removable front grille. Dealers should let you check the effects of these controls: you might prefer the way the speaker sounds with a control setting different from the one chosen by the dealer.

The changes those settings make can completely change your opinion of a speaker. A few years back, we visited a factory in Japan to evaluate a new speaker about to be introduced in the U.S. At first, the speaker sounded odd to us—clear, but with a slightly offbeat tonal balance. Then one of us changed the speaker's rear-panel control settings, and with this slight adjustment our reaction changed from dislike to enthusiasm.

Once you have the frequency balance the way you like it, listen to how the different frequencies are handled. Bass is the major consideration; in fact, bass performance is often the main difference between medium- and high-priced speakers from the same maker. You should be able to distinguish different musical tones, even down to the bottom range. Beware of "Johnny One-Note" speakers, which play the same bass drone regardless of the actual note the instruments are playing. When there is no bass in the music, you should hear none from the speaker. When the music drops below the speaker's frequency limit, it should fade away to silence, not blat out as lumpy distortions ("doubling") an octave higher. This is especially important with less expensive speakers, which usually cut off their bass at higher frequencies than expensive ones, and sometimes use such fake "bass" in a higher range to conceal the fact. Better no bass than bad bass. After all, you can always add more bass later, with a specialized bass-only speaker called a "subwoofer."

Test records with descending series of pure tones (that is, without overtones to enrich the sound and cloud the issue) are good bass tests. They let you tell just how far down a speaker's response goes. They also let you know at once, by a change in the tone color, if the speaker begins doubling.

At the higher frequencies, the main things to listen for are dispersion (an even spread of highs through the listening area) and smoothness—no "spitting," no emphasized sibilance from voices, no overemphases that make certain frequencies "zing" out at you unnaturally.

In the midrange, the main criteria are smoothness and clarity. Listen to the complex texture of orchestral or choral music, big-band jazz or the like. It should sound clear, rather than muddy. Some rock has similar sonic complexity; just make sure the song you use for this test is not one which has muddiness deliberately mixed in.

Makers of good speakers have a particular sound in mind, and know how to achieve it. All the speakers in such a manufacturer's line sound similar, with the more expensive models having better bass response, greater dynamic range, and perhaps greater smoothness. Even if you dislike the sound that manufacturer is trying for, you must admit his competence in achieving it. When each speaker in a company's line sounds different from the others, you may rightly question whether that company knows what it's doing. If such a company produces one or two good speakers, it's usually a fluke—or a sign that they've changed designers.

Listen for dynamic range. A good speaker should be able to play as loudly as you think you'll ever want it to, and then some (so you'll have some reserve capacity). Make sure that it can handle these loud passages cleanly. If the sound gets muddy at high volumes, find out whether or not it's the speaker's fault by listening to the same amp and record through another speaker, and by listening to the same speaker and record with another, more powerful amp.

The speaker should also be able to play softly without changing its tonal character. Your ear's characteristics make the tone "thin out" a bit as you turn down the volume. Avoid speakers which accentuate that tendency and make all soft music sound thin and tinny.

Listening Comparisons

A well-stocked dealer may have dozens of speakers in your price range. Don't try listening to them all at once, or you'll simply get confused. Compare two models at a time. Judge which you prefer, then play the winner against yet another model. Three to five models per listening session is plenty.

When you listen, make sure both speakers are as closely matched in loudness as possible. While major differences in volume are easily noticed, small ones often masquerade as differences in quality, with the slightly louder one appearing better. This becomes especially tricky, as the relative balance between the speakers can shift with the music; if one speaker emphasizes the upper midrange while the other emphasizes the lower middle, the first will sound a little louder on some notes, a little softer on some others. You may have to readjust the volume frequently as the music changes.

Your dealer will usually have a switch for instant comparison between speakers. Ask to operate this switch yourself, and flick it in midpassage (musically jarring though it may be) rather than at transitions between musical passages. This ensures that you'll be comparing how each speaker handles the same sonic texture, rather than trying to make sense of a comparison between one model's flutes and the other's trombones.

Don't rely on instant, or "A-B," comparisons to reveal all the differences between speakers. Other differences will show up only when you listen to both speakers at length, especially when you repeat the same long musical passage through each speaker. Don't let the dealer rush you. After all, you'll be listening to the speaker you select for a long time; you should let your acquaintance ripen a little before you take it home. (Some dealers may even let you try speakers in your home, and trade them in at full price for another pair if they don't sound the way you'd like them to there.)

Obviously, all this listening will require some cooperation from your dealer. You'll find some dealers more helpful than others, with the least help usually coming from the dealers who charge the lowest prices. That's reasonable: it costs a dealer money to maintain a showroom and staff it with enough knowledgeable salespeople to answer customers' questions; that extra cost is added to his prices. It is not reasonable, therefore (or at least, not fair) to use one dealer's facilities and time to learn what you want, then buy it from a discount dealer who wouldn't or couldn't give you that assistance. (We'll get to this again in chapter 26.)

In this chapter, we've skipped most speaker technicalities. These mean less than how a speaker sounds. But they do mean something; so we've devoted the next two chapters to them.

9 Speakers II: Understanding Speakers

Loudspeakers must impersonate all the instruments of the orchestra and of the rock band, the ringing timbres of an opera singer and the gravel voice of a country-western star, and they must do all those tonal tricks without calling attention to themselves. It takes both scientific knowledge and technical tricks to attain such naturalism. Small wonder that loudspeakers are not simply a product of straight, classical engineering but are compounded from approximately equal parts of science, art, and magic.

Sometimes, the "scientific principles" explaining why a speaker sounds good were formulated (not always correctly) after the fact. In other cases, inventors have proceeded on pure principle, disregarding the sonic results. Today, we have reached the era when even the backyard speaker designer uses computers in his work, often to good effect. But a good ear and a knowledge of basic physics remain the designer's best tools. The buyer's best tools are his own ears.

Still, ads, catalogs, and the litanies of salespeople are full of technical lingo explaining this or that attribute. Some of that information is worth knowing; it's also worth knowing what to ignore.

The two facts most worth considering in purchasing a speaker are the two least technical: its size and price. If the speaker won't fit into your listening room, it's not for you. (This may happen if the speaker itself is too large or if it is designed to work so far out from the wall that it blocks traffic.) If you can't afford it, you should also pass on to another model. But don't be too hasty to reject a speaker merely because its price gives you a jolt. It's better to buy the best speaker you can, and keep it for the long haul, than to settle for something cheaper and less satisfactory and trade up later. In the long run, buying quality is the more economical approach.

Your very first system may be an exception to that. Some speaker designers recommend starting your first good system with cheap speakers (but good equipment otherwise), living with the system for six months or so to train your ears, then coming back for better speakers and moving the old speakers elsewhere in the house.

Size determines not only where you put your speakers but how they will sound. Both small and large speakers have their points. Small ones often have great clarity of sound, are easier to place where they'll sound best, and often cost less. All else being equal (which it hardly ever is), there's still a tradeoff between a speaker's size, on the one hand, and its bass response and efficiency on the other. Small speakers tend to skimp on bass or have low efficiency—which means they gobble up more watts of amplifier power for a given sound level. Large speakers seldom suffer such constraints.

Efficiency is a function of the speaker's *dispersion* (how widely it spreads sound throughout the room) and its *sensitivity* (the loudness delivered for a given amount of amplifier power). Speaker specs list only sensitivity, expressed in dB of sound pressure level (SPL), as measured one meter in front of the speaker, with an amplifier output level of one watt. The higher the figure, the more sensitive and more efficient the speaker; most speakers have sensitivities between 86 and 96 dB.

Efficiency has advantages that may not be obvious at first: While larger, more efficient speakers sometimes cost more, they can often be used with smaller, less powerful and hence less expensive amplifiers. The money saved on the amp may make up for the additional cost of the larger speakers. A speaker with a sensitivity 3 dB greater than another model will deliver as much sound from half as much amplifier power.

Efficient speakers also tend to be more durable. The amplifier power a speaker does not convert to sound energy is turned into heat, and excess heat can damage the loudspeaker. Because efficient speakers waste less power as heat, they can absorb more power—and play louder—without risk of damage.

Efficiency also helps protect a speaker against damage from *under*powered amps. When an amplifier is asked for more power than it can deliver, it distorts, generating false high-frequency harmonics that can damage the speaker system's delicate high-frequency speakers, its "tweeters." By drawing less power from the amplifier, efficient speakers avoid this risk —a most common cause of damage to speakers.

Manufacturers often specify "minimum recommended amplifier power" figures for their speakers. Alas, these figures are often arbitrary. The best way to check is to connect a speaker to an amplifier with the same power as the one you have or plan to buy, and see if that combination still sounds clean and undistorted when you turn up the volume a bit past the loudest sound level you ever listen to.

Speaker Configurations

The most common type of speaker system consists of two or more *drivers* enclosed in a wooden box. These drivers push and pull the air to generate sound waves (figure 9–1). Your amplifier feeds a signal to the drivers' voice coils, where the varying signal generates a varying magnetic field. This acts against the field of a permanent magnet, making the coil move. The coil pushes and pulls the speaker's cone, which, in turn, moves the air and makes the sound.

A single driver would have trouble handling all the frequencies in the audible range. High and low frequencies impose opposite requirements on a loudspeaker. A good low-frequency speaker should be large to push a lot of air (and to handle the power required to move it). A good high-frequency speaker must be light (to move back and forth rapidly) and small (so that it will disperse high frequencies over a broad area, rather than narrowly beaming them). For these reasons, most speakers include two drivers: a small, light *tweeter* to handle the treble and a large *woofer* for the bass.

A speaker with just a woofer and a tweeter is called a *two-way system*. A *three-way system* adds a *midrange* driver to handle the frequencies in the middle (figure 9–2). There are also a few four-way and five-way systems on the market.

In two-way and more complex systems, a circuit called a *crossover* divides the frequencies so that each driver receives only the frequencies it's supposed to reproduce. The crossover does not slice off each driver's portion sharply, but overlaps them to some degree around a *crossover frequency* (figure 8–2).

The number of drivers in a system is not necessarily an index of quality. The fewer the drivers, the more easily they can be matched and blended; but the more drivers used, the smaller

Fig. 9-1. *Exploded view of a cone driver. The signal from the amplifier, passing through the voice-coil (wound around a small metallic tube, just left of center), generates a varying magnetic field which makes the coil move within the field of the magnet (large ring, second from right). The coil drives the cone diaphragm (at left), which moves the air. The other parts shown are primarily for support and alignment. (Courtesy of Bose)*

the frequency range each one will handle, and the better each can be tailored to its job.

Even a single-driver system has advantages: it is *phase-coherent*—that is, all the sound frequencies it radiates reach the ear at the same time (more on this in chapter 10). But, since good woofers make poor tweeters (and vice versa), single-driver systems can rarely cover the full range of sound, nor can they distribute highs as evenly as those with separate tweeters and woofers.

A two-way system gains an extended range and wider treble dispersion, but the frequency where sound "crosses over" from its woofer to its tweeter falls right among the frequencies to which the ear is most sensitive, making it difficult to keep the sound natural at that point. A three-way system moves the crossover points to less troublesome frequencies but gives the designer two crossovers to deal with instead of one.

Fig. 9-2. Three-way speaker, with grille removed, showing (top to bottom) dome tweeter, dome midrange, and cone woofer. The controls to the right vary the midrange and high-frequency levels. (Courtesy of Yamaha)

In general, a three-way speaker will handle a wider frequency range than a two-way, a four-way will do better yet, and so on. However, a well-designed two-way system will sound far better than a poorly designed or cheaply made five-way system. Moreover, as the number of drivers and crossovers increases, so does the system's cost. The problem of phase coherency also grows more complex. Some authorities claim that the differences made by coherent phasing is unimportant. Still, phase-coherent speakers often do sound clearer than others.

Phase problems occur because common drivers differ in depth. When the music covers a broad enough range of frequencies to be split between different drivers, the high frequencies, from the shallow tweeter, may reach your ear a fraction of a second before the low ones from the deeper-coned woofer. Some designers tackle this difference by using flat-fronted woofers, others by slanting or stepping the cabinet front (figure 9–3 A & B) so that the tweeter is recessed to be even with the back of the woofer. Others use crossovers that delay the higher frequencies before they reach the tweeter. Since the crossover circuits also change the phase of different frequencies, they must be designed for phase coherency as well.

Multi-way speakers often have controls, either in back or behind the grille, to adjust the output of the tweeter and, sometimes, midrange, to match the woofer's output so as to balance the sound for a room's acoustics or to adjust it for personal preferences. The manufacturer's recommended adjustment points are frequently shown on these controls. These recommended settings aren't sacrosanct (or why would there be controls?); they do make a good starting point for your own experiments in finding the tonal balance that best suits your listening.

Boxing in the Bass

The box that holds the woofer—its *enclosure*—is as important as the woofer itself. This is because the woofer cone radiates sound waves from its back as well as its front. The front and back waves are "out of phase"—that is, when the speaker is pushing the air in front, it's pulling the air in back. If the air from the back were to mix with the air in the front, the push and pull would cancel each other and smother the sound. (This is only a problem at low frequencies.)

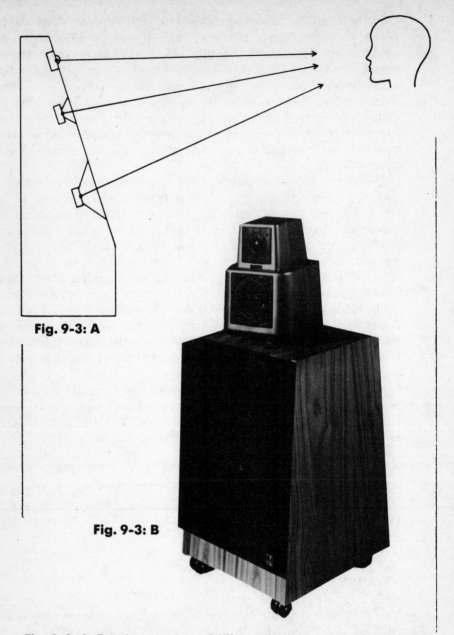

Fig. 9-3: A

Fig. 9-3: B

Fig. 9-3: A, B. *When speakers of different depth are mounted in a common vertical plane, their sounds can reach the listener at slightly different times, creating phasing problems. Mounting the speakers on a sloping plane (A) or staggering them (B) can help solve these problems. (Courtesy of Thiel [A] and KEF [B])*

Speaker designers have found three basic ways to deal with this: 1) to put the speaker on a board (*baffle*) so big that the back wave can't get around it; 2) to seal the back wave in a box; and 3) to build an unsealed box that diverts the path of the back wave. We'll say more about these techniques in chapter 10.

Speakers and Stereo

As listeners have become more aware of stereo imaging (the sense of instrument locations in space—see chapter 7), so have speaker designers. Most speakers now have all their drivers one above the other in a vertical line, as this has been found to improve imaging. Others add extra drivers for imaging purposes: one or two manufacturers add to each speaker a tweeter handling the high frequencies from the other channel, on the theory that some problems in stereo perception are caused by each ear's also hearing the signal from the speaker on the other ear's side. The signal from the extra tweeter supposedly cancels such "interaural crosstalk." Another approach is to use many drivers, facing in different directions. This enriches the image by adding controlled reflections from all around the room.

10 Speakers III: Typical and Atypical

There are nine and sixty ways to constructing tribal lays,
And—every—single—one—of—them—is—right!
                                        —Rudyard Kipling

Kipling's observation also holds true for loudspeaker systems. But while every single way is right, it can also be wrong, if not done well. And no way is perfect, so speaker designers follow a diversity of approaches to reach as close to perfection as they can. Each approach has its advantages and drawbacks, and to choose intelligently, you should have a basic acquaintance with the principles involved.

Knowing a speaker's design principles won't tell you how it sounds; only your ears can gather the evidence that counts. Still, you'll also hear so much about how speakers are designed that you may well wish to know what all those buzzwords mean. You'll find most of them defined in this chapter. If you want to know more about speaker construction, read it through. If you only want to learn what one or two terms mean, just skim the italicized key words until you find those you want.

The typical speaker system, as we said in the preceding chapter, consists of two or three drivers, a crossover to feed the proper frequencies to each driver, and a box which not only holds the drivers and crossover but helps control the bass. Usually, the woofer is a shallow cone, the tweeter a small dome, and the midrange driver, if there is one, is either another cone or dome.

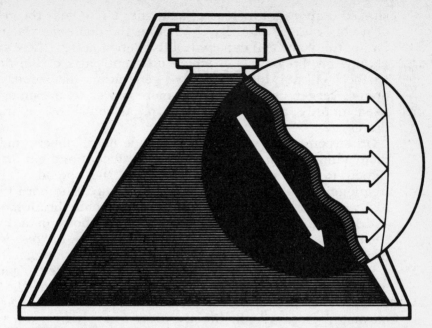

Fig. 10-1. *In the Walsh driver, the slope of the downward-firing cone converts up-and-down vibrations into lateral sound waves. (Courtesy of Ohm)*

The *cone* speaker was shown in some detail in figure 9–1. Its *voice coil* converts electrical power from the amplifier into mechanical motion, driving the *diaphragm* (cone), which in turn moves the air to generate sound. The coil moves because it is surrounded by a magnet: the current from the amplifier creates a magnetic field as it passes through the coil; the field varies with the signal, alternately pushing and pulling against the fixed field of the surrounding magnet. Most speakers work on this principle.

One variation on the cone, the Walsh driver, radiates not only front and rear but also to the sides. Its directional pattern is, in fact, a cylinder of sound radiating outward. The driver itself looks like a conventional cone driver with deep sides, and faces down into its enclosure instead of outward from its box. According to its designers, sound waves move down the cone's steep sides as circular ripples, generating a cylindrical sound wave as they travel down the slope (figure 10–1). In some speaker systems using this driver, the rear is covered so that sound radiates over an angle of only 180 degrees instead of the full 360-degree circle.

The *dome* works in the same way as a conventional cone driver, except that its voice coil drives the outer rim of a dome-shaped diaphragm instead of a smaller circle near the center of a cone-shaped one. By contacting the dome over a wider circle, the voice coil can control its motion better; there's less chance of "breakup," in which different parts of the driver surface vibrate independently, generating distortion. The dome's larger coil can handle more power, too. Domes are used mainly as tweeters, and occasionally as midrange drivers.

Other common tweeter types include horn, ribbon, and orthodynamic. *Horn tweeters* are very efficient and can be designed to give excellent control over the spread of high frequencies, both horizontally and vertically. The horn is not really a driver but a device to control and smooth the air motion a driver produces; the driver behind the horn in a home speaker may be any of several types; one is made of "piezoelectric" elements that flex in response to electrical signals.

In *ribbon tweeters,* a thin metal ribbon, suspended in a magnetic field, takes the place of both the voice coil and the diaphragm of cone or dome drivers. As a result, the magnet's field moves the entire ribbon directly, instead of driving a voice coil which only contacts the diaphragm along a circle. This, plus the ribbon's lightness, gives many ribbon tweeters low distortion and excellent transient response (the ability to follow rapid sounds, such as guitar plucks or drumbeats).

Another tweeter type, sometimes called *orthodynamic,* uses a thin, flat diaphragm with a flat voice coil printed or etched onto it. Its action and properties are like those of ribbon; JVC, in fact, calls their version a Dyna-Flat ribbon, while others refer to this type as a "leaf" or use such trade names as Infinity's EMIT and Wharfedale's Isotweeter. (One reason the type is so little known, though widely used, is that each manufacturer has a different name for it.)

Yet another variant is the Heil AMT (Air-Motion Transformer) driver. It, too, uses a film with a flat voice coil printed on it. But instead of moving as a flat sheet, it is pleated, and is arranged in a magnetic field that makes the pleats contract like those of a squeezed accordion, shooting out air the way you'd shoot a pea by squeezing it between your fingers.

The more points at which a driver's diaphragm is driven, the less likely it is to experience "breakup" distortion. Some manufacturers tackle the problem by modifying conventional cone designs. They may make their speaker cones of stiffer, less resonant materials or fill the hollows of the cones with rigid foam. They may replace the cone with flat diaphragms of such stiff, light materials as aircraft-type metal honeycomb. Or they may drive a single, flat diaphragm with several strategically located voice coils.

Avoiding breakup is another reason for the popularity of the dome, ribbon, and leaf tweeters. As we'll see later, similar techniques, and others, are used to solve the same problem in other frequency ranges, too.

Baffles and Boxes

In the last chapter, we mentioned three ways to keep waves leaving the back of a woofer from canceling the waves leaving its front: mounting the speaker in the center of a very big "baffle" board, enclosing it in a box that sealed the back waves in, and enclosing it in a box that releases some of the back waves in a controlled and useful fashion. Most speakers use box enclosures.

Large enclosures that box in the back waves are called 'infinite baffles," because they act more or less like a flat baffle of infinite size. Smaller enclosures that box in the waves are called "acoustic-suspension" or "air-suspension" types, because the springiness of the air within the box is used as part of the woofer's suspension system.

Because they don't use the energy coming from the rear of the speaker cone, these designs reduce speaker efficiency—the amount of sound delivered for each watt of power produced by the amplifier. To avoid such waste, some designers put carefully designed vents in their enclosures, utilizing the speaker's back wave. If done correctly, the path length from the rear of the cone through the vent will be just long enough to make the front and rear waves in phase with each other, reinforcing the sound at the frequencies where the speaker most needs help. (In some designs the vent is covered with a "passive radiator," essentially another woofer with no voice coil or electrical connection to the amplifier. This should not be considered an extra woofer but merely a sophisticated version of the vent.)

In the past, vented, or "bass-reflex," enclosures had a poor reputation. (This may be why the type has so many other names: "Helmholtz-resonator," "tuned-port," and "ported" enclosure.) Designed by crude trial-and-error methods, many of them added false resonance to the bass. Today, the basic design of vented enclosures can be accurately calculated beforehand. These calculations cover size, efficiency, distortion, and low-frequency response—not just how low the speaker goes, but the shape of its response curve at low frequencies.

The possible variables in vented-speaker design were explored and formulated by Neville Thiele, an Australian acoustician, about twenty years ago. In some of the designs derived from Thiele's work, only part of the frequency shaping is done by the speaker and cabinet, with the rest handled by an external "equalizer" box connected to the sound system's amplifier. Such speakers can be much smaller than unequalized speakers with similar performance. However, the speaker and its custom equalizer must be designed together for this process to work.

Occasionally, it is possible to correct slight low-frequency deficiencies with accessory equalizers (see chapter 24). However, the results are never as precise as those from custom-matched speaker/equalizer systems, and you run a risk of damaging the speaker by feeding it too much bass—especially if your system does not include a sharp, low-cut (or "rumble") filter to eliminate subsonic frequencies. This is important, as bass-boost circuits also usually boost these inaudible frequencies. While these frequencies are too low to be heard, they can still overload your speakers.

Horn speakers are the most efficient of all speaker designs, requiring only a small fraction of the power typically needed for closed-box systems. A good horn should have a long, gradual taper. Since this would ordinarily result in horns too large for even the great halls of a mansion, the sides of the horn are folded back on themselves several times, and the horn is often placed in a corner, so that the room's walls and floor act as extensions of it. The resulting speakers are still rather large, but manageable, and their complicated carpentry makes them expensive. But the real reason for their limited popularity today is stereo: it is often difficult to find even one free corner where one can put a horn; finding two on the same wall, the right distance apart for stereo, is even harder.

The *transmission line* speaker, sometimes called a *labyrinth* (figure 10–2), also sends the back wave on a complex path out of the speaker box. But the object here is not to make the back wave audible (as in the reflex) but to squelch it through absorption in the padded lining of the labyrinth. The result is often good sound, but low efficiency.

Boxes, Barrels, and Pyramids

Lately, designers have been changing the traditional shapes of box speakers. One innovation is to taper the box. This is done

Fig. 10-2. *In a transmission-line enclosure, the back wave is gradually absorbed as it passes through a softly-lined labyrinth.* (Courtesy IMF)

to make the speaker phase-coherent, as mentioned in chapter 9; but that's not the only reason. Air in a box resonates, undesirably favoring some frequencies at the expense of others. The more even its dimensions, the stronger its resonance. If the speaker tapers, its dimensions constantly change, preventing strong resonances by spreading them over many frequencies instead of concentrating them at one or two.

Tapering is also one of the tactics used against *diffraction*—high-frequency reflections from the speaker cabinet which muddy the treble and the stereo image. Tapering helps because it makes the cabinet narrower near the tweeter, reducing the area from which sound can bounce. Other anti-diffraction tactics include rounded or beveled cabinet edges, grilles without side frames to reflect sound, and soft areas surrounding the tweeter.

Some cabinets are curved, often into a cylinder or barrel—usually to minimize panel vibrations more than to prevent diffraction. When a speaker cabinet vibrates, its panels act like random extra drivers, producing odd effects on frequency response and phasing. The more rigid the panels—whether due to the cabinet's shape, thickness, or internal bracing—the less the cabinet will vibrate. When you rap the panels of a well-designed speaker cabinet, you should hear a short sharp "thwock!" rather than a hollow "clonk."

Other designers have shaped their systems to keep the woofers as close as possible to the nearest wall, either by keeping the box relatively shallow (figure 10–3A) or by mounting the woofer on the side or top of the box (figure 10–3B). This is to prevent interactions between the sound from the woofer and the reflections of that sound from the wall behind the speaker, which can cause variations of anywhere from 6 dB to 20 dB in a speaker's response.

Variations on the Theme

A small but significant number of speaker systems use neither cones nor domes nor boxes. They take an entirely different tack, using broad, flat diaphragms far larger than conventional cone speakers; the surfaces of these diaphragms are driven at all points, like those of ribbon and leaf tweeters.

In fact, some speaker companies (such as Apogee) make ribbon speakers that cover the full frequency range. There are also full-range speakers using the same principle as the orthodynamic tweeter, with a voice coil unwound and laid down on the large diaphragm in a snakelike pattern, working against the fields of bar magnets laid in strips (figure 10–4). (The Magneplanar is the best known of this kind.)

The oldest and best known of these flat-surface speakers is the electrostatic type, such as the Quad. Here the speaker is basically one large diaphragm, suspended between two oppositely charged electric grids. The signal is fed to the diaphragm, varying its electric charge, attracting it first to one grid and then the other. This design, like the other two, was once confined to tweeters but is now being applied to full-range systems.

Yet another type is the BES Geostatic. Here a molded plastic diaphragm is moved by several voice coils. The diaphragm is divided into sections, each responsible for a different frequency range.

All these types have much in common. Their diaphragms can't move very far, so those diaphragms must be big in order

Fig. 10-3: A

Fig. 10-3: B

Fig. 10-3: A, B. Frequency irregularities due to interactions between sounds from the woofer and those reflected from the wall behind it and the floor can be minimized by keeping the woofer close to those surfaces, by making the speaker cabinet flat (A), or by mounting the woofers on the cabinet sides, near the bottom (B). (Courtesy of Boston Acoustics [A] and Allison [B])

Fig. 10-4. *Planar speakers, like these Magneplanars, are tall and thin and take up little room, but should be several feet from the rear wall, as shown.* (Courtesy of Magneplanar)

to move enough air. This makes the speakers big enough to serve as their own baffles, keeping low-frequency waves at the back of the speaker from interfering too severely with those at the front. Consequently, such speakers are not enclosed in boxes. They often surpass other designs in tonal clarity but usually lack deep bass. They tend to beam their high frequencies narrowly because of their size (for good dispersion, a tweeter must be smaller than the sound waves it produces). To prevent such beaming, some planar designs have small, independently driven tweeter sections.

They are also *dipoles*—speakers which radiate sound both front and rear. The sound from the front of the speaker reaches you directly, while the sound from the back reaches you by reflection from the walls, floor, and ceiling of your room. The resulting sound depends a good deal on the room and how the speakers are placed in it. The reflected sound reaches you a fraction of a second after the direct sound, which can add depth and spaciousness or simply muddy the sound, depending on how well the speaker is placed. With dipole speakers, stereo images tend to be extremely wide, and the apparent location of instruments is more likely to remain fixed in the room as you move around; with ordinary speakers, when you move to one side, the image is likely to collapse into the nearer speaker.

There are logical reasons behind all these diverse speaker designs. Good and bad examples of each type abound. Your ears, not your prejudices should govern your choice.

Within each basic design approach, speaker designers must reconcile three factors—size, efficiency, and the ability to reproduce low bass. The better a speaker is in any of these areas, the worse it is in the others. For example, a small speaker can either have low efficiency and good, deep bass or high efficiency and poor bass—and efficient speakers with deep bass tend to be big.

Nor can inefficient speakers usually handle as much power as efficient ones. This plus inefficiency narrows the range between the minimum power needed for reasonably loud sound and the maximum the speaker can handle, expecially in the low bass. If you like very loud sound, small speakers may be a poor choice for you.

Some systems get around this problem by using small "satellite" speakers which are designed to handle only the frequencies from about 100 Hz or 200 Hz on up. A single, large "subwoofer" handles the lower frequencies (figure 10–5). Low frequencies are relatively nondirectional, so little stereo effect is lost by having both channels of bass come from the same speaker, and the fact that the bass and treble come from different places isn't too apparent if the crossover frequency is low and the subwoofer is placed between the two satellites.

This system has several advantages. It usually costs less than two full-range speakers with equivalent bass performance. Because the satellites are small, they can more easily be placed where they'll sound best in a given room. And efficiency can be high because the small speakers handle no low bass and the bass speaker can be large enough to do its job.

A few speakers use electronics in other ways than the equalizers mentioned earlier. Some have "room equalizers," allowing you to make several basic tone adjustments to match the speaker's response to your room's acoustics. Others have circuits which limit the input to the speaker when there's danger of the speaker being damaged by incipient overload. Still others use feedback circuits to monitor the speaker's output and compare it to the input signal. If the two don't match, the speaker is distorting or failing to reproduce some frequencies. A signal is then fed back to the amplifier to effect a correction. Speakers of this kind usually come with special amplifiers.

Fig. 10-5. *Satellite speakers, with a matching subwoofer.* (Courtesy of Acoustic Research)

Luckily, you don't have to remember everything you've encountered on this dizzying tour of loudspeaker design principles. But it will give you a basic idea of available options and design considerations, and what they mean to you. It won't make you an expert but will help you nod appreciatively instead of gaping like a goldfish at the technical terms you encounter.

11 Amplifiers I: A Sense of Power

The amplifier is the heart of any sound system. Through it pass the signals from every program source in the system—tape, phonograph, AM, FM, CD, and video—en route to the loudspeakers.

An amplifier builds up the weak signals from these sound sources, making them powerful enough to drive the loudspeakers. In low-priced systems, the amplifier is usually invisible, because it's built into a *receiver* (figure 11–1), which combines, in one unit, the functions of an amplifier and tuner. Expensive systems are more likely to use "basic" or "power" amplifiers (figure 11–2), which have few or no controls and whose only function is to make weak signals powerful and feed them to the speakers. Such amplifiers are meant to be used with separate *preamplifiers* which contain the controls, such as volume and input selection. There are also *integrated amplifiers* (figure 11–3), which combine the functions of the power amp and preamp.

The form that is right for you depends, again, on your specific needs. A receiver does the work of an amplifier, preamplifier, and tuner, while taking up less space and costing less than the three components it replaces. But it's also less flexible: when you buy a receiver, you can't pick the features and performance of each section separately, nor can you trade in the sections separately if one part becomes outdated or if you want to upgrade that section's performance. For most listeners, these restrictions aren't particularly bothersome.

A receiver may not be a good choice, however, when your amplifier and tuner needs don't match. In most receivers, both amplifier power and tuner quality tend to rise as you move to more expensive models. That's fine for most users. But you'd be better off with separates if you could get along with a modest amplifier, but lived where FM reception was poor and a better tuner was needed. The same would be true if you needed a powerful amplifier but only a modest tuner (for instance, if you lived in a city, near all the FM stations you wanted to hear).

If you want a separate amplifier or tuner (or don't want a tuner at all), you still have to decide between an integrated amplifier and a separate preamp and power amp. Integrated amplifiers are more compact and less expensive than comparable separates. Like receivers, though, they limit your choices. If you want a control-studded preamp section but only a modestly powered amp, or a simple preamp and high amplifier power, you'll have to buy separates. In the highest ranges of power, price, and quality, you'll need to buy separates in any case.

Separate amplifiers and preamplifiers give you greater choice, but at greater expense. But if you can afford a separate power amplifier and preamplifier, there are practical advantages to be gained. If you want high power, for example, you'll usually have to buy a separate amp to get it. Most high-power amplifiers are so big that building preamp or tuner sections into them would make them impractically bulky. Even with small amps, separates can have a slight performance edge— theoretically, it's possible for preamp performance to be adversely hampered by an amplifier (especially a powerful one) in the same box. And you might simply want to have as much flexibility as possible in making your choices, purchasing whatever amp and preamp you think best, even if they're different brands.

Amplifiers aren't perfect, but they come closer to perfection than any other components in the hi-fi chain. As a result, their specs (other than power) don't tell you much; the imperfections we know how to specify are mostly tamed, while the faults we haven't tamed we cannot yet measure. Even so, we'll talk about specifications later, so you'll understand them when they're thrown at you.

How Much Power Do You Need?

The main difference between amplifiers (but not the only one) is the amount of power they deliver. The more power, the

Fig. 11-1. A receiver can usually be recognized by the presence of both a tuning dial and a prominent volume control. (Courtesy Onkyo)

Fig. 11-2. A preamplifier (top) and a power amplifier. (Courtesy of NAD)

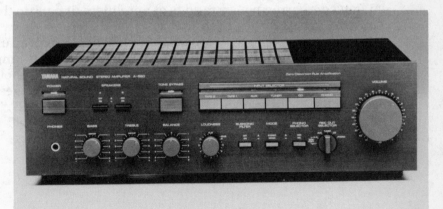

Fig. 11-3. An integrated amplifier combines both preamplifier and power amp, and frequently resembles a bulky preamp. (Courtesy Yamaha)

better, in most cases. But the more powerful the amplifier, the more it costs. So you want enough power without expensive excess.

How much power you really need depends on several factors. A principal one is your speaker's efficiency. The more efficiently the speaker converts your amplifier's power into sound (see chapter 8), the less amplifier power you need to reach a given sound volume. Some common speakers require up to a hundred times more power than others to achieve the same sound output level (an efficiency difference of 20 dB).

The bigger your room, the more power you need. Double the room's volume, and you double the power required to fill it with music. Fill it with padded, sound-absorbent furniture, and you might double your power needs again. If you keep your listening down to background-music levels, you need a lot less power —if you reproduce rock music at the deafening levels typical of rock concerts, you need a lot more.

Unfortunately, efficiency as such is never listed on speaker specification sheets. You can deduce it from the speaker's rated sensitivity (see chapter 9) and recommended minimum and maximum power ratings, but that's all. Assuming that a speaker's rated sensitivity is the same as its efficiency, we'd get the following power requirements for an average living room of about 3,000 cubic feet (see figure 11–4, page 76).

Note how fast the power requirements shoot up: raising the level 10 dB (which only makes the music sound twice as loud to us) raises the power required by a factor of ten—and raising the level 20 dB multiplies the power required by one hundred. Lowering speaker efficiency by 10 dB also multiplies the power required tenfold—and even an efficiency loss of 3 dB doubles the power requirement.

When comparing power ratings of amplifiers, it pays to think about the ratio, rather than the absolute difference between them. For example, a 20-watt amplifier is twice as powerful as a 10-watt one, a significant difference; but a 100-watt amp is only slightly more powerful than a 90-watt one, even though the difference is also 10 watts. It has therefore been suggested that amplifier power be measured not in watts but in "dBW"— the difference in decibels between the output power and one watt:

Watts	dBW	Watts	dBW	Watts	dBW
1.0	0	10.0	10	100	20
1.25	1	12.5	11	125	21
1.6	2	16	12	160	22
2.0	3	20	13	200	23
2.5	4	25	14	250	24
3.2	5	32	15	320	25
4.0	6	40	16	400	26
5.0	7	50	17	500	27
6.3	8	63	18	630	28
8.0	9	80	19	800	29

Table 11-1. *Amplifier power in watts vs. dBW.*

Like many worthwhile ideas, this one has never really caught on.

The main thing to remember when comparing the power of amplifiers is that an amplifier must be at least 50 percent more powerful than another—and preferably 100 percent—before the difference can be considered significant.

That still doesn't answer the question of how much power is enough. Figure 11–4 doesn't quite tell us, because the figures there are only for average sound levels. But music is full of peaks which, for brief instants, require more amplifier power. If you're listening to a phonograph record at a level that requires an average of 5 watts from your amplifier, the rule of thumb is that those peaks will require about ten times as much power—i.e., 50 watts. Compact Discs, whose peaks are less restrained, might require 100 watts or more for those brief instants. If your amplifier can't deliver that power, those peaks will be distorted—but the distortion will last only for the duration of the volume peak.

Rules of thumb are just that, though. Music contains many small peaks which require less than 50 or 100 watts to reproduce, and occasional ones which require a good bit more. A modest amplifier will reproduce most peaks without distortion and will only distort an occasional, brief climactic moment. Yet even a very powerful amp might still distort a peak now and then.

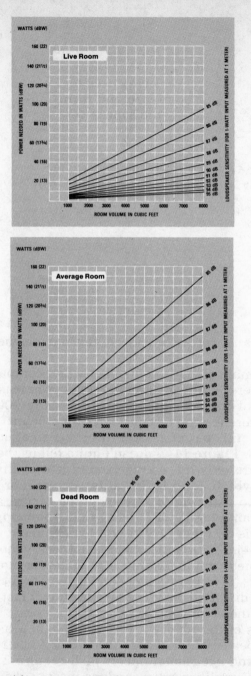

Fig. 11-4. Amplifier power requirements for typical rooms and speaker sensitivities. (Courtesy of *High Fidelity* Magazine)

Many amplifiers have meters which show you how much power they're delivering at any moment. If the speakers in a showroom are connected to such a metered amplifier (most showrooms can easily arrange this), you can see at a glance how much power is being used for any sound level. Because of differences in room size and furnishings, this is not a totally accurate guide to the power you would need when playing those speakers at home; but it gives you some idea.

In our own homes, we've noted the average power levels shown on our amplifiers' meters. In a small bedroom, using fairly efficient speakers, power levels usually run about 1 watt or less for TV talk and dramatic shows (which have a small dynamic range), between 5 and 10 watts for music. In a large living room, using less efficient speakers playing digital Compact Discs with extremely wide dynamic range, we've seen peaks of several hundred watts when listening full-blast.

You probably won't consciously notice the difference between modest and high-power amps unless you've really skimped on amplifier power. But your unconscious mind reacts to it; you may feel like turning down the volume a bit so that fewer peaks are big enough to strain the amp, or get tired of listening sooner than you expected, due to "listener fatigue."

Up to a point, more amplifier power will let you listen at a louder level, because you'll be able to turn up the volume more before you sense distortion. But when the sound is loud enough for you, you will turn up the volume no further. At that point, the only difference you'll note between an amplifier that can deliver just enough power and one that has power in reserve will be less listener fatigue; you'll listen longer and more happily. Ample power means cleaner, more pleasurable sound.

How Much Power Are You Getting?

For all these reasons, the amplifier specifications which require your closest attention are those relating to power. That, after all, is what you buy an amplifier for.

But some people look *only* at the power rating. As a result, a few years back some manufacturers found ways to con buyers by raising power ratings without actually raising power. At that point, the government stepped in and regulated amplifier power ratings—the only hi-fi specification to receive official attention. Today, amplifier power must be stated in terms so stringent that the buyer, rather than the manufacturer, always gets the benefit of the doubt. This may make amplifier power ratings seem unnecessarily complex and hedged with qualifications. But those details are there—by law—for your information and protection.

A typical stereo amplifier's power specification therefore reads like this:

> 50 watts per channel, minimum continuous power, both channels driven, into 8-ohm loads, 20–20,000 Hz, at no more than 0.015% total harmonic distortion.

This is a mouthful, but all of it is necessary to show how much power the amplifier really can deliver.

Taking it from the top, we see that the amplifier can actually deliver 100 watts—50 from each of its two stereo channels. *Continuous* (or *average*) describes the time frame over which the power is measured. Since any audio signal varies continuously from 0 to a peak value, we measure the average power over the length of the wave, rather than its momentary (and misleading) peak value. (Average power is also sometimes miscalled *rms,* for *root-mean-square,* a mathematical term used in voltage measurement.) *Continuous power* means that this is the amount of power the amplifier can put out for prolonged periods (several minutes), not just for an instant.

We measure power with both channels driven at once because measuring channels one at a time would be misleading. With most amplifiers, one channel can borrow a bit of power from the other if some of the second channel's power wasn't being used, making the borrower channel seem more powerful. But to measure only that first channel's power would be unrealistic, since, in music, if the sound is loud in one channel it's also likely to be loud in the other one; thus full power is often needed in both channels at the same time.

Most amplifiers can deliver more power into a speaker whose impedance (see chapter 8) is 4 ohms than into a speaker with an impedance of 8 ohms. (More power doesn't necessarily mean louder sound in this case.) But since the 8-ohm test is the more stringent one, and since 8-ohm speakers are most common, the 8-ohm figure must be stated on home amplifier spec sheets. (Car-amplifier spec sheets usually give the 4-ohm figure, because virtually all car speakers have 4-ohm impedances.)

A good amplifier should be able to deliver its full power over the entire range of audio frequencies, from 20 Hz to 20,000 Hz, as in the example above. Some amplifiers can only deliver full power over a more limited range, such as 40 Hz to 18,000 Hz;

this is not too much of a problem at the treble end, where full power is rarely required, but it is a problem at the bass end, where most amplifier power is actually used.

Many good amplifiers can deliver full power over a wider frequency range, such as 10 Hz to 50,000 Hz. Theoretically this improves performance within the audio range and gives assurance that full power will be available at all audio frequencies. Amplifiers rated as being able to deliver their full power only over the range from 20 Hz to 20,000 Hz can usually still cover a wider range at less than full power. In that case, the amplifier might list a *power bandwidth* of 20 Hz to 20 kHz and a *frequency response* of, say, 5 Hz to 100 kHz.

An amplifier's distortion varies with the power it's delivering (which is a function of how far you turn up the volume and the strength of the signal being amplified). The more distortion you can tolerate, the more power you can squeeze out of an amplifier—up to a point. Beyond that point, power stops increasing when you turn up the volume or increase the input signal—but distortion keeps increasing. If you graph an amplifier's power versus distortion (figure 11–5), you'll usually see that its distortion is fairly low at most power levels, but begins rising rapidly once a certain power level is reached. The amplifier's rated power is usually right at the corner in the distortion curve (10 watts, in our figure).

(The manufacturer has some leeway in choosing a power rating; the amp in figure 11–5, for instance, could well be rated as delivering either 10 watts at 0.5% distortion or 15 watts at 2%. In practice, the maker usually chooses some value that's a multiple of 5 or 10 watts—25-watt and 30-watt ratings are common, while 27-watt ratings are rare.)

Federal Trade Commission regulations specify that the distortion rating should be the maximum the amplifier produces at its rated power and all lower power levels. The figure given is for total harmonic distortion (THD). The figure for intermodulation distortion (IM) is usually listed, too; even if it's not, it's normally close to the THD figure, which means it's fairly low.

Knowing what all these specifications mean in detail isn't all that important. But keep in mind that only a power rating which includes all this information is meaningful (or legal, for that matter), that the stated distortion should be low (below 0.5 percent), and that power bandwidth should run from at least 20 Hz to 20,000 Hz.

Most of the time, in any case, the amplifier will be loafing along at a lot less than its maximum rated power—and less than its maximum rated distortion, too.

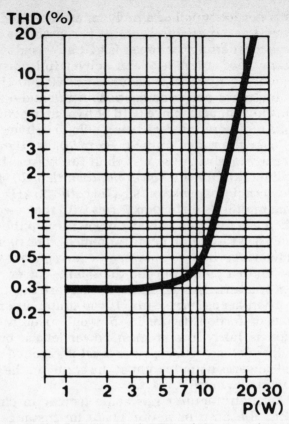

Fig. 11-5. *A graph of power vs. distortion for a typical small amplifier. Note how distortion is quite low up to the rated power point, then shoots up sharply.*

Supplementary Specifications

Reputable makers of amplifiers usually tell you more about an amplifier's performance than merely its power output and distortion at that power level. Some manufacturers list more performance factors than others, often on the basis of what they consider most important or what they think *you* will. Here are some of the additional specifications you may find:

Dynamic headroom tells you how well an amplifier will handle brief musical peaks requiring more than its rated maximum power. It is expressed as the ratio (in dB) between an amplifier's rated, continuous power output and the amount it can put out for 0.02 seconds without distorting noticeably.

Amplifier designers disagree about how much headroom is

desirable. Some feel that by sacrificing ability to handle peaks beyond the amplifier's rated power, the amp can be made to sound "tighter" and more accurate between peaks. Others feel that this is not the case, or that the great increase in peak ability is worth small tradeoffs elsewhere.

As a result, the specifications for some amplifiers proudly state that the amps have 0 dB of headroom, while others claim as much as 6 dB (i.e., these amps can briefly deliver four times their rated power). Most amplifiers fall between 2 dB and 3 dB; 50-watt amps with such headroom have peak capabilities of 80 and 100 watts, respectively. Dynamic headroom is useful, but probably most useful when the amplifier's continuous power is low.

Total harmonic distortion and *intermodulation distortion* (see chapter 6) are lower on amplifiers and preamplifiers than on any other type of component. In this respect, most amplifiers are so good that their specs tell you little about how they sound. For example, if an amplifier with 0.001 percent distortion sounds better than one with only 0.1 percent distortion, it's probably not because of its lower distortion. For a power amplifier, distortion (of any kind) should be no more than 0.5 percent.

Signal-to-noise ratios (S/N) are usually higher in amps and preamps than other components. They should be as high as possible, with figures around 75 dB a rock-bottom minimum.

The damping factor measures the amplifier's ability to control the speaker's motion. Technically speaking, it's the ratio between the amplifier's output impedance and the speaker's input impedance. The figure (often stated only for low frequencies, where it matters most) usually ranges from about 40 (short for a ratio of 1 to 40) up. In practice, though, the resistance of the speaker cable changes this ratio sufficiently so that very high damping factors make little difference.

Slew factor and *Slew rate* measure how fast an amplifier can react to signals. The theory behind these measurements is that amplifiers will distort, briefly, when processing signals more rapidly than they can comfortably handle, a phenomenon known as *slewing-induced distortion (SID)*. Some designers believe that the fast signals (including transients such as drumbeats and guitar plucks, or tones within the signal that are above the audio range) may cause SID in "slow" amplifiers, which can't handle the high frequencies involved. Other designers, though, feel that nothing is gained by being able to handle frequencies much beyond the audio range, and that the best way to prevent SID is to filter out such frequencies.

Slew rate is the more commonly cited version of this rating, though its meaning (which is expressed in volts per microsecond), varies with the amplifier's power or output voltage rating. A slew rate of 80 V/μS, for example, would be far more remarkable in a 30-watt amp than in a 200-watt one.

Slew factor, the more informative but less used version of this rating, is a ratio between the highest frequency an amplifier can handle without slewing and the highest audio frequency (20 kHz). A slew factor of 5, for example, means that the amplifier could handle frequencies up to 100 kHz (20 kHz x 5) without slewing, and means the same thing regardless of the amplifier's power.

Several specifications relate to an amplifier's inputs. *Sensitivity*, for example, tells how strong a signal is needed to drive an amplifier to a specified output level (usually one-half volt for preamps, one watt for amps) with the volume turned to maximum; the lower, the better. *Maximum input level* tells how strong a signal you can feed in before distortion begins; the higher the better. *Input impedance* tells how much the amplifier will load down whatever device is feeding the signal to it; this figure should also be as high as possible. For the most part, the only one of these specs worth paying much attention to is maximum input level.

These figures vary with the type of input, and are most critical with phono inputs. We'll hear more about that when we get to cartridges, in chapter 16.

Separation applies only to stereo performance, and describes the difference in dB between a signal fed into one channel and the amount of that signal leaking into the other. Stereo *crosstalk* is basically the same thing. In practice, the two terms are often used interchangeably. Once in a while, though, you'll find someone referring to crosstalk as the amount of leakage between inputs—the amount of tuner signal you hear, for example, when you're listening to your Compact Disc player. Although this is actually a more serious problem than inter-channel signal leakage, it's rarely covered in the specs. If you run into this problem, you can solve it by turning off the undesired signal source or turning down the source's output level control (if it has one).

Crosstalk and separation figures should be as high as possible. Ideally, they should be about as high as the signal-to-noise ratio, though they are almost never that good.

But specifications are hardly the whole story. After power, buyers usually pay most attention to an amplifier's control facilities. These are surveyed in the next chapter.

12 Amplifiers II: A Sense of Control

The amplifier section doesn't just power the speakers—it's also the stereo system's nerve center, where the main controls adjust the sound. These controls can alter the sound level, tonal quality, and many more things. All of these features are useful, but you may not find all of them necessary. Only you can tell which ones will serve your purposes.

In the most elaborate systems, two separate components handle the power and control functions: the power amplifier drives the speakers and the preamplifier selects the signal source and adjusts the sound. In most home systems, though, the power amplifier and preamplifier are part of the same component—an integrated amplifier or a receiver (an integrated amplifier with a radio tuner). We'll use the terms amp or amplifier and preamp interchangeably, to avoid having to say "receiver, integrated amp, or preamplifier" every time.

A preamplifier can get by with only three controls: a power switch, a volume control, and a source-selector switch. (If all the sources have their own volume controls, the amp section can get by with the selector switch alone.) Such spartan systems do exist. But most preamps have more controls than just these basic ones, and there's a surprising variety of them.

Sound-Level Controls

The control that raises and lowers the sound level may be labeled "volume" on some amplifier systems and "loudness" on others. The name does make a difference: *Volume controls* simply raise and lower the sound level. When the level goes down, our ears become far less sensitive to low frequencies and a bit less sensitive to high ones; the sound seems thin and distant. *Loudness controls* compensate for this by automatically adding more bass (and, sometimes, a bit of treble) as the level is turned down. The amount of compensation needed depends on the difference between the original sound level of the music in the studio or concert hall and its level in your room. With just enough compensation, the sound is quieter but otherwise natural. Add too much compensation and the sound becomes a little overrich, or boomy; add too little and the sound stays thin.

Unfortunately, most loudness controls give you too much or too little compensation. With these controls, the amount of compensation depends on where you set the volume control—which has only a rough relation to the sound level in your room, since room sizes and speaker efficiencies vary so much. This fixed compensation level is designed for "average" rooms and speakers, not necessarily for yours. Too little compensation won't help enough, but won't hurt, either, but since too much compensation causes boominess, the control panel should have a loudness switch to turn the compensation off. Don't buy an amp with loudness compensation that can't be shut off. (Portables and table models designed only to be used with specific speakers are an exception, since their designers are aware of the speaker efficiency involved, and can assume from the low price of such systems that they'll be used in average rooms.)

A few preamps let you match the loudness compensation to the actual sound level, with separate volume and loudness knobs. You use the loudness knob to set the amount of compensation that your room and system need, then use the volume control to adjust sound level thereafter.

Stereo systems also require a *balance* control, to adjust the relative right/left sound levels. The control is used mainly to adjust for circumstances such as speakers placed at different distances from the listener, as few recordings are imbalanced. The balance control is therefore often inconspicuous—a ring around the volume control or a small knob, for instance.

Some volume controls are adjusted in small steps rather than in a continuous sweep; some listeners find such controls easier to adjust, while others find it harder. On expensive preamps, stepped controls are often switches with separate positions for each volume level; such switches allow very precise matching between channels, without which the left/right balance can shift slightly as you change volume settings. On medium-priced equipment, stepped volume controls are more often ordinary controls, which click through a series of detents to give them the feel of the more expensive type. In either case, make sure the steps are closely spaced (no more than 1.5 dB apart, preferably 1 dB or less), so that you'll never have to choose between a setting that's a bit too loud and one that's a bit too soft.

The *muting switch* immediately cuts volume by 15 dB or 20 dB (a large amount) when pressed. It gives you a handy volume reduction when you want to answer the phone or hear who's at the door, and an equally handy way to restore your original volume level. The muting switch can also help, sometimes, if your system's fixed loudness compensation level is too strong; with the muting on, the sound level where the loudness compensation starts will be 15 dB or 20 dB lower.

Program Selection

Selector switches let you pick which program source you'll listen to: phono, tuner, video, CD, aux, etc. All but the phono inputs are *high-level* ones, designed for signals with amplitudes of a volt or two. High-level inputs can be used interchangeably—you could put the CD player on the tuner input, if you liked. The Aux (auxiliary) inputs are a sign of this: they're provided in case you want to add a program source the amplifier designers didn't think of (Compact Disc or video sound, for instance).

"Video" (or "VCR") and "Compact Disc" are new designations for what are generally plain high-level inputs. However, a growing number of receivers includes switching for both the audio (sound) and video (picture) outputs from videocassette recorders, videodisc players, and TV tuners. So a front-panel switch position labeled "Videodisc" or "VCR" may switch both audio and video signals. No harm will be done if you accidentally plug video signals into audio jacks, or vice versa, but your screen will stay dark and your speakers silent until you correct things.

Phono inputs are *low-level* circuits, designed for signals of a few millivolts (thousandths of a volt) or less—the output of a phono cartridge in a turntable. Such signals must be preamplified to match the level of the high-level signals before they can be fed to the amp; the circuits which do this give the preamplifier its name.

Phono cartridges come in two basic types: moving-magnet (with output levels of a few millivolts) and moving-coil (with output levels about one-tenth as great). Most preamps have *moving-magnet (MM) phono inputs*, but a growing number have *moving-coil (MC) inputs* as well. In the latter case, the selector switch may have both MM and MC positions, or there may be a separate MM/MC selector switch on the front or rear panel. On preamps having two phono inputs, one may be only for MM and one only for MC cartridges, or one or both inputs may be switchable for use with either type. Moving-coil cartridges can also be used with preamps having only MM inputs, if a *step-up transformer* or a *pre-preamplifier* (also called a *head amp*) is plugged in between the cartridge and the preamp.

Plugging a cartridge into the wrong input type won't harm anything. If you plug an MC cartridge into an MM input, the output signal will be weak; if you plug an MM cartridge into an MC input, the sound will be very loud and often quite distorted. If you plug a phono cartridge of either type into a high-level input, the sound will be very weak and very shrill. But once things are connected properly again, these problems disappear.

Phono inputs have another distinguishing property: *RIAA equalization*. For technical reasons, records are made with the bass cut and the treble boosted and played back with a complementary boost and cut to make the frequencies equal again. Both the recording and playback equalization follow a standard issued by the Recording Industries Association of America (RIAA). The so-called "new RIAA" standard is a nonstandard attempt to define equalization at very low frequencies, which the RIAA standard does not cover.

Tape decks have high-level outputs, but there's rarely a tape position on the main selector switch. Instead, signals from the tape deck usually come in through a separate *tape monitor* switch. This allows you to listen to the output from the tape recorder while you're making a recording.

It works like this: when you record, whatever signal you've picked with your preamp's selector switch (or with the separate *record selector,* if your preamp has one) is fed to the tape recorder. This feed takes place before the signal goes through the preamp's controls, so that you can adjust tone or volume without affecting the recording. That same signal also goes to the "off" side of the monitor switch; with the monitor off, you hear the same signal that's going to the tape deck.

With the monitor on, you hear the signal coming from the

tape deck. If you're recording and all is going well, the signal should sound identical to the signal you hear with the monitor off. If you hear a different signal, then the deck is playing a tape instead of recording it, and you must start the recording over again. On "three-head" decks (see chapter 20), you can not only tell whether the deck is recording or not, but also hear how well it is recording, and compare the original and recorded signals by flicking the monitor switch.

If the tape deck is switched off, no sound will come from your system when the monitor switch is pressed—a common cause of worry until the problem is spotted. If your amplifier lights up but you hear nothing, the tape monitor and volume controls are the first things to check.

Preamps with more than one tape monitor circuit often allow *dubbing* (copying) tapes from one deck to another, just by setting a switch. You can usually do this while monitoring either deck or while listening to something else entirely. Some such preamps let you dub from either deck to the other one, while others only let you dub in one direction. If you don't have two tape decks, you can connect an equalizer or other signal-processing device (see chapter 24) to the unused monitor circuit and use the dubbing switches to process the signal going to or coming from your tape deck.

Many amps and preamps, however, have *external processor loops* (sometimes marked "EPL") specifically to handle such add-on sound-altering accessories. Like the tape monitor, the EPL is a front-panel switch that lets you choose between a signal coming from within the preamp or an altered version of that signal, which has been fed out of the preamp and through the accessory before returning. You can also use an EPL as an extra tape-monitor loop, if necessary.

Tone Controls

In an ideal world, all recordings, all speakers, and the acoustics of all rooms would be perfect, and the sound you hear at home would be both an accurate and pleasing rendition of the original performance. But this is not an ideal world. Some recordings are too shrill, from distorted or excessive highs, while others sound dull because there aren't enough highs. Some records sound too boomy from excessive bass, while others sound thin from a bass deficiency. And your system or (more likely) your room's acoustics can also cause frequency imbalances.

That's why most preamps have *bass* and *treble tone controls*. If you have too much or too little bass or treble, you can adjust these controls until things sound the way you want them to. Well-designed bass and treble controls affect only their assigned frequencies and leave the middle frequencies alone (figure 12–1); you can get the effect of raising the middle tones by lowering both the bass and treble ones, and vice versa.

Here, too, some variations are available. Some preamps have three tone controls (bass, treble, and midrange). Some have five controls, referred to as a *five-band equalizer,* a setup allowing more precise sound control but requiring more finicky adjustment to achieve it.

Some preamps have no tone controls at all, on the theory that every extra circuit in the preamp can degrade the sound a little. For the same reason, many preamps which have tone controls to correct improper frequency balances also have *defeat* switches to remove the tone circuits from the signal path when you're not using them.

Tone controls may have other switches or knobs governing their actions. Often the *turnover* frequencies, at which the tone controls start working, can be selected by a small switch, giving you a choice of how much or how little the midrange will be affected. For example, using a lower turnover on the bass control lets you emphasize a cello's low notes without making its upper notes sound too warm, while a higher turnover adds warmth, if that is needed. Some controls go even further with *parametric* adjustments, which let you vary both the turnover frequencies and the steepness of the control curves.

Most tone controls today are ganged—that is, a single knob controls both stereo channels. Some preamps, though, have individual tone controls for each channel. Ganged controls are easier to use when correcting the frequency balance of a recording but are difficult to use when correcting for room acoustic problems, which may not be the same in both channels. A compromise design uses individual controls which are *clutched* together; you can turn both controls by turning either one, or you can turn one separately by holding the other still.

Bass boost switches usually raise the lowest frequencies by a fixed, moderate amount but leave the upper bass for the bass tone control to handle. This is designed to compensate for the reduced bass output of most speakers.

Filters, like tone controls, alter the signal's frequency balance. But while tone controls cut or boost large areas of the tonal range gently, filters only cut sharply and do so at the frequency extremes.

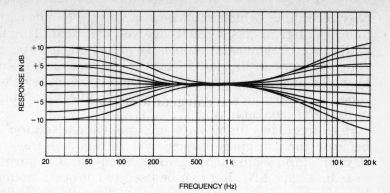

Fig. 12-1. *Typical bass and treble tone-control curves. (Courtesy of NAD)*

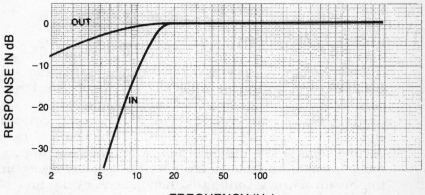

Fig. 12-2. *The action of a low-pass "rumble" filter. (Courtesy of NAD)*

At the low-frequency end of the scale are *subsonic* (or "rumble") filters (figure 12–2). These cut out very low frequencies, chiefly from turntable or record rumble (see chapter 15); it's best to cut at 20 Hz or below, though some of these filters start cutting at 30 Hz.

Subsonic frequencies can't be heard. But your power amplifier can waste a lot of its power amplifying them, and speakers can be driven into distortion (and sometimes even damaged) by attempting to reproduce them. For this reason, you should usually switch your low filter in and leave it there (especially if your tone controls are boosting the bass), except when you play recordings which you know have very low bass in them and the filter makes a difference you can hear. This is especially true if, when the filter is switched off and you remove your speakers' grille cloths, you can see your woofers moving slowly in and out, a sure sign that there are subsonics present. Bass' boost switches often have subsonic filters built in, too, to protect the speakers.

High-frequency filters are sometimes called "scratch" filters, because their original purpose was to diminish the scratchiness of worn records. They remain handy for that purpose and to reduce tape hiss, but can be used to cut other troublesome high frequencies, such as distortion from old or badly made recordings or from poor FM reception. Such filters generally cut frequencies above 10 kHz or 15 kHz, or are switchable between such frequencies as 8 kHz and 15 kHz.

Front-Panel Miscellany

Noise reduction systems are found on a few preamps, using *DNR, autocorrelator,* or other circuits which can lower the noise from any source by a moderate amount.

Stereo-mono mode switches, as you'd expect, cut out the stereo effect, turning the signal into mono. This is useful in cutting some noise and distortion when listening to poor FM reception or worn records, but it's close to a last resort, unless the broadcast or recording is monophonic in the first place. Mode switches may have additional settings, such as *reverse stereo* (for a few old recordings which have their channels reversed), or *left* and *right* (to feed single-channel sources, such as portable cassette recorders, through both channels of the listening system).

Headphone jacks allow you to listen without disturbing others, or to hear when others are making noise that would otherwise disturb you. The jacks on the front panels of receivers or integrated amps usually have enough output to drive any pair of headphones—sometimes even enough for two pair (in which case, two jacks are usually provided); those on preamps may have trouble driving some inefficient headphones very loudly. Test your phones and your chosen preamp before buying, if you can.

Since the speakers don't need to be on when you're listening to headphones, there should be a switch to turn them off. On preamps, that switch usually cuts the output to the power amp; on integrated amps and receivers, it's usually part of the *speaker switch.* That switch also usually lets you select either or both of two pair of speakers, so you can have sound in two rooms.

Front-panel tape inputs and outputs are very useful if you frequently plug portable recorders or other transient components in and out of your system.

Human Engineering

While we've occasionally referred to controls as "knobs," not all of them are these days. On many preamps, knobs are being replaced by "slider" controls, pushbuttons, and rocker switches—partially for styling reasons, to give a modern, flat look to the front panel, but for functional reasons, too.

Knob controls give you a good grip and a wide range of adjustment in a small amount of panel space. (The bigger the knob, the more finely you can adjust the control.) Slider controls are handy when you want to compare several related control settings at a glance (which is why they're used in most multiband equalizers) and when you want to relate a control setting to a specific direction (left-right balance, for example).

Rocker switches, or up/down buttons, don't control the sound directly, as knob and slider controls do. Instead, they control an electronic circuit inside the component, which in turn controls the signal. This can result in cleaner sound, because the signal is not fed all the way to a front-panel control and back, possibly picking up noise en route. This electronic signal-handling circuit is also easier to operate by remote control than conventional, knob controls. But the controlling circuit adjusts the signal in steps, not continuously: if the steps are too coarse, you may sometimes have to settle for slight misadjustments; if the steps are too fine, making large adjustments seems to take forever, and you're liable to hold the control down too long and overshoot your setting.

Some people like to have lots of controls, while others are intimidated by them. To suit both types of listener, some amps and preamps have panels that can be closed to hide all controls except the volume, selector, and one or two other basic ones.

Indicator lights, helpful and otherwise, abound on many models. Lights which show you which switches have been set are quite useful, especially if you're trying to figure out which ones you've set wrong; they're most helpful if they're close by the switches they correspond to rather than all grouped in one spot. Power meters (usually strings of LEDs—light-emitting diodes—these days) tell how much power the amplifier is delivering; that information is academic, for most people, though it's fun to know. It does come in handy, though, when you're trying to decide whether the silence you hear is caused by a dead amp or by disconnected speakers. Some amplifiers have display panels which spell out switch settings. These, too, are fun, but hardly more informative than lights by each switch. If indicators are important, make sure they're not so far recessed that you can't see them if the component isn't right at eye level.

Rear-Panel Features

From the switches on the front panel you can usually guess what input and output jacks you'll find on the rear one. However, some receivers and integrated amps also have preamp-out and amplifier-in jacks. These are normally connected together but can be disconnected (by flicking a switch or removing a short cable) so that you can insert signal-processing accessories like crossovers (see chapter 24) between the two, or hook in a more powerful amplifier later.

The *AC convenience outlets* on the back allow you to feed electric power to your other components without snarling your system in extension cords. There will usually be both switched outlets (controlled by the front-panel power switch) and unswitched ones. The latter are for use with certain turntables and tape decks which can be damaged if their power is shut off while they're running. (Consult your turntable or tape-deck manual to see if you have this kind.) Everything else—including most modern turntables and tape decks—can be plugged into the switched outlets. Just make sure that the front-panel power switch is rated (in the preamp's spec sheet) to handle the total current or wattage of the load you've connected to it.

We've given much attention to the speakers, amp, and preamp because they are vital parts of every system. But they're useless without program sources to feed them the signals that they control, amplify, and convert to sound. Now it's time to cover those signal sources—beginning with that mysterious new one, the Compact Disc.

13 The Compact Disc (and Other Digital Wonders)

As we have mentioned, there are two basic kinds of sound recording: analog and digital.

Increasingly, new phonograph records and cassettes are made from digitally recorded master tapes, which have been turned into analog recordings, playable on ordinary turntables and tape decks. There is, however, one purely digital system commonly available for home use: the Compact Disc, or CD.

The CD itself (figure 13–1) is a rainbow-silvered disc of plastic only 4.7 inches in diameter—smaller than a 45-rpm "single" record. It's not played by a needle dragged through a groove but by the pure light of a laser beam reading its information. Because light beams cause no friction, the disc won't wear out or deteriorate, no matter how often you play it. It yields better sound than even a brand-new LP or tape, and far, far better sound than tapes and records that have been played a lot. Besides, it's the most convenient and efficient sound storage medium ever devised.

So you'll probably want to add CD to your stereo system. But do you want it right away? Here are some pros and cons.

What's on the Records

Thousands of CDs are now available, something for every imaginable taste. That sounds like a lot, but it's actually just a drop in the bucket compared to the number of LP records or even prerecorded cassettes. A trip to any record store will show

Fig. 13-1. *A Compact Disc player and some discs.* (Courtesy of Magnavox)

you that. But then, cassettes have a head start of some twenty years, and stereo LPs have been around even longer. Even so, the number of available CDs is growing fast, and virtually every record company you've ever heard of now offers at least some CDs.

The Compact Disc has become an international standard— partially because the audio industry was smart enough, for once, to pile onto a single bandwagon. But the CD's success is due even more to its convenience, durability, and sonic excellence.

CD's Convenience

Convenience starts with the CD's small size, which not only saves storage space but opens up new uses that LPs can't compete for—such as portable players to hang over your shoulder (figure 13–2) and in-dash players for the car (figure 13–3). (The size of a car's dashboard radio slot was one of the factors considered when the CD's size was set.) The disc is recorded only on one side, so you don't have to flip it over halfway through.

A CD can hold up to seventy-five minutes of music, enough for long works such as Beethoven's Ninth Symphony. For longer works, such as operas, the convenience grows: three CDs can hold as much as five LPs; and those three CDs require only two interruptions to change discs, while ten LP sides require nine interruptions.

Compact Disc still cost more than LPs, though the price gap is shrinking fast. Discs which use the CD's full capacity (such as the Beethoven's Ninth Symphony) already cost less than the same music does on LP.

The CD system was designed for automation, adding still more to its convenience. All CD players are automatic, to varying degrees—more like cassette decks than phonographs in how they work and look.

That automation starts with disc loading and play. You push a button to open the disc compartment, place the disc inside, and close the compartment again. Depending on which button you pushed to close it, the player will either start playing the disc at once or wait for you to tell it which tracks on the disc you want to hear or which to skip. Many players even let you *program* those tracks into whatever sequence you please.

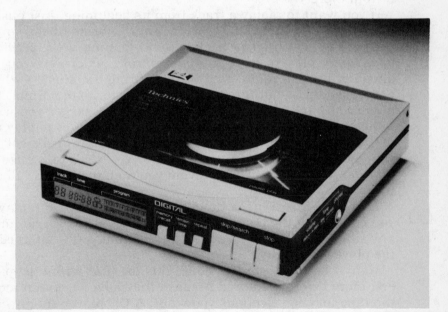

Fig. 13-2. *A portable Compact Disc player, to be used with headphones.* (Courtesy of Technics)

Fig. 13-3. *A Mobile CD player. (Courtesy of Sony)*

(This is not like programming a computer: With CDs you just key in the numbers of the tracks you want, and the player takes it from there.)

If you want to replay a track from its beginning, just push a button. Do the same thing if you want to jump ahead to the start of the next track or back to the beginning of the previous one. Many players have *audible search*, which lets you zip ahead or back at high speed while hearing the music—which is speeded up (about three to ten times faster than normal) but at correct pitch. This helps locate specific passages you want to hear. A growing number of CDs can also be set to play the first few seconds of each track, or each programmed track, so you can find the one you want even if you don't recognize its name or if vision problems prevent you from reading the album notes.

There are also *repeat* functions. Depending on the player, you can repeat the entire disc, the tracks you've programmed, any single track, or a section of a track that you've marked in the player's memory.

Many cassette recorders do all this too. But with tape players, more time is required because they have to search along the tape for the selections you want. A CD player simply consults a computerized table of contents at the start of the disc, then zips across the disc to the next track you want (a basic advantage of the disc shape over tape). Furthermore, tape's audible fast cue and review features raise the pitch of the music to a screech when speeding it up, even though their search functions are slower.

Besides, tapes hold only audio information; CDs hold that and a good deal more. For example, since the tracks on classical CDs tend to be fairly long, some have *index* points coded where significant passages start within a track. An opera, for example, might have one track per act and index marks for every scene or aria. With some players you can go straight to any of these indexed points, just as you can to the beginning of a track, simply by keying in its number and pushing a "go" button.

There's also room on the disc for other codes, as yet unused. Future CDs (and by "future" we mean only two or three years) may use that information space for song titles, sing-along lyrics, opera librettos, song translations, or even a series of still pictures, to be displayed on the player itself or on your TV screen. Some CD players already have output jacks for this purpose. And, as yet another link between CD and the TV screen, there are already players which use one laser to play both CDs and LaserVision videodiscs.

CD players also have *displays* to keep you posted on the operation of their various features. The more expensive the player, by and large, the more elaborate and informative the display. Lower-priced models may tell you only which track is currently playing. Others may tell you how many tracks are on the disc, how long they last, how long the entire disc is, how much playing time has elapsed since the beginning of the disc or the current track, and how much remains—all helpful when taping. The display may also indicate what selections you've programmed for play and how many are left.

Some players show on their displays how all their switches are set, so you can read all operating information in one place. Other players put little lights on each switch, which makes that information easier to read from across the room.

Players also differ in the *number of selections* you can program them to play automatically, ranging from none to ninety-nine. With the still-rare multidisc automatic changers, you can program in the disc as well as the track number, so you can set up a whole evening's listening flexibly with just a minute or so of button-pushing.

This hardly exhausts the list of CD conveniences. Most of the more expensive players have *remote control;* the remote-control unit for some players can also be used on other audio or video components from the same company.

A few players have *pitch controls,* which raise or lower the record's pitch to match that of the instrument you play, if you want to play along with the disc. Unlike the pitch controls on some turntables and tape decks, those on CD players don't change the tempo when they change the pitch.

Like most tape decks, some CD players have *timer start switches,* which start play as soon as power is fed to the player. With this and an external timer, you can program a player as a musical alarm clock—an expensive substitute for a clock radio, but at least you'll know exactly what music you'll hear when it switches on.

If you tape CDs for use in your car or portable cassette player, you'll probably find them among the best-sounding tapes you own. Several features of the players are designed to make such taping easier. Some players have *calibration-tone generators,* which put out a tone at the same level as the strongest signal that can come from a CD. This helps you set the level controls of your tape deck before recording. Some players can insert a few extra seconds of silence between tracks as it plays, so that a tape deck's music-search function will be able to sense the silent gap between musical selections, and the start of each.

The *auto-pause* function found on some CD players serves several purposes. When you're taping individual selections from different CDs, it saves you from accidentally taping the track which comes after the one you want. (Players which automatically stop after playing a single, programmed track are of equal help when taping.)

Some CD players have *compressor circuits,* which can be used to narrow the dynamic range between the loudest and softest signals on a CD. This lets you record a CD with a wide dynamic range onto tape, whose range is narrower. It also keeps the sound from becoming too dramatic for quiet listening. This is especially useful when making tapes for use in the car, where road noise often drowns out quiet passages.

Future CD players may also have *expander circuits* to make the swings between loud and soft more dramatic, in case you feel the performance is too tame. If recordings took full advantage of the CD's dynamic range, there'd be no need for the expander. But few CDs do use the entire dynamic range available, for two reasons. One is because the noise in the average home would obscure quiet passages that can be heard in the concert hall. The other is because CDs are often made from the same basic master tapes as LPs, to simplify life for the record companies. As CDs account for more of their business, record companies will probably produce separate master tapes with a wider range to match the digital medium. At that point we'll need compressors, for times when our homes are noisy or we're not listening with full attention.

We've described these features in general terms because different manufacturers give these features different names. The more convenience features a CD player has, the more convenient it becomes to use—up to the point where the number of buttons and display indicators overwhelms you. Even then, careful design can make the controls easier to understand.

Your tastes and circumstances will govern which features you'll want. For example, programmability means more to pop-music listeners, whose discs contain many short songs, not all of which may interest you at a given time; classical-music listeners tend to listen to a disc from beginning to end. Remote control is more helpful if your system's components are far from your listening chair than if you can reach the front-panel controls from where you sit. Players which load from the front can be stacked under other components if you prefer, while top-loading players may be more convenient if you prefer to place your player on a low cabinet or table.

CD Durability

A CD is a lot less vulnerable to damage than an LP: it's made of harder plastic and the recorded information is not on the disc's surface, but inside, where the transparent plastic shields it from harm.

This is possible because nothing touches the actual recording. The laser merely looks at it. The beam focuses on the recorded inner surface, and an optical system reads the light reflections from that surface. The plastic of the disc material is actually part of the optical system, narrowing the laser spot as it passes from the disc's surface down to the recorded layer. As a result, all but the worst dirt and scratches are so far out of focus that they are invisible to the player's optical system. And since the disc surface is glassy-smooth, not grooved like an LP's, most dirt is easy to get off. Just wipe gently with a clean, damp, soft cloth.

But CDs aren't invulnerable. While dirt wipes off, scratches don't. Minor scratches don't usually affect play. Bad ones can cause distortion, add noise (usually a ticking sound), or make the laser skip or lose its place. Dents and scratches on the label side can be even more serious, because the information layer within the disc is protected only by a thin and fragile lacquer coating on the label side, as compared to the thick, tough plastic below the information layer. The players can compensate for many problems caused by dirt or damage, but not all of them. It pays to pamper CDs. They're getting cheaper, but they're still not cheap.

Do CD Players Sound Alike?

There *are* differences between the sound of different CD players. But those differences are very subtle—so much so, that even experts have trouble hearing them. What differences there are stem mainly from the players' *filtering,* their *error-correction* circuitry, and their *analog output* sections.

When a digital signal is turned from a hail of numbers to a stream of sound, ultrasonic frequencies creep in, which are not audible but can cause audible problems. These frequencies must be filtered out. Filtering them from the analog output signal requires complex filters (sometimes called *brick-wall* filters, because they sharply attenuate the undesired frequencies). These filters can affect the phase response of the sound. If some of those undesired frequencies are filtered from the digital signal first, then only mild analog filters are needed to finish the job. Many expert listeners feel this technique of using digital filters together with analog ones, improves the sound.

While analog systems try vainly to eliminate errors such as noise and distortion, and then hope for the best, digital systems acknowledge that errors will occur and take steps to limit their effect. Minor errors can be completely corrected. If the errors are too large to be corrected, they can be concealed, as the player computes and fills in approximately what the correct signal should be. The better the player, the less it errs in reading data from the disc, the more errors it can correct, and the fewer it must conceal. Unfortunately, there are no specifications for this, so it must be inferred from test reports which tell how well the player can handle special "obstacle-course" test discs and from whatever differences you can hear when comparing players.

After the digital data has been read, error-corrected and converted into analog form, the signal must go through ordinary analog circuits in the player's output section. Some player manufacturers lavish attention on these circuits, while others throw in just enough cheap parts to do the job. This, too, can subtly affect sound quality.

Tomorrow's CD—and Beyond

In a few years, you may even be able to record CDs at home, as easily as you now record tapes. The first recordable CDs may be "write-once" discs that cannot be erased and reused, but re-recordable discs should follow.

Recordable discs will probably encourage the use of CD as a storage medium for computer data and programs; that could begin even before the medium becomes recordable. Standards for such use are already being established.

But you can already record digital sound at home—though on tape, not disc. Even before CD arrived, there were PCM converters, which record studio-quality digital sound onto home videocassette recorders, and a few complete recorders using videocassette tapes. Coming soon will be digital recorders using small tape cassettes, roughly the same size as today's regular cassette tapes.

What all these systems have in common is digital technology. The advantages (and disadvantages) of that are the next chapter's subject.

14 The Digital Difference

Digital sound is easy to appreciate but hard to understand. Full of paradoxes, it approaches perfection by giving up all hope of ever reaching it and mirrors nature by working in ways that nature never does. The very idea of it goes against the grain. But it works.

The claims made for digital sound seem unbelievable: flat frequency response from below 20 Hz all the way to 20 kHz; virtually no noise or distortion; no wow and flutter at all. It sounds like snake oil, until you hear the sound itself. Then you believe it.

For the first century or so of recorded sound, we've been making models or "analogs" of sound—modeling its tiny air-pressure fluctuations in fluctuating electrical currents, magnetic fields, or wiggles in a record groove. It was logical: since sound, like everything else in the real world, is a seamless, continuous process, model it in a seamless, continuous medium. The problem was ambiguity: the model and the original were too much alike, so the machinery couldn't tell the medium's defects from the original's.

A phonograph, for instance, can't tell the jagged edge of a record scratch from a recorded pistol shot, or the roar of a rough or dirty record surface from the roar of applause. Only an ultrasophisticated computer—like the one between your ears—can manage that.

A digital recording avoids these problems because it isn't a model of the sound, but a blueprint, based on millions of precise measurements. The medium is just a computerized sequence of numbers, so the medium's defects can't be mistaken for those of the original—and, like all numbers, the recording can be checked for accuracy.

Since sound and our ears are both analog, digital recording requires that the signal first be turned into digital and later returned to analog form. So it's possible to record something digitally, then turn it back to analog for radio transmission or to put it on a phonograph record. It's also possible to record something in analog, then digitize it to put it on a digital medium like the Compact Disc. There are reasons to do both.

The signal always starts out as an analog, the output from the microphones (figure 14–1). It then goes through an *analog-to-digital (A/D) converter,* which measures its amplitude more than forty thousand times per second and records those voltage samples as numbers.

When the recording is played back, each of the numerically encoded voltages is reconstituted by the player, then held constant till the next sample comes in. This gives the signal a "stair-step" appearance when graphed. Another circuit then smooths out the stepped wave pattern into a replica of the original sound wave. These playback circuits form a *digital-to-analog converter (D/A).*

How good a replica it is depends on how detailed the blueprint is, how faithfully it's transmitted, and how well the reconstruction is done at the playback end. The amount of detail mainly depends on the number of samples per second (which controls frequency response) and the number of binary digits, or "bits" per sample (which controls noise and distortion). Fidelity of transmission and reconstruction depend on "error-correction" systems and on the accuracy of the playback D/A converter circuits.

Sampling Rate and Frequency Response

Most sound waves are complex mixtures of simple sine waves. We only need to record two points per cycle of such a wave's highest frequency to be able to reconstruct the wave in playback.

You can't make do with fewer than two points per wave cycle, though. So the *sampling frequency* (the number of times the signal is measured per second) must be high enough to ensure at least two samples for every wave of every audio frequency—at least forty thousand samples per second for an audio band going up to 20,000 Hz (called the *Nyquist limit,*

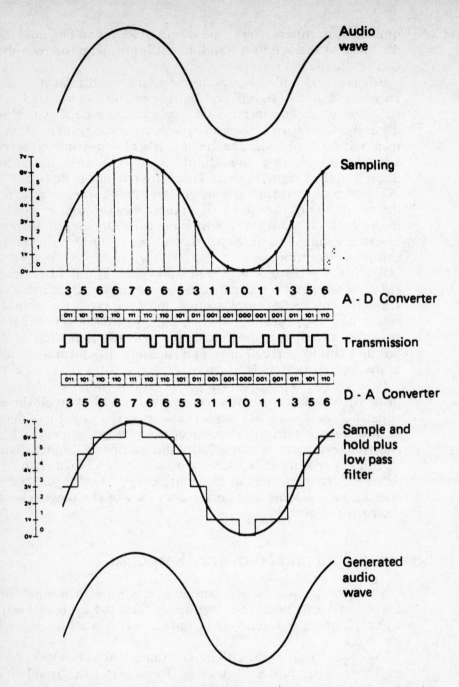

Fig. 14-1. *In digital recording, the original sound wave is measured at more than 40,000 sampling points per second, and the wave height at each point recorded as a number (B). In playback, the sampling points are recreated, then the curve between the points is smoothed to duplicate the original wave (D). (Courtesy of Philips)*

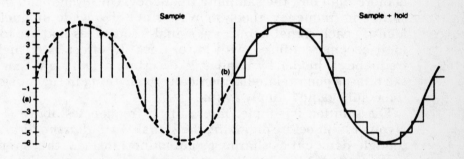

Fig. 14-2. A more detailed view of the process by which the original signal samples change from discrete points to the stair-step signal. The process uses a sample-and-hold circuit, which stretches each sampled point by holding its value until a new sample value is read.

after its discoverer). In practice, we go a little higher, for two reasons.

One reason is that if a signal frequency was exactly half our sampling frequency, an accident of timing could make us miss it altogether. This would happen if the sampling points in figure 14–1 fell right on the points where the wave crossed its zero axis; then we'd get two zero samples, which would make the decoding circuits assume the wave wasn't there. If our sampling frequency is a little higher, we avoid this problem— if we don't detect one cycle of the wave, we'll catch the next (real-world sounds last for many cycles).

The second, and even more important, reason is a phenomenon called *aliasing*, which occurs when the signal frequency is more than half the sampling frequency. Once you reach the sampling frequency, the system runs out of ways to uniquely identify each signal frequency; signal frequencies that are too high become confused with lower ones. In effect a too-high frequency is hidden by an alias, like a criminal lying low. Since the aliases don't relate harmonically to anything in the music, the result sounds simply awful.

The solution is simple: filter out all frequencies above the Nyquist limit before digitizing the signal. *Anti-aliasing filters*, though, don't cut as sharply as guillotines; instead, they gradually "roll off" the frequencies they're rejecting, in a rounded but steepening curve. Raising the sampling rate to make them twice the highest desired signal frequency allows for the gradual filter roll-off. In Compact Discs, for instance, the sampling frequency is not 40 kHz (twice 20 kHz), but 44.1 kHz.

In analog recording, there's theoretically no limit to high-frequency response. In practice, response drops off at very high (and very low) frequencies. And these practical limits are constantly being expanded. In digital recording, the upper-frequency limit is fixed and predictable, deliberately set at 20 kHz. But there's no roll-off at frequencies just below the limit, and no roll-off at any frequency in the deep bass. This is one way in which digital gives up the possibility of perfection for a fixed limit that ensures accuracy where it counts.

Distortion, Noise, and Bits

The other fixed limit in digital systems comes from the number of digits used to encode the signal samples. Digital systems measure in steps, but the analog signals they're measuring are continuous. An analog signal that ranges between +1 and −1 volts goes through an infinite range of values between those points, but a digital system can record only a finite number of those values. The more digits it has, the more steps it can distinguish and the more closely it can match its readings to the variations in the original signal.

Because digital systems use finite means to record infinite signal variations, some mismatch is inevitable, and every such mismatch adds noise and distortion to the signal. While noise and distortion in analog signals can also be considered cases of mismatch between original and recording, the amount of the mismatch is unpredictable. In a digital system, the size of the mismatch is completely predictable: one-half the difference between digits, or steps. Any signal less than half a digit away from one "legal" value is recorded as that value—more than half a digit away, and it is recorded as the next one.

Digital systems use the same binary number systems as computers; that is, each digit only has two possible values, 0 or 1, instead of the ten-value range (0 to 9) of our decimal number system. Each digit added doubles the number of possible values the system can handle: a one-digit number has two values (0 and 1); a two-digit number has four values (00, 01, 10, and 11—which are the binary equivalents of our familiar 0, 1, 2, and 3); a three-digit number has eight possible values; and so on.

So every time a digit is added to a digital recording system, the amount of its inaccuracy—and, therefore, its noise and distortion—is cut in half. This increase in accuracy is equivalent to cutting noise and distortion by 6 dB; so you can roughly gauge a digital system's dynamic range by multiplying its digits, or bits, by six. For example, a fourteen-bit system has 84 dB of dynamic range, and a sixteen-bit system (such as the Compact Disc and studio digital recorders) has 96 dB. Since distortion and noise are lumped together in this figure, it's sometimes referred to as the "signal-to-error ratio."

Again, once you've set the number of bits in a system, you've forever limited its dynamic range. And that limit is unrelenting. Slight signal overloads don't cause slight increases in distortion, as they do in analog. In digital systems, they cause sudden, intolerable distortion. Weak signals, no stronger than the system's noise, don't play hide-and-seek with that noise—they're simply not recorded at all. But though the digital system's dynamic range is firmly limited, its limits are far wider than those of most analog systems. At 96 dB, those limits are wide enough to accommodate the entire dynamic range of music. And any noise you do hear is likely to be from the master tape, not added by your home playback equipment. No analog system can make that statement.

Handling Errors

Every time you copy or transmit a signal, you degrade it. In analog, this limits frequency response and adds noise and distortion. In digital, it imposes no such degradation, no such limits. In analog, a copy of a copy of a copy of a copy is a far cry from the original. In digital, the nth-generation copy is equivalent to an original.

This is partially due to the nature of the digital signal itself. An analog recorder has to follow an infinite range of signal values. A digital recorder only has to look for two signal values, the value that stands for 0 and the value that stands for 1.

That search could be as simple as looking for north or south magnetic fields on a tape, regardless of their strength: north is 1, south is 0. In practice, it's a little more sophisticated: the system counts as a "1" anything within a certain range of north field strengths, as a "0" anything within a certain range of south field strengths. The signal doesn't have to be precisely right, as long as it's in range. The system's response to out-of-range signals is neither 1 nor 0 but "How's that again?" In analog, whatever isn't signal is noise, because the system can't tell them apart. In digital, whatever isn't signal is ignored— the two are so different that they can't be mistaken for each other.

This still leaves problems. In reality, there's enough noise, enough missing bits, and other errors that "How's that again?" is fairly common. *Error codes* solve that problem.

There were error codes before there was digital recording— they go back at least as far as double-entry bookkeeping (which was invented in the thirteenth century). Consider the simple-minded ledger in table 14–1:

	Net Cash	Business	Personal
	$123.80	$123.80	
	$ 66.75		$ 66.75
	$145.20	$ 42.86	$102.34
Totals:	$335.75	$166.66	$169.10

Table 14-1. *"Double-Entry" error coding.*

There's a one-cent error in the "Personal" total, but any book-keeper could find it in seconds. That's because the Net Cash column and the Totals line act as error codes. If all is well, the entries in every line add up to equal the Net Cash entry for that line, and all the entries in each column add up to equal the total underneath. If the totals of one row and one column don't match, the error will be found where that row and column cross. Digital systems use more complex error codes, to catch the possibility of more than one error occurring in a group of numbers, but the principle is the same.

From time to time, errors occur which are too big to be corrected. When that happens, the equipment playing the recording averages out the last trustworthy sample and the next one, and assumes that the values which can't be determined lie on a line between the two. Such "error concealment" isn't completely accurate, but it's usually not too far off, reducing the sound from great to merely okay. If the error becomes so bad that it can't be concealed successfully, the player will usually silence itself, stop, or skip the affected passage.

Error correction and concealment also prevent or minimize signal degradation when signals are copied digitally. Error-correction reconstructs the original signal on the new recording, making it just like the original—or better, because its errors have been corrected. Only if the recording has been damaged is there likely to be much error concealment; where there is, the digital copy is not quite as good as the original, but still fairly close.

Digital has another virtue—no wow and flutter. The tiny speed variations that cause wow and flutter in analog tape recorders and disc players are also present in digital ones. But you never hear them. That's because as samples are read off the recording, they're not fed directly to the digital-to-analog converter. Instead, they're fed into a buffer circuit, which smooths out the speed variations until the pulses are timed with the invariant precision of a quartz clock.

Confusions and Controversies

Analog phonograph records and cassettes are often made from digital master recordings so that the vast majority of listeners, who don't yet own CD players, can enjoy the performance on those digital masters. Those masters may lose some of their quietness, dynamic range, and freedom from distortion when they're transferred to analog, but those analog records and tapes will still be quieter, wider-ranging, and freer from distortion than recordings made from most analog master tapes. So record companies take pains to tell you that these are "digital" LPs or cassettes. What they forget to tell you is that those recordings are completely compatible with analog turntables and tape decks.

Compact Discs are often made from analog masters, too, because there are still far more analog than digital masters in the record-company vaults. Such CDs may not have all the digital advantages, but they will reflect the virtues of the analog master tapes better than LP records or cassettes can do. Analog-mastered CDs also preserve unique musical performances on discs that won't wear out.

Many listeners want to know whether a Compact Disc was made from an analog or digital master, and some record companies mark their new CDs with a three-letter code to indicate this. The first letter is "A" if the original master tape was analog, "D" if it was digital. The third letter is always "D," because the CD is an analog medium.

The second letter shows whether or not the recording was ever processed in an analog mode. Record companies often use analog equipment when they need to mix channels, change the frequency balance, or add reverberation to a recording. Since there's still little digital equipment available to do these things, studios frequently must convert the signal back to analog to feed it through the processors they already have, then redigitize it for use as a CD master. In the process, the signals pick up noise and distortion, sometimes audibly.

Despite the virtues of digital, some digital recordings sound shrill or otherwise unpleasant. There are three schools of thought about this.

One says that the digital idea is great, but that its limits have been set too low. A faster sampling rate, and perhaps more digits would make digital recording sound good, because we can hear more and better than conventional hearing tests suggest, enough to sense the limits of today's digital systems.

The second school believes that digital is inherently so artificial that it can't sound good under any circumstances. This group cites many defects: the sound is, they say, somehow dispiritedly flat; it doesn't let you follow the tune.

The third group points out that digital can't be all that bad, intrinsically, because so many digital recordings sound splendid. If many other digital recordings don't, then it must be the individual recording's fault, not the system's. The probable culprit is the use of microphone techniques which emphasize the highs. While this helps override the high-frequency roll-off found in analog recording, it doesn't work in digital, where there's no roll-off to counteract the treble emphasis.

We belong to the third group. For us, digital works fine much of the time. There is improvement yet to come, not only in recording technique but also in the D/A converters used in digital players, and in the other digital-player circuits which handle the signal while it's in analog form.

As to intrinsic problems, we haven't heard them. This suggests there are none, but does not quite prove it. When a system brings so much improvement to the traditional problems we've learned to listen for, it takes a while to learn to listen for whatever new faults might lie in wait. But we don't really expect any.

If there is a problem, it's the challenge made to the system's amplifier and speakers, to deliver all the sound quality—the full bass, clean treble, and full dynamic range—that digital offers.

15 The Phonograph I: The Turntable

> The reports of my death have been greatly exaggerated.
> —Mark Twain

"The phonograph is obsolete." Depending on your age, you may have first heard that opinion expressed when home tape recorders arrived, in the early fifties, or when the cassette arrived in the sixties, or you may be hearing it for the first time now, with Compact Disc on the scene. It's an easy statement to make, but a hard one to make stick, as one look around a record or a hi-fi store will show you.

There are still plenty of reasons to make the phonograph the cornerstone of your stereo system—and, admittedly, several reasons why you might choose to do without it.

The main reason for the phonograph is the prevalence of records. A phonograph will play the records you and your friends now have, it will give you the widest choice of new recordings for some years to come, and will let you buy recordings (not to mention players) for less money than its chief competitors, the CD and the cassette. Even when Compact Discs become more readily available than records (which is some years off), there will still be recordings available in LP that aren't issued in CD form—records whose sales may justify continued production from existing molds but don't justify the costly transfer to CD.

The phonograph is as much a marvel of technology as CD, but a marvel of a different kind. It exemplifies old technology brought to astonishing levels of refinement, as opposed to new technology whose advantages are already evident despite its still rudimentary development. Even after a century, the phonograph is still being improved—but the more refined it becomes, the harder it is to improve it further. That, if anywhere, is where the age of the existing, analog recording system has begun to show.

The phonograph's main vice is that it's self-destructive. The music is recorded as wiggles in a groove, and played by dragging a stylus through that groove (figure 15–1). Every time the record is played, it wears down a little. How much it wears depends on how clean it is, how many times it's been played before, and the condition of the equipment playing it.

To play a record, you need five things: a *turntable* to spin the record, a *cartridge* to track the wiggles in the groove and turn them into an electrical signal, an *arm* (or *tonearm*) to hold that cartridge in place over the record, an amplifier to beef up that signal, and a speaker to turn it back into sound. We've

Fig. 15-1. *The roots of the phonograph go back a century, but its technology is surprisingly sophisticated.* (Courtesy of Shure)

already covered the last two and will deal in the next two chapters with the cartridge and arm. For the present, we'll consider the turntable, whose task is more intricate than simply going around in circles.

Automation

The first thing to consider is the degree of automation you need: manual, semi-automatic, or automatic.

With *manual turntables* you must put the arm down on the record when you start play and lift it off again when the record ends. That's a double nuisance, and most people are quite willing to pay a few extra dollars for more automated models.

The only aid most such turntables give you is a *cue control*, which lets you raise and lower the arm gently with a lever, instead of touching the arm itself. This lowers the risk of your dropping the arm onto the record or dragging it across a groove or two.

The least expensive turntables in a maker's line are likely to be manual ones. Curiously, the most expensive turntables are often manual models, too. There are two reasons for this. First, automatic turntables have gotten a bad name among perfectionists, who buy the most expensive equipment. This is because, long ago, the linkages between arms and automatic mechanisms impeded an arm's progress across a record. But that reason is no longer valid.

A better reason why high-priced models are manual is that audio connoisseurs often prefer to choose their arms and turntables separately, to be sure of getting what they feel is the best of each, and it's hard to automate an arm designed to be used on a variety of turntables.

Semi-automatic turntables only require that you put the arm down at the beginning of the record. When the record ends, the arm will automatically lift off and return to its rest position, and the turntable will stop. This eliminates the nuisance of having to leap up and lift the arm when the record is finished.

Having to put the arm down at the start is less of a nuisance than having to pick it up at the record's end, because you can choose when to do it. Still, setting the arm down in just the right position takes a keen eye and a steady hand, so most arms have *cueing controls* which cushion the descent into the groove, letting you set the stylus down without risk of damage.

Automatic turntables eliminate having to do even this. You need only put the record down and push a button—the turntable does all the rest. If you want to play some inside track instead of starting at the disc's beginning, most automatics, like manuals, let you move the arm across the record to a given track and lower it with the cue control, preventing accidental record scratches. A few automatics are also *programmable,* with sensors to detect the beginning of each band and controls to let you select which bands you want to play and, sometimes, the order in which to play them.

One type of automatic that's becoming almost extinct is the *multi-play* turntable, or *changer*. With a changer, you can load a stack of about half a dozen records, push a button, and do nothing more until it's time to flip the stack over and play the second sides.

While this sounds handy, there are drawbacks: a changer can sound its best on only one disc in the stack; its arm tilts from the optimum angle to play those records stacked higher or lower. And one warped record in the stack can make the discs above it slip or wobble when played.

A changer won't turn over a record to play its other side. But there are single-play turntables which do play both sides of the disc. These models don't turn the disc over but have separate arms to play each side. The discs do not lie on a platter but are clamped at their label areas, so they are less solidly supported than they would be on conventional turntables. Two-sided models often sit vertically, to save space.

There are times when it's simpler to play a record manually, such as when you only want to listen to one particular cut or track in the middle of the disc. Virtually all automatics let you do this, too—just pick up the arm, start the motor (if it doesn't start itself), and put the arm down at the beginning of the track you want to play.

Most turntables are *top-loading:* you raise the lid and set the record down. A few automatic models, however, are *front-loading* (figure 15–2), with dust covers which open from the front and, sometimes, motorized drawers which slide out for easier record loading. Such turntables can be stacked with other components, wherever you find convenient; you needn't always put the turntable on top. However, with such turntables, when you play only specific cuts on a record, you may need extra light to find the track. With programmable turntables, of course, this is no problem: they'll find the track for you.

Fig. 15-2. *Front-loading turntables such as this can be stacked with other components.* (Courtesy of Sharp)

Turntable Performance and Construction

A turntable's main job is to turn the record at a steady and accurate speed, without vibration. Although that seems easy, it isn't. No turntables do it perfectly, but the good ones come close.

Unsteady speed introduces *wow and flutter,* aberrations whose names reflect their effect on the music. Slow speed variations (below about ten variations per second) produce wow, which makes the music rise and fall in pitch. Steady tones then sound like a wobbly "wowowowow." Faster speed variations produce flutter, a more tremulous effect which blurs the music and, at its worst, makes music sound gargly, as if under water. Slow piano music (or a steady test tone, preferably about 3,000 Hz) shows up wow and flutter perceptibly. On a really good turntable, you'll hear neither while playing such test material. If you can make out even a trace of wow and flutter on such tests, you may consider the turntable barely acceptable. If you readily notice wow or flutter on faster, less-revealing music, pass up that turntable and pick another.

While the ear is more sensitive to flutter than to wow, the two are usually lumped together as one specification. There are several ways of measuring wow and flutter. Depending on the measuring system used, as much as 0.08 percent (unweighted) may be acceptable, and 0.05 percent is excellent.

Speed accuracy is less important, unless you are one of the rare people with a sense of absolute pitch which lets you tell whether the note being played is an A, an A-sharp, or an A-flat. In any case, many turntables have *pitch controls,* which allow you to raise or lower the record's speed by about 6 percent, enough to change its pitch by a semitone. This control is more often used by musicians who want to play along with the record, for tuning a record to the same pitch as their instruments. It can also be used when taping long records (a speed increase of 6 percent can squeeze a forty-eight-minute record onto a forty-five-minute tape side, if you don't mind the change in pitch and tempo), or just to make music sound either a bit more or a touch less brisk.

If you like to tape records, you should also check that the turntable's speed does not drift much over time, or you'll find the beginning of the record's second side slightly different in pitch than the end of side one. And if your area has unsteady line voltage, you might check hi-fi magazines for test reports on the turntables you're considering, to see if low AC line voltage will affect their speeds.

Vibration comes from the turntable's driving motor and can affect the music in two ways. Low-frequency vibration causes *rumble,* a growl that sounds as if a large truck had been idling outside the recording studio. You'll only hear this when listening through speakers with good bass response. (For a test of rumble, listen to the silent grooves between record bands, at the loudest listening levels you're ever likely to use.) Rumble can be a problem even when you cannot hear it, because your amplifier and speakers are wasting their signal-handling capacity on these inaudible low tones. When selecting a turntable, check for inaudible rumble by taking one speaker's grille cloth off to see if its woofer cone is moving slowly in ways unrelated to the music.

Some poorly made LPs have rumble recorded in their grooves, so don't condemn a turntable on the basis of just one disc. Try a few, then use the disc with the lowest rumble for your tests. If no turntables in your price range pass this test, then make sure your amp or preamp has a subsonic filter (see chapter 12), which cuts these low frequencies.

Higher-frequency vibrations are more difficult to hear directly. But if music seems clearer on one turntable than another, lower vibrations may be the reason. A turntable's vibration is measured by its signal-to-noise ratio (S/N), which should be as large a number (positive or negative) as possible. Again, there are several ways of measuring this which can't be compared directly. For example, a good turntable might have an unweighted S/N of −38 dB, but weighted S/N figures of −56 to −78 dB, depending on the weighting system used (see chapter 6), such as ANSI, CCIR/ARM, DIN A, DIN B, etc. However, you can compare measurements made with the same weighting system; differences of 1 or 2 dB are usually not significant, but differences of 5–10 dB or more are.

Not all turntable-generated noise comes through your speakers. Sometimes the turntable's motor can be heard, a minor annoyance you can hear if your room and music are quiet, or you normally sit near your turntable.

As usual, audible results—freedom from wow, flutter, speed inaccuracy, drift, and vibration—mean more than the drive, suspension, and other methods used to achieve them. But those methods are still worth consideration.

Belt drive is simple and inexpensive. The turntable motor turns at a fairly high speed (usually 300 or 1800 rpm) for speed-smoothing momentum. The motor drives the turntable platter by a belt, which reduces the speed to the speed of the record. The belt absorbs most of the motor vibration so that it won't reach the platter. The belts should be replaced every few years—they most often don't cost more than a few dollars and are usually easy to change.

While many turntables operate at only 33⅓ rpm, the speed of LP records, most also operate at 45 rpm (for singles and a few superfidelity albums), and occasional models can also handle the old 78-rpm discs as well. If a belt-drive turntable operates at more than one speed, that speed may be changed by changing the motor's speed or by shifting the belt from one motor pulley to another. Belt-shifting is most common on low-priced turntables using *synchronous motors* whose speeds are controlled by the AC power-line frequency, but it is also used on some very fine expensive ones.

The other way to change turntable speed is to change the speed of the motor itself. This requires that the motor have *electronic* speed control (sometimes called *servo* control) to regulate its speed. This makes the motor's speed independent of the power-line frequency. More expensive turntables may add either *phase-lock-loop (PLL)* or *quartz-lock* speed controls, which are more elaborate, but more precise.

A good electronically controlled motor will usually have less flutter than a synchronous one, and makes it easy to incorporate pitch control and a *strobe* light as a speed indicator so that you can easily reset correct pitch. Turntables with digital speed-readout displays almost always have electronic speed control.

Direct-drive turntables always have servo-controlled motors, which turn slowly, at the speed of the record itself. With these, the platter rests directly on the motor shaft, which simplifies construction and probably increases reliability. Vibrations are transmitted directly to the platter, but because the motor turns so slowly, those vibrations are low enough in frequency to cause no problems. (Belt-drive advocates counter that, while this takes care of rumble, it makes high-frequency vibrations more bothersome unless great care is lavished on the design.) Wow and flutter are also usually lower on direct-drive tables because the platter and motor are so tightly coupled to each other.

In either type of design, the round *platter* which supports the record is usually made fairly heavy (anywhere from 3 to 60 pounds), with its mass concentrated at its outer rim so that it will act as a flywheel, turning with as much momentum as possible. This smooths out speed variations. Heavier platters have greater speed-smoothing effect but, because of their inertia, also take longer to come up to speed. They also put more strain on their support bearings, which can lead to rumble. Design techniques to prevent this raise the cost of turntables with extra-heavy platters.

Most platters are made of metal, usually nonferrous, since the magnets in some cartridges are attracted to iron or steel. But platters have also been built from glass, ceramic, and mixtures of plastic and stone or concrete, to suppress resonance. If you flick your fingernail against a platter, you should hear a click, with a minimum of ringing—the clearer the ring, the worse the platter resonance.

How the record sits on the platter is also important. Usually, there's a rubber mat, cut away a bit near the center to clear the record's thicker, center label area and a bit smaller than the disc's diameter to clear the record's raised edge. This shape gives you a better grip on the record's edge to lift it after playing. More important, it couples the record firmly to the platter so that it won't pick up sound vibrations from your speakers and transmit them back through the cartridge to the amplifier and through the speakers again. Some mats are made of special vibration-damping material; some are electrically conductive, to drain static electricity. If you don't like your turntable's mat, you can usually change it.

A few turntables use vacuum systems, weights or clamping devices to ensure that the record is in firm contact with the mat, to help control its vibrations. At least one vacuum device and many record clamps or weights are available as accessories and fit most turntables. These devices are also helpful in dealing with warped records, making them easier to track.

Turntable suspensions also affect what you hear. The suspension's job is to isolate the turntable from external vibrations—primarily footsteps on the floor and soundwaves from the speakers (*acoustic feedback*) and, in belt-drive designs, from motor vibrations. It is also used to level the turntable, which some types of tonearm require.

The simplest suspension is a set of rubbery or springy feet supporting the turntable and arm. In belt-drive designs, the motor is usually mounted on rubber bushings, too, for isolation. Sometimes the feet can be "tuned" to respond to different frequencies, so as not to resonate at the same frequency as the arm and cartridge do.

There are also ways to make the base itself resist vibration. The simplest is to make it very heavy, or of a nonresonant plastic compound. Even so, the turntable base and its dust cover (especially if the cover is left up during play) can act like sails to catch soundwaves. So the best suspension designs isolate the working parts from these exterior ones.

In the simplest of these isolation systems, the arm and platter are mounted on a floating top plate, which is spring-mounted on the base. However, even this top plate can pick up vibrations. More sophisticated designs mount the platter and arm to a *subchassis* which hangs on springs beneath the top plate. A few of the most expensive belt-drive turntables have their motors mounted on a separate chassis.

You can check a turntable's sensitivity to vibration in the store. Play a record, setting the amplifier's volume control as high as you can comfortably listen. Then switch the turntable off, so the arm and cartridge rest on the stationary record. Without changing amplifier control settings, use your middle finger to sharply rap the turntable base, dust-cover top, and the shelf on which the turntable stands. The weaker the "thump" you hear coming from the speakers when you do this, the better the turntable's isolation. If the thump does not end sharply, but rings like a bell, skip that turntable model.

Last but not least, check the turntable's controls. Are they easy to reach? It's best to have them outside the dust cover, so that you can reach them while the record plays, without risk of bumping the needle in the groove when you raise the lid. Do all controls move smoothly, without jiggling the turntable? Does the dust cover open smoothly and stay open? Is there provision for tightening it should it wear loose over the years? How far from the wall must the turntable be to allow the dust cover to open, and is your shelf deep enough to allow that?

Like many jobs that look easy, just going around in circles isn't hard. The hard part is to do the job precisely, and with maximum convenience. Of the three parts of the phonograph, the turntable makes the least difference to the sound (though it does make some) and the most to the convenience. Now it's time to consider the part that affects the sound the most, the phonograph cartridge.

16 The Phonograph II: Giving Records the Needle

The turntable doesn't play the record; it just spins it while the cartridge does the playing. The wiggles in a record groove aren't music until the signal hits the speaker, and until the cartridge translates those wiggles into a signal, there is none.

Turning motion into signal makes the cartridge, like the speaker, which turns signal into motion, a *transducer*. And as a transducer, your cartridge, like your speaker, will put its own sonic fingerprint on everything you hear through it (though probably not to the same degree). The fingerprint may be small, but it's still significant.

The only working parts of the cartridge you can see are its mechanical ones: the tiny, diamond stylus (or needle), whose point actually traces the groove; and the cantilever which holds the stylus and transmits its vibrations up inside the cartridge (figure 16–1). Invisible inside is the generating system which turns those vibrations into an electrical signal. The body holds the other parts and governs how the cartridge can be mounted.

Cartridge *bodies* are of three basic types. The most common type, shown in figure 16–1A, has small mounting ears that are fastened to the tonearm with screws, while four wires from the arm are individually attached to small pins at the back. Gaining popularity fast are *P-mount* cartridges (figure 16–1B), which simply plug into matching P-mount arms and fasten with a single screw. These cartridges often come with eared adapters for mounting in other arms as well. Some cartridges are built into headshells which attach directly, without tools,

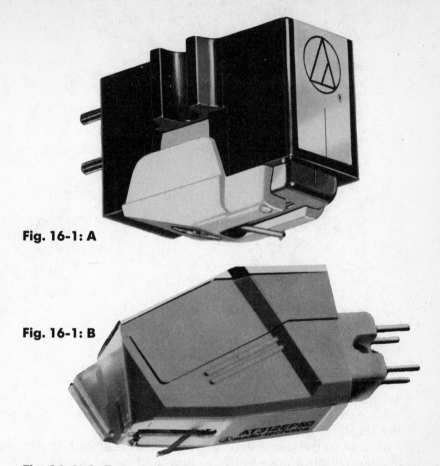

Fig. 16-1: A

Fig. 16-1: B

Fig. 16-1: A, B. *Typical phono cartridges. Most cartriages (A) are mounted by screws through ears along each side of the cartridge body. P-mount cartridges (B) plug directly into the arm, then are secured by a transverse screw (note the hole just ahead of the connecting pins). (Courtesy of Audio-Technica)*

to certain common kinds of arm (figure 16–2). The latter two types are far easier to mount; we'll discuss their other advantages and disadvantages in the next chapter.

The cartridge body types you can use are mostly limited by your arm. The type of *generating system* you can use is controlled more by your preamp. The two most common types of cartridge generators are the moving-magnet (MM), which can be used with most preamps, and the moving-coil (MC), whose low output usually requires an extra voltage step-up stage either in or before the preamp. If your amp, preamp, or receiver

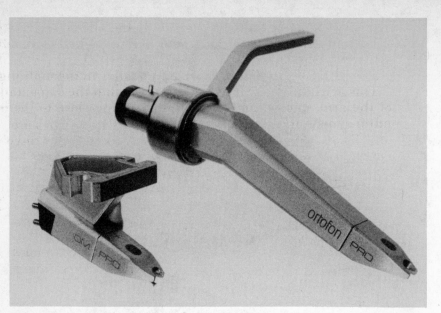

Fig. 16-2. *Standard-mount and integral-shell versions of a cartridge.* (Courtesy of Ortofon)

has an input selector position marked "MC," you can use it with moving-coil cartridges directly; if not, you can still use such cartridges if you add a *step-up transformer,* or a *pre-preamplifier* (often called a *head amp*).

To add to the confusion, there are also high-output MC cartridges which don't require a step-up device, medium-output MC cartridges which require a step-up for some preamps but not others, and even a few low-output MM cartridges which must be used with step-up devices or MC inputs. These oddball types are usually identified clearly by their manufacturers and dealers. Of other types, most plug into regular MM preamp inputs.

Most cartridges generate their signals by moving a magnetic field though a coil (the common *moving-magnet cartridges* and the less common *moving-iron, induced-magnet,* and *variable-reluctance* types). All these cartridge types are comparatively low-priced; can track even very loud, heavily modulated records; and have plug-in styli that are easy to replace (figure 16–3). Their main demonstrable weakness is that their frequency response depends upon an electrical property called "capacitance" in the arm, preamp, and the cables between the two. With too much capacitance, the cartridge's response will have a high, bright peak in the midtreble (about 10 kHz) and drop off to nothing well before 20 kHz is reached. With too little capacitance, the high-frequency response will start rolling off gradually above a frequency in the midrange.

This is usually easy to correct: just see that the capacitances of the arm, cables, and preamp input come close to the optimum capacitance for your cartridge. These properties are usually listed on the spec sheets for the components involved (though not with inexpensive cables, which can run as high as 45 to 60 picofarads, or "pF," per foot; arm capacitance, if not stated, is usually 50 to 100 pF). Simplifying things still further, many preamps have adjustable input capacitance, and you can cut cable capacitance by shortening the cable—just make sure it's long enough to reach your preamp.

In *moving-coil cartridges,* the cantilever moves a coil within the field of a fixed magnet or magnets. To keep its mass from loading down the cantilever's motions, the coil must be very light, hence very small. The coil's size limits the cartridge's output (the reason a step-up device is needed), but it also makes the cartridge less sensitive to load capacitance.

However, the problems of making delicate, flexible, low-resistance connections to the moving coil make changing styli difficult. With most MC cartridges, when the stylus wears out or breaks, you don't just plug in a new stylus—you send the entire cartridge for repair. With some brands, this can take weeks; other companies let the dealer take your cartridge (and some money) in exchange for a new or rebuilt cartridge. Either way, you can't replace the stylus without removing the entire cartridge, and you must carefully realign the cartridge in the arm when reinstalling it.

Because many people feel that moving-coil cartridges sound better than any other kind, they put up with the nuisances of low output and styli they can't replace at home. Moving-coil lovers say the MC type is smoother, truer, more accurate, and less distorted—enough so even to outweigh the moving-magnet's superior ability to track tough records. But, like most lovers, they don't always agree on their reasons.

Either you hear such a difference or you don't. What really matters is how good a given cartridge—of either type—sounds to you. The differences between MM and MC cartridge types are no greater than the differences between the sounds of individual cartridges within each type. And as both MM and MC cartridges improve, it becomes more difficult to distinguish one type from the other. However, the MC cartridges seem to be advancing faster, with some models offering higher output,

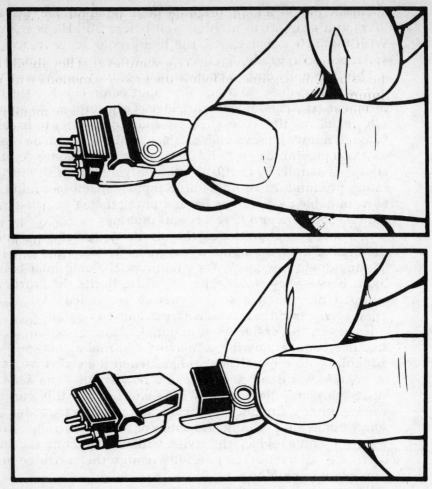

Fig. 16-3. *Replacing a cartridge's stylus is usually just a matter of unplugging it and plugging in a new one.* (Courtesy of Shure)

user-replaceable styli, and greater trackability than before. Ignore the controversy and just go by the sound.

That "trackability" we just mentioned is the ability to follow the fine twistings and turnings of the groove. That's where the cartridge's mechanical parts, the stylus and cantilever, come in.

At low frequencies trackability is most affected by *compliance*, the force needed to deflect the stylus. Compliance is usually expressed by a measurement such as "10^{-6} dynes/centimeter" (or pascals per millinewton, which amounts to the same thing). Up to a point, the lower the compliance, the better. How low that point is, as we'll see in chapter 17, depends on your tonearm.

At higher frequencies, trackability is most affected by the *moving mass* of the stylus and the cantilever. They should both be as light as possible, to follow the groove's motions with minimum inertia.

This is why the *cantilever* is not just the simple metal rod it may appear to be. If it is made of metal, it's often a hollow tube (figure 16–4), usually tapered or stepped to narrow it at the stylus end. Some hollow cantilevers even have tiny vibration dampers inside them.

More expensive cartridges often use exotic cantilever materials: boron, beryllium, titanium, carbon fiber, alumina ceramic, even ruby, sapphire, or diamond. The idea, in each case, is to make the cantilever as light as possible for low inertia, while still keeping it as stiff as possible so it will accurately transmit the stylus's motions to the generating system.

Another way to achieve low mass with high rigidity is to keep the cantilever short. But this involves a trade-off: the shorter the cantilever, the more the stylus moves in an arc instead of straight up and down or from side to side, the way the cutter moved when making the master disc; this causes slight distortion.

The *stylus* is always made of diamond, because that's the cheapest material for the job. It outwears all other known materials, saving on stylus replacements and record wear alike.

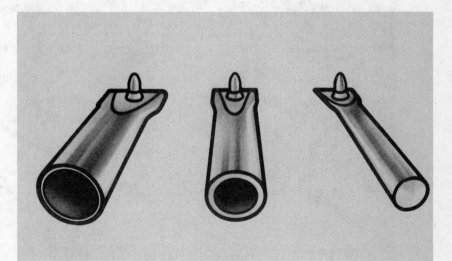

Fig. 16-4. *Hollowing a stylus cantilever tube (center) and thinning its walls (right) improve its ratio of stiffness to effective mass. (Courtesy of Shure)*

However, even diamond styli wear out—and no wonder: a stylus is dragged through nearly a mile of groove for every hour you use it. It's under immense pressure, too: its contact area is tiny enough to translate a downward force of two grams or less into a pressure of several tons per square inch!

But if the stylus material is always the same, its mass is not, because of differences in mounting and construction. In lower-cost cartridges, the diamond is usually bonded to a metal stub which is then mounted in the cantilever. Better cartridges use nude diamonds, saving the weight of the metal stub. One cartridge manufacturer cites a weight of 0.28 milli-ram (0.00001 oz.) for a bonded stylus tip, but only 0.08 to 0.015 mg for nude styli. Some stylus shanks are even trimmed into squared-off shapes to lower the moving mass further. Squared-off shanks are also easier to orient precisely when mounting. With the newer stylus shapes, this makes a major difference.

The shape of the stylus tip also affects trackability. Originally, all styli were *conical,* with rounded-off tips. Since only the tip of the stylus is small enough to fit into the record groove, the tip radius defined the stylus size—normally 0.7 to 0.5 mil

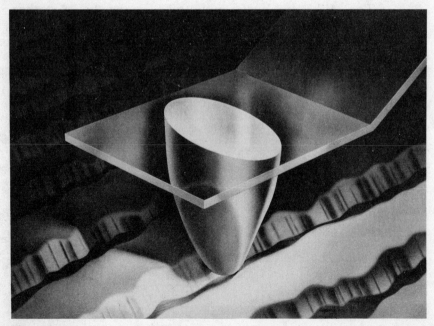

Fig. 16-5. *Only a small portion of the stylus tip actually traces the wavy modulations of the record groove.* (Courtesy of Shure)

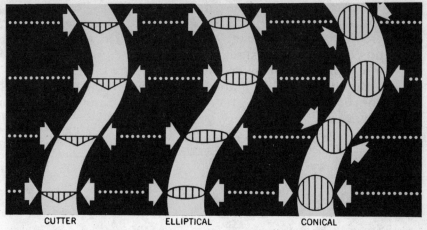

CUTTER   ELLIPTICAL   CONICAL

Fig. 16-6. *A stylus contacts the groove at two points. A round stylus's contact points (right) can shift relative to those contacted by the cutting stylus (left), causing distortion. A narrow stylus shape (center) follows the cutter's path more accurately.* (Courtesy of Shure)

(thousandths of an inch) for stereo discs. Even at this size, however, the tip is too blunt to properly follow the groove's finer contours.

The groove carries two signals, for the right and left channels, one on each of its 45-degree sloped sides. That makes the groove path rather complex, swinging from side to side and growing deeper or shallower according to the signals' interaction (figure 16–5). The sharp-edged recording stylus which cuts the master record contacts the groove at two points along a line that always points straight toward the center of the record (figure 16-6).

A conical playback stylus also contacts the groove at two points. But, as figure 16–6 also shows, the line between these points isn't always aimed along a radius. When it isn't, each side of the stylus "reads" a different section of the groove, which causes *tracing distortion.*

It also causes *pinch effect,* making the conical stylus rise and fall in the groove even when the groove itself stays level. This happens when the cutting stylus moves from side to side sharply, as it will on high frequencies. The groove's width along the cutter's radial line stays constant. But to a conical stylus, whose points of contact now lie on a different line, the groove seems narrower, and the stylus rides up. Since a stereo cartridge reads vertical as well as horizontal signals (each 45-degree groove wall is half vertical, half horizontal), pinch effect produces more distortion.

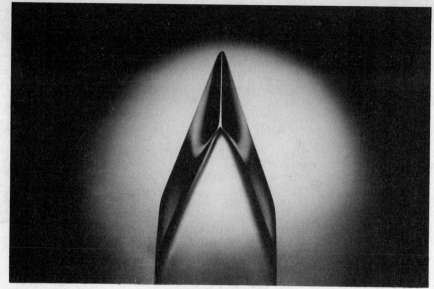

Fig. 16-7: A

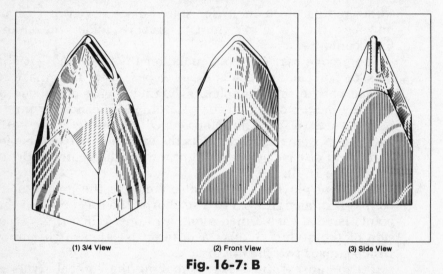

(1) 3/4 View   (2) Front View   (3) Side View

Fig. 16-7: B

Fig. 16-7: A, B. *Cartridge manufacturers offer many stylus shapes designed to trace the groove accurately with minimum record wear. Among the newest are the Van den Hul (A) and micro ridge (B). (Courtesy of Adcom [A] and Audio-Technica [B])*

Narrower styli can follow the cutting stylus's path better, with less tracing distortion and pinch effect. Such styli may be *elliptical* (like the one in figure 16–5), or of such newer, sharper-edged types as the *Shibata, Hyper-Elliptical, Van den*

Hul (figure 16–7A), and a complex ridged design called various names by various manufacturers (figure 16–7B).

The sharper edges of these styli (as seen from above) would normally increase the pressure of the stylus in the groove by reducing the area over which the cartridge's downward force acts. However, these styli are complexly shaped so that their edges will have longer, though narrower, areas of groove contact, spreading the force to decrease the pressure (figure 16–8).

Obviously, for these styli to work properly, they must be very accurately oriented to the groove. Otherwise, they sound worse than conical styli. This is another area where square-shanked diamonds help, by allowing the diamond to be precisely oriented in the cantilever. Drilling minute square holes into thin cantilevers, especially cantilevers made from brittle materials like beryllium, is not exactly a job for Black and Decker; many manufacturers drill with lasers.

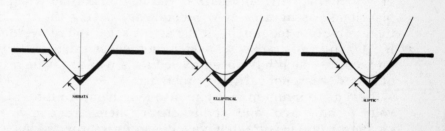

Fig. 16-8. *Three stylus shapes, as seen from the front. The longer the contact line, the lower the contact pressure and groove wear, one reason for the popularity of long-contact (Shibata, van den Hul, etc.) stylus designs. (Courtesy ADC)*

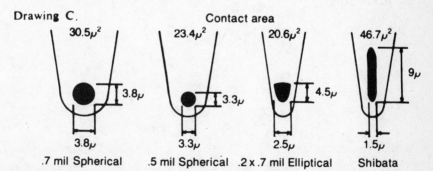

Fig. 16-9. *As seen from the side, the long-contact stylus shows an additional advantage: its "footprint" is narrower, and so better able to track small, high-frequency groove details. (Courtesy of Audio-Technica)*

Cartridges and Record Wear

Diamond styli wear out, but vinyl records wear out even faster, so it pays to know how to limit record wear.

The lower the stylus pressure, the less the record wear. That pressure is not just a matter of the *tracking force* in grams that you set your tonearm for, but also of the stylus contact area over which that force is spread—a factor which, alas, is never quantified in spec sheets. In general, though, cartridges which require less tracking force (a figure which *is* given on spec sheets) tend to wear records less.

Even so, the best tracking force to use is generally closer to the cartridge's rated maximum than to its minimum, because the higher tracking force assures good tracking under more extreme conditions. This doesn't affect only sound accuracy: the better a cartridge's tracking, the less it will wear down records; its stylus will hug the groove walls smoothly instead of ricocheting between them. If you hear distortion when you play loud passages on new records, try raising the tracking force a bit (not too much—if the stylus sags, you're overdoing it); if it still "mistracks," consider another cartridge. Distortion on records which have been played for a while may be a sign of record wear, not cartridge problems.

Preventive maintenance can also lengthen record life: keep your records and your stylus clean (there are many good cleaners), and be sure to have a dealer check your stylus with a good microscope from time to time. Check the stylus after about five hundred hours of playing time, again at one thousand hours, and every hundred hours or so thereafter. A worn stylus is easy to replace—the records it chews up may be irreplaceable.

17 The Phonograph III: Putting the Arm on Records

A record groove is a moving target: it recedes from the record's outer edge in toward the label and even moves up and down a bit where the record is warped (figure 17–1). Keeping the cartridge on target and in the groove is the job of the tonearm.

Most arms are built into turntables at the factory; but you can, if you prefer, buy a separate arm and turntable and put them together (or have the dealer do it for you—it's an exacting job). Either way, you need to know what you're getting, both in terms of overall quality and of how well your arm and cartridge will work together.

The technical-sounding points discussed under "Tracking and Skating" may seem academic, but they affect how your arm or turntable will sound. The sections on "Arm Handling" and "Setting Up" are less abstract.

Tracking and Skating

A tonearm is more than just a stick on a swivel with wires extending from the cartridge position and a weight at one end to balance most of the cartridge's weight at the other. (The remaining weight, a gram and a half or so, provides the tracking force that keeps the stylus in the groove.) One of the most obvious differences from the simple stick is shape: most modern arms are bent, or *offset*, about 25 degrees (figure 17–2), to prevent a problem known as *tracking error*.

Tracking error occurs because a pivoted arm's swing across

Fig. 17-1. *Tracking warped records without skipping requires a properly matched arm and cartridge.* (Courtesy of Shure)

the record twists the stylus in the groove. As a result, the motions of the playback stylus don't quite duplicate those of the cutting stylus, which moves straight across the disc when making the record. This error causes some distortion.

If the arm is mounted so that the stylus swings just a little past the record center, this error will be large but can then be made fairly constant. If the arm is then bent just enough to compensate for this constant error, the error will become small again.

But that bend, the *offset angle,* means that the stylus is being pulled in two directions as it tracks the record: along a line from the stylus to the arm's pivot and in the direction of the offset head. These forces pull the stylus away from the center of the groove, a problem called "skating." As a result, pivoted arms have *antiskating compensators,* which provide a gentle force in the opposite direction. The skating force varies with the tracking force and stylus shape (it's greatest for narrower stylus tips), so the antiskating dial usually is calibrated for both stylus types and the expected tracking-force range.

Linear (or *radial*) *arms* (figure 17–3) move, as their name implies, straight across the record's radius—hence, no arm offset, no skating compensation, and very little tracking error. Theoretically, the tracking error should be zero; in practice, a linear arm has some tracking error much of the time but constantly corrects itself to keep that error very small—much less than a pivoted arm's. The pivoted arm is always changing stylus angle, too, but much more slowly; some listeners feel that they hear the effects of the linear arm's more rapid angle changes.

Fig. 17-2. Most turntables have pivoted arms; note offset angle of the cartridge mount. (Courtesy of Technics)

Fig. 17-3. Radial arms, which track in a straight line across the record, eliminate tracking error. (Courtesy of Revox)

Tracking Force

How much tracking force you need depends on your cartridge; how much you get depends on how you adjust your arm. There are four common ways to adjust tracking force. With the most common one, *static balance,* you adjust a counterweight at the back of the arm until it just balances the cartridge, set a sliding dial on the weight to zero, then turn the weight until the dial shows the desired tracking force.

Static balance is simple, reliable, and light; the only catch is that the system goes slightly out of balance if the turntable is tilted. Most turntables have leveling feet, and a few have built-in bubble levels so you can correct any tilt; both the feet and the levels are available as separate accessories.

The *dynamic balance* arm design requires no leveling. You balance the arm to match the cartridge's weight, then apply tracking force with a built-in, calibrated spring. This solution is slightly less reliable (spring forces change over time; gravity doesn't), but it lets you track at any angle—even with the turntable upside down!

The cheap solution is to use a spring for counterbalancing as well as tracking force. You'll find this only on very inexpensive, low-fi turntables, as it is highly susceptible to the effects of tilt or external shock.

The fourth solution is used in *P-mount* arms. P-mount cartridges all weigh about 6 grams, so there's no need to provide a balancing adjustment. The ones that require slightly more tracking force than usual are made correspondingly heavier; those requiring a bit less are made a little lighter. You just plug in the cartridge (its pin locations are standardized to fit a plug in the arm—no little wires to fuss with) and tighten one screw to hold it firmly in position.

With any arm design, you can only apply proper tracking force with cartridges whose weights fall within a certain range (2 to 11 grams, for one typical tonearm). With the P-mount system, this is taken care of for you. With other types, make sure before buying that the tonearm you want will accept the cartridge you want to use with it.

Mass and Inertia

As you've probably gathered from brief references so far, an arm's mass, or weight, matters. The lower its mass, the less inertia it has, and the more easily it and the cartridge can follow the groove when the record warps up and down. With too much inertia, the arm lags behind the record's curve, making the stylus dig in for an instant, as a warp bulges the record up; the arm and cartridge then keep rising—sometimes just diminishing tracking force, sometimes jumping the groove entirely—as it passes the warp's crest.

To lower arm mass, the arm tube may be made more slender, constructed of lighter materials, or both. The headshell, into which the cartridge fastens, may be lightened by perforating it (as in figure 17–1), making it of very light materials, or even trimming it to a vestigial mounting surface, as in figure 17–2. This same figure shows another lightening technique, used mainly in expensive arms: the joint which makes part of the arm detachable for easier cartridge mounting is placed back near the pivot (locked in by a small thumbscrew atop the arm), where its inertia is least effective, rather than in the usual position just behind the headshell. Some arms have no detachable parts, to reduce mass even more (though this makes changing cartridges more difficult).

This same arm illustrates another way to lower arm mass. Many heavier arms are J- or S-shaped, with the offset bent into the arm shaft, and the headshell straight. If the arm is made straight, and the offset is bent into the neck of the headshell, the arm can be a little lighter.

Radial arms are usually quite light, for several reasons: they're fairly new and therefore use the latest technology, they're always straight, and they're usually shorter than pivoted arms. However, since they're shorter, they swing through a sharper arc when they move up and down on record warps. This can produce *warp wow,* an audible speed change as the arm rides up and down.

Mass and Resonance

When an arm and cartridge track a record, the system acts as a weight (the arm and cartridge) resting on a spring (the stylus). Like any weight on any spring, this system has a resonance—at some frequency, even a slight amount of energy can vibrate the arm, altering the sound and possibly even throwing the arm into the next groove.

So it's important to set that resonance at a frequency where there isn't much to make it vibrate—between 8 Hz and 16 Hz, and preferably between 10 Hz and 12 Hz (figure 17–4). Below

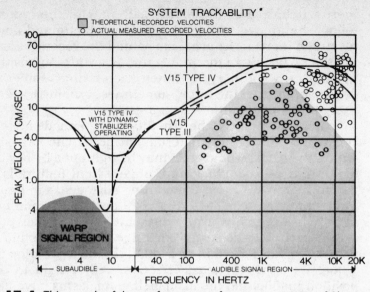

Fig. 17-4. *This graph of the performance of two generations of Shure's V15 cartridges shows why the combined resonance of a cartridge and arm (the dip in the cartridge curves) should be about 8 to 12 Hz: if the resonance is lower, record warps could excite the resonance and cause mistracking; if the resonance is higher, the signal on the record might. (Courtesy of Shure)*

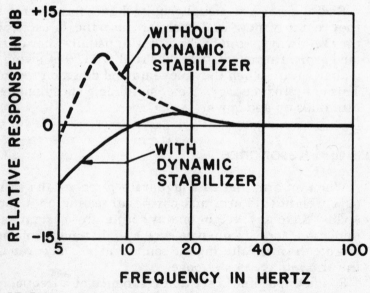

Fig. 17-5. *How damping reduces resonance. (Courtesy of Shure)*

those frequencies, the resonance can be excited by footfalls, groove warp, and other extraneous vibrations. Above that range, it can be excited by sound frequencies cut into the record or carried to the arm and record by sound from the speaker (acoustic feedback).

Since the resonant frequency depends on both the stylus's springiness, or *compliance,* and the mass of arm and cartridge that the stylus bears, making the cartridge more compliant means that you also have to make the mass lower. The lower the mass and the higher the compliance, the lower the resonant frequency; and vice versa.

Arm and cartridge manufacturers don't give you much help in finding the right combinations. Arm makers rarely specify recommended cartridge compliances and weights, and cartridge manufacturers seldom recommend the optimum arm masses. Many arm makers don't even specify their arms' *effective mass* (the portion of arm mass that actually affects tracking)—but if you do have that information and know the cartridge's mass and the compliance, you can figure out the combination's resonant frequency from table 17–1.

Another way to handle resonance is to damp it, so that its energy is absorbed before it has a chance to affect tracking audibly. The results can be quite dramatic, both in terms of measured resonance and observable tracking (figure 17–2). The arm/cartridge resonance can be damped at the cartridge, but is usually damped at the arm. Some arms do this with floppily mounted, *decoupled* counterweights. Other arms are damped by vanes which pass through oil-filled troughs, moving easily at the slow pace of the groove's progress toward the record center, but resisting faster vibrations.

The arm has resonances of its own, besides the one it sets up with the cartridge, which can be excited by acoustic feedback from the speakers. Arm designers use such tricks as tapering the arm tube, filling it with damping material, and making it of resonance-damping substances such as carbon fiber compounds. You can judge how effectively an arm is damped by noting how much handling noise comes through the speakers when you put the arm onto its rest.

Arm Handling

Even if you get an automatic turntable, you'll probably wind up handling the arm at some point, if only to set it down on a passage in the middle of a record band or take it off in midband

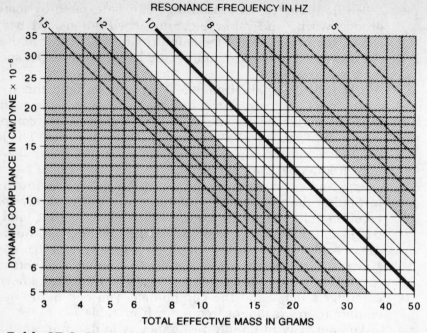

Table 17-1. *Tonearm/Cartridge-matching graph. If the horizontal line representing your chosen cartridge's dynamic compliance, and the vertical line representing the sum of the cartridge's weight and your chosen arm's effective mass, do not meet in the white area, the combination's resonance will not allow proper tracking. (Courtesy of* High Fidelity)

because the phone is ringing. Most arms have *finger lifts* on their headshells and *cueing* devices to raise and lower the arm.

The cueing device is usually actuated by a small lever near the base of the arm or by a button on the front control panel (as in figure 17–2), which raises and lowers a platform under the front of the arm. In the better arms, the cueing motion is damped so the arm won't bounce on the way up or drop sharply into the groove when lowered. Check to see that if you interrupt play with the cueing lever, the arm will come back to the same groove it left. Whether it will or not also depends a lot on the turntable's suspension.

Make sure the arm itself is comfortable to handle: it should move lightly, easily, smoothly (a sign of low-bearing friction), but not so lightly that you feel afraid it will slip from your fingers and go skittering across the disc. It helps if you can get a good grip on the finger lift and if the turntable gives you a place to rest your hand while doing so.

Reading Tonearm Spec Sheets

If you're buying a turntable with a built-in arm, the first arm specs to look for are its effective mass and the range of cartridge weights it can accept. This tells you what cartridges it will work with.

If you're buying a separate arm, you also need to know its dimensions; they tell you what turntables it will fit. Subtract the *overhang* (the distance the stylus's path goes past the turntable center) from the *effective length* (the distance from pivot point to stylus—usually about 9 inches to 10+ inches, or about 225 mm to 280 mm) and you know how far from the turntable center the arm mounting hole must be. Now find the mounting hole size to see if it will fit. Then check the arm's overall length to make sure the counterweight behind the pivot won't hit the inside of the dust cover; check the height, too, if the dust cover is low. Make sure there's some way to adjust arm height, since not all cartridges are the same size.

Lateral tracking error should be as low as possible, especially at the inner grooves. Bearing friction should be as low as possible too. The range of cartridge tracking forces should be at least 0 grams to 3 grams, which should handle all modern cartridges.

Arm capacitance is important if you use moving-magnet cartridges, the most common kind. The lower the arm's capacitance, the more cable you can use between it and the preamp, which can prove a great convenience in some setups. The main thing is to be sure that the sum of the arm, cable, and preamp input capacitances match your cartridge's requirements.

Setting Up

There are three parts to setting up an arm: mounting the arm itself (if it isn't premounted to the turntable), installing the cartridge, and making the signal connections.

It's important that both arm and cartridge be mounted precisely right (especially with line-contact or Shibata-type styli) for the best tracking and best sound. This means that the arm

---

must be set the proper distance from the turntable center, and the cartridge must be mounted at precisely the right angle and position in the headshell. Separate arms come with templates to help you drill their mounting holes correctly, and all good arms come with alignment gauges to help you get the cartridge in the right place.

Alignment gauges may be designed either to lie on the turntable while you make your adjustments or (if the arm is built into the turntable) to snap onto the headshell. If you don't have such a gauge, you can buy accessory arm-alignment gauges. If the gauge tells you to angle the cartridge slightly in the arm shell, do it—many arms require this for proper tracking.

A few tips on cartridge installation:

Before starting, remove your cartridge's stylus (if it is removable) or put the flip-down or removable stylus guard over it. Leave the stylus protected until you get to the final setup, for which the cartridge must be in place.

Make electrical connections to the back of the cartridge before mounting. To help you plug things together properly, most cartridge pins and arm wires are color-coded (usually white and blue for left signal and ground respectively, red and green for right signal and ground). If there's no color code, consult your arm and cartridge manuals to see which pins and wires are which. *Never* solder the wires to the cartridge—use the clips on the arm's lead wires. If those clips are too small for the cartridge pins, gently enlarge them with a pin or stiff wire slightly smaller than the cartridge pins. If the clips are too large, place them over the cartridge pins and gently squeeze them shut with a needle-nose pliers. If the result isn't tight enough, remove them from the pins and squeeze them shut a little more *by hand* (plier pressure could shut them altogether).

Both arms and cartridges usually come with screws for cartridge mounting. Use whichever screws are the right length, provided that, if they must thread into the headshell instead of into a separate nut, their threads mate properly with those of the hole they go into. Never force a screw where it doesn't want to go.

It's best to set the cartridge in place, tighten its attachment screws until it's snug but can be moved with a little effort, then make your final adjustments before tightening. Recheck after tightening, to be sure the cartridge hasn't moved.

Arm height and cartridge angle are important, too. Arms are designed to track best when they are parallel to the record surface. Most arms can be raised and lowered a bit so they'll track level with cartridges of different height. If the arm height isn't adjustable, shims (small positioning wedges) may be provided so you can match the cartridge depth to the arm height instead of vice versa. Most cartridges are designed to work their best when their tops are mounted flush with the headshell of a level arm; but a few aren't, in which case you may be instructed by the cartridge maker to tilt the cartridge with shims.

It's also important that the stylus point straight up and down as seen from the front of the cartridge. A few degrees of tilt can reduce stereo separation by up to 15 dB with a good cartridge, slightly less with one whose separation isn't that exacting to begin with. To check for stylus tilt, put a small mirror on the turntable and rest the stylus on it. As seen from the front, the stylus and its reflection should make a single, straight line. If the line bends at the mirror surface, the cartridge should be straightened. Some headshells can be twisted to straighten the stylus angle; if yours can't, insert small shims of paper between the headshell and the cartridge to level the stylus.

If you have no alignment tools, protractors, gauges, or instructions, you can usually approximate correct alignment by setting up the cartridge so it's square and level in the headshell and the stylus is far enough out to pass about ⅛ inch to ¼ inch beyond the turntable center if you swing it that far. But before doing that, sit down and write to the arm's manufacturer or importer, requesting instructions on how to align it properly, or put an accessory alignment gauge on your "urgent" shopping list. The difference between approximate and accurate alignment will be clearly audible, and is well worth the trouble.

If you don't trust your ability to handle such finicky precision tasks, don't be ashamed to ask your dealer for assistance. On the other hand, not all dealers take as much care in getting things precisely right as you would. As you grow more confident with your system, you might want to check the dealer's work with an alignment gauge (the one that came with the arm or an accessory gauge) and readjust as necessary.

The signal connections are usually a simple, plug-in job. The cable either plugs into the arm or is permanently attached to it, while the other end goes into your system's phono inputs (remember to use the MC input, if any, for moving-coil cartridges). Turn off the amp or set it to another input before plugging so that you don't get loud blasts of noise through your speakers as you plug. The plugs that go into the amplifier are usually marked to show which is left and which is right; if it's not spelled out, the red is usually the right channel.

The thin, black wire without a plug is a ground wire, which usually should be attached to the ground screw on the back of your preamp; if there is no such screw, loosen one of the screws on the preamp's back panel just enough to let you wrap the wire around it, then tighten it down again. Set your preamp's selector to "phono" before doing this, and check whether hum increases or decreases with the ground connected (it usually decreases). With a separate tonearm, it sometimes pays to connect the arm ground with the turntable (some turntables have ground screws for this purpose); experiment and see.

18 Music from the Air: Tuners, FM and AM

Radio is a bargain: put a tuner in your stereo system and it will bring you music free, forever, without your spending a cent on new recordings. How much of a bargain it is depends on where you live—how many stations carry your kinds of music and come in clearly; but it's still a bargain, almost anywhere.

You can't control the kinds of music your local stations carry, but you can control how clearly they're received. All you need is a good tuner (or a receiver with a good tuner section) and a good antenna for it. Just how good depends on your location.

FM? FM/AM? or More?

When you're picking a tuner, the first question to ask yourself is whether or not you want it to receive AM as well as FM broadcasts. All stereo tuners can pick up FM, a medium with fairly high fidelity (50 Hz to 15,000 Hz with low noise and distortion), stereo sound, and a fairly limited reception range (typically 60 miles to 90 miles—see figure 18–1). Many tuners can also pick up AM broadcasts, which have fairly low fidelity but carry farther (at night, some AM stations cover half of the country). Some stations are now broadcasting AM in stereo, too, and most will follow in the next few years. Now that stereo TV broadcasting is here, some tuners and receivers also have TV-sound reception.

By and large, AM and FM stations carry different kinds of programming. More FM stations carry "serious" music (clas-

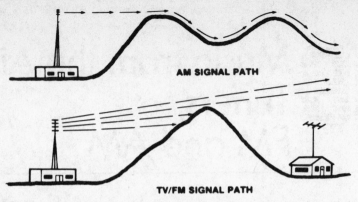

Fig. 18-1. AM broadcasts carry farther than TV or FM. (Courtesy of Winegard)

sical, jazz, serious rock), though there's also a lot of plush "beautiful music" on "easy-listening" FM stations. AM is heavier on talk (news, sports, and late-night phone-in shows), its musical content largely consisting of Top-40 popular, country and western, and more "easy listening."

This split may be due less to FM's higher fidelity—most radio listeners never consciously note that difference—than to the fact that it's in stereo. Now that AM is going stereo, it may start carrying more music, and stations may start paying more attention to the quality of their sound. (AM could sound much better than it does today, just as it did before FM grew so popular.)

However, the Federal Communications Commission has authorized not one but several technical systems for stereo AM, and progress is slow while stations and receiver makers try to figure out which one to adopt; it does no good to broadcast something no one can receive or build receivers for a system no one's broadcasting. As of this writing, the Motorola C-Quam system seems to have the lead among radio receiver manufacturers; however, some receivers (including portable and car models) are equipped to receive all the competing systems, which makes them the safest (though most expensive) bet for now.

If AM reception is important to you, listen carefully to the AM as well as the FM sections of the tuners or receivers you're considering. The AM sections of many quite expensive tuners and receivers are not as good as those of decent table radios. We hope the advent of stereo AM will make manufacturers, as well as listeners, more conscious of AM's possibilities.

The sound that TV stations broadcast has always been better than the small speakers of TV sets could demonstrate. Now that TV stations have begun transmitting stereo, some tuners and receivers are equipped to pick up *TV sound,* too. If that interests you, check whether the tuner is equipped to receive those programs in stereo or whether it requires an adapter (and, if so, whether that adapter is available and how much it costs). Also, make sure it will pick up all the channels you want to receive. All such tuners pick up the VHF TV band (channels 2 to 13); not all pick up the UHF band (channels 14 to 83), and few are equipped to pick up cable channels (A through W, and so on).

Tuning Systems: Digital and Analog

The stations that announce themselves as "94 on your FM dial" or "Stereo-100" are getting behind the times. The pointer-and-dial *analog* tuning systems (figure 18–2A), which show where a station is located along the broadcast band and its approximate frequency, are giving way to *digital* dials (figure 18–2B) that show the station's frequency precisely—which makes it harder to think of a station at 101.7 as "Stereo 102."

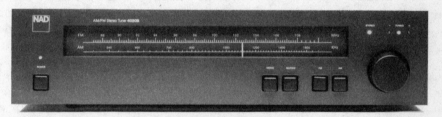

Fig. 18-2: A

Fig. 18-2: B

Fig. 18-2: A, B. Analog (A) and digital (B) tuners. (Courtesy of NAD)

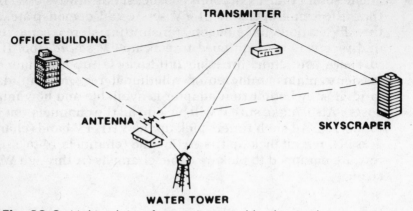

Fig. 18-3. *Multipath interference is caused by the simultaneous reception of reflected signals.* (Courtesy of Winegard)

Digital dials give you more precise information in less panel space. Whether they're more convenient or not depends on how you think of stations—as "94.3" or "down around 94 someplace." At one time, only expensive tuners had digital frequency displays; now even cheap models often have them.

Those displays usually—though not always—signify true digital *frequency-synthesized* tuning. Digital tuners move in steps up and down the dial, stopping only on those frequencies which stations might be using, and never on the frequencies between. Most digital FM tuners jump from 99.1 to 99.3, for instance, without ever stopping uselessly on 99.225. Some, however, make smaller jumps—of 100 kHz or even 50 kHz, instead of the 200-kHz width of an FM channel. This is useful when listening to FM over some TV cable systems, which shift station frequencies.

Frequency synthesis makes tuning easier, in some ways: you're always either right on a station's frequency or so far off that you can't possibly be fooled into a slightly mistuned signal. On the other hand, if the tuner is a trifle misadjusted, it will be slightly mistuned for all stations, and there's nothing you can do about that, short of returning your tuner for repairs.

With analog tuning, you dial in the signal, nudging the knob till you get the best possible result. Under some conditions, stations can sound best when slightly mistuned; all analog tuners, but only a very few digital ones, allow you to mistune. You can also zip quickly back and forth along the dial, a heavy flywheel behind the tuning knob keeping the knob spinning even after you release it. Some analog tuners have digital dials; the tip-off is a continuous-tuning knob, usually with a heavy flywheel that keeps the knob spinning after you let go of it.

There are slight intrinsic differences in performance. It's easier to make analog tuners a bit quieter (digital dials generate some interference signals), but frequency-synthesizer tuners are less likely to drift off frequency as they warm up. The main reason for digital's adoption, though, is probably the number of new features it makes practical.

With analog tuners, you turn the knob to get your station, varying the frequency to which the receiver is tuned. A very few analog models offer *preset memories* for pushbutton tuning of a few favorite stations, but setting the memory buttons to those stations is a bit awkward, and the settings tend to drift.

With digital, all tuning controls are really switches, linked only to electronic circuitry. This gives the designer many options. The main, manual tuning control may be a rotary switch that clicks off one station at a time, or a rocking or turning switch that keeps changing stations as long as you hold it down. The preset station memories are easier to set and more stable (though some memories are *volatile,* forgetting their frequencies if the tuner is unplugged for long); there are often more of them; and the ones on AM/FM tuners tend to hold two stations apiece, one on each radio band. You may also be able to punch in a station's frequency directly, like dialing a pushbutton phone.

And those are just the manual controls. Most digital tuners have *seek tuning,* jumping to the next station when you press a button. Many also have *scan tuning,* which samples every station on the dial for a few seconds, until you find one you want to hear and stop the process. There may also be a *memory scan,* which similarly samples only the stations in the preset memories. Bidirectional seek or scan, which can work up or down the dial, is more convenient, but rarer, than one-way seek.

All this automation is made easier by digital, because the process is all-electronic, with no moving parts except for the switches. This is also why you'll find digital tuning on tuners and receivers with remote control.

Whichever tuning system you purchase, make sure you'll be able to read the dial when you put your tuner into your home system. Consider whether the tuner will be at or below eye level, and how well it can be read at that angle. If you'll want to check it from across the room, make sure it's large and contrasty enough. If direct sunlight will fall on it, make sure it will still be readable under those circumstances.

Meters, Lights, and Such

Digital display panels can show more than frequency numbers—a lot more. Tuners have appeared which can be programmed to show the station's call letters as well as its frequency; in Europe, they're exploring systems which allow stations to feed this information to specially equipped tuners, which will display it without programming by the user.

Tuners have also long used meters to help you zero in on the signals you want. Originally, these were true meters, with moving needles; now, they're as likely to be lines of *LED*s (light-emitting diodes), more and more of which illuminate as signal strength rises. This new type is easier to read from across the room, but true meters can show infinite gradations, while the number of gradations an LED array can show is limited by the number of spots it can illuminate separately. This doesn't mean that a 5-LED array can only show five different values; on some such displays, intermediate values can be shown by having the highest illuminated spot glow weakly or flicker.

Meters—real or LED—are most often used as *signal-strength indicators*, for both FM and AM tuning. These are some help in telling weak from strong stations and in aiming the antenna.

Don't be surprised, though, if the best-sounding signal doesn't come from the same direction as the strongest one. This situation can occur when you get *multipath interference* —the same phenomenon that causes "ghosts" on television. Multipath occurs when a signal and its reflections reach you from several directions at once (figure 18–3), as often happens in cities or near hills. The bounced signals, having traveled a longer distance, arrive an instant later than the direct one, causing interference as if they came from another station on the same frequency. You may get best results by aiming your antenna to pick up one lonesome reflection instead of the original signal and six blurry carbon copies.

Some tuners (few, alas!) therefore have *multipath indicators*—either meters (nearly always of the needle type, to be sufficiently sensitive to minor differences), built-in *oscilloscopes*, or rear-panel jacks to feed external oscilloscope indicators.

Center-channel meters show when a station is tuned in dead-center or which way to fine-tune to get it there. They're very useful with analog tuning systems, but of no use with digital tuning, which cannot usually be fine-tuned by hand. Fine-tuning is a subtle process, so LED arrays are never used as center-channel indicators, though a single LED may show when tuning is correct.

Oscilloscopes are both more subtle and more expensive indicators than meters. So those very few tuners with built-in oscilloscopes usually use them to show all aspects of tuning: signal strength, multipath, and center-channel accuracy (often all at once). The oscilloscope may also show you other information, such as the strength of signals on nearby channels (an aid in aiming antennas for minimum interference), what your audio signal looks like (more entertaining than informative), and how much stereo separation is in your audio signal (more informative than entertaining).

Additional lights, or other indicators, usually just show you at a glance how various controls are set. Which brings us to the controls in question.

Tuner Controls

The only controls a tuner absolutely cannot do without are a tuning control and (unless it's FM-only) an AM/FM selector. But plenty of others are worth having.

Most of these, like the meters, deal with common reception problems. For example, FM noise and interference are worse in stereo; while tuners automatically switch to mono when the radio signal grows weak, many also have manual *mono/stereo switches,* for use when the signal is strong but plagued by interference. Switching to mono cuts down the problem by cutting out the stereo—effective, but drastic. Since these problems are also most audible at high frequencies, some tuners have *high-blend circuits,* which diminish stereo separation almost entirely at the highest audio frequencies but leave it more or less intact in the midrange; you still hear stereo, but with less noise. Usually, the high-blend circuit's action is either fixed or varies with the signal strength; a few very sophisticated tuner designs also vary the blend in proportion to noise, distortion, and other areas of signal quality. Home tuners may let you select different degrees of high-blend; car tuners, to save panel space and help you keep your mind on driving, don't.

Many tuners have *local/distant*, or *Lo/DX*, *switches*, to help cope with the differences between strong and weak signals. Not all of these switches do the same thing. Some Lo/DX switches only affect the scan or seek tuning modes, so they'll either stop at most stations or only at strong, local ones. Other such switches change the tuner's sensitivity (either directly or by reducing the signal level coming in from the antenna). Putting the tuner in its less-sensitive, "local," mode often reduces multipath problems, preventing the tuner from picking up the weaker signal reflections; it also helps prevent distortion caused by *overload* from ultra-strong signals—usually from broadcast stations in the immediate neighborhood.

Some tuners also have *bandwidth* switches. These control the range of frequencies that can pass through the tuner's *i.f.* (intermediate-frequency) *circuits*. When there are no strong signals at nearby frequencies to interfere with the station you're listening to, you set the i.f. bandwidth to its "wide" position for the cleanest possible sound and best stereo separation. When there are interfering signals, you set it to "narrow," which rejects much of the interference, at a small cost in other aspects of sound quality. A few tuners switch bandwidth automatically, and a very few have three bandwidth positions.

A few analog FM tuners have *AFC*, or *automatic frequency control*, *circuits*. These perform automatic fine-tuning, homing in on strong signals as soon as you have them almost tuned in, and correcting if the tuner or the station drifts off frequency (neither much of a problem these days). But if you try to tune to a weak station when there's a strong one next to it on the dial, AFC will try to retune from the desired station to its stronger neighbor; for that reason, if the tuner has AFC, it should also have a switch to turn it off.

Two other controls are used not to get more stations but to selectively reject some you might not want to listen to. The *muting switch* cuts off output from the tuner if the radio signal falls below a preset level. This prevents a blast of noise if you tune to a frequency where there's no station or only a very weak one. But most tuners let you shut the muting off, so you can pick up those weak signals if you feel the program content is worth the noise, and so you can use interstation noise as a test signal (see chapters 8 and 19). A *stereo-only switch* mutes out any stations which aren't transmitting in stereo or which are coming in too weakly for stereo reception. This is useful, perhaps, if you care about stereo more than about program content. Often the functions of these two switches are combined, on the assumption that you won't be able to listen with pleasure—even in mono—to stations so weak they fall below the muting level.

Some tuner controls cater to the few FM stations which broadcast with Dolby noise reduction (described in chapter 19), then change their signal's high-frequency response so that it will sound normal on tuners which do not have Dolby noise reduction. Some tuners do have *Dolby decoders* built in. And some tuners which do not provide for the use of external decoders by letting you select the tuner's *deemphasis* (high-frequency roll-off) curve to match what the station is doing. When listening to Dolby-encoded broadcasts and using a Dolby decoder, switch the tuner to 25 *microseconds;* for all other listening, use the standard 75-µS setting.

Other controls help in taping off the air. The *MPX filter* cuts very high frequencies from the tuner's output to keep the recording from being affected by an inaudible 19-kHz "pilot" tone present in all FM stereo broadcasts. These filters can also cut down, very slightly, audible highs, so most tuners let you switch them off. A few other tuners get rid of the tone by *pilot cancellation,* applying an equal but oppositely phased tone to neutralize it.

On the AM side, you're likely to find few of these controls. Tuners which receive stereo AM broadcasts will have stereo/mono switches, may sometimes have switches to match reception to the various AM-stereo broadcast systems (at least until the late 1980s, by which time sanity and standards may have arrived) and may possibly have stereo-only switches.

Local/distant switches on AM/FM tuners usually work on both bands. Bandwidth controls are found on a very few AM sections, and we've seen AM muting controls once or twice in our lives too. Dolby, deemphasis, and AFC switches are for FM only.

Record-calibration switches change an FM tuner's output to a steady tone at the tuner's average output level. Your tape deck's recording level is correctly set when the deck's meter reads 0 or near 0 on that tone.

To help you record programs you're not around for, one or two tuners have built-in *timers* for on-off and, sometimes, station switching at the times you select. Some which don't have timers built in will collaborate with external ones, changing stations in preset sequence each time they're turned off and on, or in response to signals from matching timers.

Level controls may have two purposes: to ensure that the tuner's output is neither too strong nor too weak for the preamp input it's connected to (rarely a problem, in any case), and to adjust the output from the tuner's built-in *headphone jack,* if there is one.

Rear-Panel Features

Like most audio components, tuners have their controls conveniently in front and their connections out of sight in the rear. FM antennas using flat, two-conductor wire are attached to the *300-ohm* antenna terminals, a pair of screws about ¾ inch apart. Antennas using round *coaxial cable* (so-called because one conductor is a tube wrapped about the other, and both have a common axis) are attached to the *75-ohm* antenna terminals, which may consist of either two screws (usually one of the two 300-ohm screws plus an added screw between the two 300-ohm ones) or a threaded metal nipple called an "F" connector.

Too many people use the rear-panel FM-antenna inputs only with the T-shaped plastic antenna that was included in their tuner or receiver. These are better than nothing, but not much. We'll cover better alternatives in the following chapter.

Most tuners have AM antennas built in but usually also have screw terminals for external AM antennas. You'll receive the best signal with a good external antenna, next best with a *loop antenna* attached to the tuner, worst with the *ferrite rod* found on most tuners. The more you can move and adjust the antenna, the better your chances of getting a good signal. Rod and loop antennas look like handles; they are not. Use them as such, and you'll be lucky if you only break the antenna, without dropping and breaking the tuner too.

One or two companies make antennas which can be tuned to match the frequency the tuner is receiving—a real help in cutting down interference. If your tuner maker has such antennas, there may be special connections for them.

There will always be at least two audio output jacks—sometimes four, if the tuner offers both fixed- and variable-level outputs. Similar jacks are, very rarely, provided for external oscilloscopes or for AM-stereo adapters. If you buy such a tuner for AM-stereo use, make sure the adapter is available, and buy it quickly—external adapters won't be with us long.

Tuner or Receiver?

Most of what we've said about tuners in this chapter, and all of what we'll have to say about them in the next one, applies equally well to tuner sections of receivers (combination tuner/amplifiers). A few receivers even use the same tuning circuits as the same company's separate tuners.

So should you get a receiver or a separate tuner?

As usual, it all depends. If you want the ultimate in features and performance, from amp, tuner, or both, you'll need separates. If space and cost are your major considerations, you may prefer a receiver.

Between these two extremes, your choice depends a great deal on the particular tuner and receiver models you're considering. The usual argument about separates versus integration apply here: you need separates if you need more from one half of the amplifier-tuner duo than from the other, or if you think the march of progress in one area will make you want to trade in half the system before you grow dissatisfied with the other.

But today there are a few features you'll find only in receivers, which may sway your choice. You're more likely to find remote control available in a receiver than a tuner (and least likely to find it in an amp)—which is a consideration, if you want to change volume or stations without getting up from your chair. (On the other hand, why not set the system up by your chair in the first place?) Many receivers also incorporate audio as well as tuner information into their displays for a result that's flashy, impressive, and sometimes even readable.

And several receivers—but few amplifiers and no tuners, as yet—now incorporate switching facilities for video as well as audio signals. That's handy if you plan to integrate your audio and video entertainment systems.

Whether you decide on a tuner or receiver, by deciding which of the features in this tempting smorgasbord you really need, which ones you'd like to have, and which you can easily live without, you'll narrow your choices among the nearly two hundred models on the market. Ultimately, your decision should rest on the tuner's performance—the subject of the next chapter.

19 Measuring Tuner Performance

Tuner specifications sound arcane but tell you a lot about how the tuner will perform. The importance of each specification, however, varies with your listening situation, as indicated by table 19–1 (adapted from one in *Stereo Review*):

	Situation			
Specification:	City	Suburb	Country	Car
Sensitivity	C	B	A	A
Capture Ratio	A	B	D	B
Selectivity	B	C	D	C
AM Rejection	A	B	D	A
Spurious-Response Rejection	A	B	D	A
Image Rejection	C	C	D	D

Table 19-1. *How the importance of FM tuner specifications varies with conditions (A = very important, B = important, C = useful, D = not critical). For specifications above the line, the lower the number the better; for those below the line, the higher the better.*

Sensitivity is the most talked-about tuner specification but not always among the most important, as the table shows. There are three ways of specifying sensitivity. All three tell how strong a radio signal the tuner needs to achieve a given level of performance. The lower the number, the less signal needed, so the more sensitive the tuner. As you can see from figure 19–1, tune stronger the radio signal, the lower the tuner's noise and distortion, until they've gone as low as that tuner lets them. (Audio output also increases with increasing signal strength but soon reaches a maximum, the point of *FM limiting*.) As you can also see by comparing the two graphs, on a good tuner the graph is steeper, reaching a good level of performance at a lower signal level and reaching a higher ultimate level of performance on strong signals.

The three basic sensitivity figures are measured at different points on the curve. *Usable sensitivity* is the signal level at which noise and distortion in mono are 30 dB lower than the audio output signal—just barely usable, in fact: you could make out the program but wouldn't enjoy listening to it under these conditions. Ignore this specification unless it's the only one you have for comparison—and then wonder why the tuner maker didn't provide more meaningful numbers.

Those numbers are the *50-dB quieting sensitivity* figures for mono and stereo. These are the radio signal levels at which noise is 50 dB below the audio output, a decent, listenable minimum. As you can see from figure 19–1, noise and distortion for any given signal strength are usually a lot higher in stereo than in mono, so it takes a much stronger signal to reach the 50-dB quieting level in stereo listening. Since you'll probably do most of your listening in stereo, the stereo figure is the more important of the two. (If the tuner specs state the *stereo threshold*—the signal level below which the tuner automatically switches to mono—it should probably be somewhere between the mono and stereo 50-dB sensitivity figures and always well above the "usable" sensitivity level.)

Obviously, the further you are from stations, the more sensitivity you need. Hence its greater importance for country listening and for listening in cars, which can travel far from stations.

Sensitivity figures may be stated in terms of signal voltage (in *microvolts*, or μV) or signal power (measured in *dBf*—decibels above one trillionth of a watt). There are two measures because the voltage for a given signal power level varies with the type of antenna—a 20-dBf signal measures 5.5 μV on a 300-ohm antenna system, but only 2.75 μV on a 75-ohm one. If you compare sensitivity figures in dBf, you're always comparing apples with apples. If you're comparing them in μV, you must either be sure both are measured across the same impedance or that you double the 75-ohm figures to make them comparable to the 300-ohm ones. There's a conversion table at the end of this chapter.

Figures given for a tuner's *signal-to-noise ratio* and ultimate *distortion* are usually given for a still higher signal level, 65 dBf, as shown in figure 19–1. As with any component,

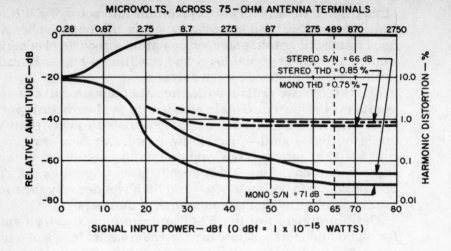

Fig. 19-1. *Reception quality vs. signal strength for two FM tuners of differing quality. (Courtesy of Audio)*

S/N should be as high and distortion as low as possible. Distortion is frequently specified only at 1 kHz, but the official tuner-measurement standard requires that it also be shown at 100 Hz and 6 kHz; it's normally a bit higher at those frequencies, especially at 6 kHz, but should still be well below 1 percent. On tuners with wide and narrow bandwidth selectors, you'll find distortion a bit higher in the narrow i.f. (intermediate frequency) mode.

Capture ratio measures how much difference, in dB, is needed between two signals on the same frequency before the tuner can latch onto the stronger one and reject the weaker (a useful FM trait which AM lacks); the lower the capture ratio is, the better. In the city a capture ratio of at least 2 dB— preferably nearer 1 dB—will help reject multipath interference. In suburbs, capture ratio also helps deal with multipath. In the country, it's usually not important—except if you're equidistant from two stations on the same frequency, when it becomes vital. When cars go from city to country, they run into both problems, hence capture ratio's importance there.

Where capture-ratio measures the ability to discriminate between desired and undesired signals on the *same* frequency, *selectivity* measures the ability to discriminate between a desired signal and others on *nearby* frequencies.

Because the FCC tries to space stations to minimize interference, the most common problem is from alternate-channel signals—those 0.4 MHz (two FM channels) away. Most tuner spec sheets therefore list *alternate-channel selectivity,* which should be as high as possible (definitely above 50 dB and preferably 80 dB or better—some go above 100 dB). High selectivity may, however, give a tuner higher distortion and a lower capture ratio, so check those specifications, too. That's one of the trade-offs of wide versus narrow i.f. bandwidth—in narrow-band mode, selectivity goes up (by about 20 dB or more), but distortion rises.

Adjacent-channel selectivity is less frequently stated, in part because the problem of adjacent-channel interference (from stations within 0.2 MHz of the desired one) is less common, and in part because the numbers read so much worse—typically 10 dB or less. A few good tuners, with narrow-bandwidth modes, can achieve higher figures, around 40 dB. If you have an adjacent-channel interference problem, consider selectable i.f. bandwidth mandatory.

A number of tuner specifications relate to the rejection of other unwanted signals. Like selectivity, these should all be as high as possible; figures of 60 to 70 dB are fairly typical, though figures of 100 dB or more can be found on the better tuners. Confusingly, a given figure may have any of three names, such as "AM rejection," "AM suppression," or even "AM response."

AM suppression reflects how well the tuner can shrug off the effects of fluctuations in signal amplitude caused by multipath, slight mistuning, signal fading, and passing airplanes.

Spurious-response rejection measures the tuner's ability to withstand such strong signals as those found within a few miles of a broadcast transmitter—hence its importance in the city (and in cars, which may drive by transmitter sites). A tuner with poor spurious-response rejection may overload on strong signals, causing *cross-modulation*, cluttering the dial with duplicates of the strong station's signal, which can then interfere with others that you want to hear. Some spec sheets list cross-modulation, or *r.f. intermodulation distortion*, the spurious responses themselves rather than the rate at which they are rejected; these figures, of course, should be as *low* as possible.

Image-response rejection shows how well the tuner can reject signals in the aircraft band. This is chiefly important to those who live near airports or under airport approach paths.

I.f. rejection measures the tuner's ability to reject signals at the same frequency as its internal "intermediate-frequency" amplifier—usually 10.7 MHz. *Subcarrier rejection* indicates how well the tuner can ignore background-music, computer-data, or foreign-language signals which some stations piggyback onto their signals to earn extra money.

Stereo separation has the same meaning in a tuner as in any other component: how well it keeps the two stereo channels unmixed. Separation figures are typically lower for tuners than for any other component except phono cartridges, typically 40 dB to 55 dB at 1 kHz, but as high as 60 dB in exceptional cases. If only one separation figure is given, it is usually measured at 1 kHz, in wide-band mode. At higher or lower frequencies, and in narrow-band mode, separation usually decreases slightly.

Frequency response is usually given as 30 Hz or 50 Hz to 15 kHz (the upper limit of FM transmissions). The better tuners also specify how strict a tolerance, in dB, applies to this spec.

You'll find fewer and less impressive specs pertaining to a tuner's AM sections, but their names, at least, should be familiar. *Usable sensitivity* should be as low as possible. Sensitivity figures in microvolts (μV) apply to signal strength at the tuner's external-antenna jacks; figures in microvolts per meter (μV/m) apply to the signal strength in the air, as measured at the tuner's built-in antenna. Since antennas differ, there's no way to compare the two.

The rest all mean about the same (but measure lower) than their FM equivalents. These include: *noise, distortion, selectivity, image response,* and *i.f. response.*

The Signal Comes First: Antennas

There are two ways to upgrade radio reception. The expensive way is to buy a better tuner. But you can often do as well, for far less, by improving the signal being fed to the tuner you already have. All you need is a good, well-sited antenna.

Most tuners come with an antenna of sorts, a T-shaped affair made of antenna lead-in wire. This will pick up strong signals, and can be aimed (if you tape it to a stick for rigidity) to emphasize desired signals and reject some undesired ones. However, a TV rabbit-ear antenna costs little, is easier to aim, and looks better in your living room; get the simplest, most durably constructed rabbit ear you can, as extra knobs and dials have little effect.

For a little more money, you can get indoor antennas with shorter elements which pick up less signal but take up less space and are combined with amplifying circuits to make up for the signal loss. Some of these antennas are far more directional than rabbit ears, making it easier to aim them to receive only the signals desired. A few can also be tuned to a narrow band of frequencies for even better rejection of unwanted signals; one or two also have remote inputs which allow them to be tuned by some tuners or receivers from the same makers, a useful gimmick.

Bodies reflect radio signals, making the signal patterns in your room change when you move. So the antenna direction which works best when you're standing there, adjusting it, may not work when you're sitting down across the room. So if you can find one of the rare indoor antennas with remote control, snap it up—it's well worth its extra cost.

For best results, an antenna should have as unobstructed a path to the station as possible—in other words, high up and outdoors, if you can manage it. Omnidirectional outdoor antennas need no aiming, but therefore can't be aimed away from undesired signals. Directional antennas generally give the best reception. This is no problem if all your signals come in from one direction, but that's rarely the case. More often you'll need either a remote-control antenna rotator or, if only two directions are involved, two differently aimed antennas on the same mast. Highly-directional antennas also have the strongest pickup, so these types are often sold for use in "fringe" areas. However, their directionality makes them worth considering for the multipath-laden city, too, if you're allowed to put an outdoor antenna up.

Putting up outdoor antennas is a skilled and hazardous job —you're probably best off hiring a professional. If you do it yourself, take precautions against falls, and be *very* careful that you don't bring your antenna into contact with electric lines. If you put the antenna up in warm weather, make sure you leave enough slack in all the cables and guy-wires so they won't snap when winter's cold contracts them.

The best antennas for FM are those designed specifically for FM reception. Nearly as good are those made for both TV and FM use (FM falls in the middle of the VHF TV band). To share such an antenna between TV and FM, use a *TV/FM splitter,* a low-cost gadget which feeds each receiver only its proper signal. If an antenna is marked for TV use, with no indication of FM, be wary—some TV antennas have circuits which cut out FM signals to prevent the possibility of their interfering with TV reception.

Antennas with *300-ohm* transmission lines use flat antenna wire, which is easy to snake under rugs and through windows and which will connect directly to most FM tuners. But this flat wire can also pick up interference between the antenna and your tuner. Antennas with *75-ohm* transmission lines use round, shielded cable, which is lumpier but has less interference pickup. Most tuners now have 75-ohm inputs too (some European ones have only 75-ohm ones). You can mix 300- and 75-ohm devices by putting an inexpensive *matching transformer* at the 300-ohm end of the system. But use such transformers only where you need them. It wastes signal strength to run the signal from a 75-ohm cable through a transformer to a tuner's 300-ohm input if that tuner also has a 75-ohm input.

Remember, when aiming your antenna, that the strongest signal is not always the best. If you get cleaner sound from a signal which registers lower on your tuner's meter than a less clean-sounding one, aim your antenna at the former.

Setting up a proper antenna may seem like an exhausting job. But once that antenna is firmly anchored on your roof, it will pull an endless bonanza of music from the sky.

Microvolt to dBf Equivalents

Microvolts (75-ohm)	Microvolts (300-ohm)	dBf
0.50	1.00	5.20
0.55	1.10	6.03
0.60	1.20	6.78
0.65	1.30	7.48
0.70	1.40	8.12
0.75	1.50	8.72
0.80	1.60	9.28
0.85	1.70	9.81
0.90	1.80	10.31
0.95	1.90	10.78
1.00	2.00	11.22
1.05	2.10	11.64
1.10	2.20	12.05
1.15	2.30	12.43
1.20	2.40	12.80
1.25	2.50	13.16
1.30	2.60	13.50
1.35	2.70	13.83
1.40	2.80	14.14
1.45	2.90	14.45
1.50	3.00	14.74
1.75	3.50	16.08
2.00	4.00	17.24
2.25	4.50	18.26
2.50	5.00	19.18
2.75	5.50	20.01
3.00	6.00	20.76
3.25	6.50	21.46
3.50	7.00	22.10
3.75	7.50	22.70
4.00	8.00	23.26
4.25	8.50	23.79
4.50	9.00	24.28
4.75	9.50	24.75
5.00	10.00	25.20
5.50	11.00	26.03
6.00	12.00	26.78
6.50	13.00	27.48
7.00	14.00	28.12
7.50	15.00	28.72
8.00	16.00	29.28
8.50	17.00	29.81
9.00	18.00	30.31
9.50	19.00	30.78
10.00	20.00	31.22
10.50	21.00	31.64
11.00	22.00	32.05
11.50	23.00	32.43
12.00	24.00	32.80

Table 19-2. *Microvolt to dBf equivalents (cont. on next page).*

Microvolt to dBf Equivalents (*Continued*)

Microvolts (75-ohm)	Microvolts (300-ohm)	dBf
12.50	25.00	33.16
13.00	26.00	33.50
13.50	27.00	33.83
14.00	28.00	34.14
14.50	29.00	34.45
15.00	30.00	34.74
15.50	31.00	35.03
16.00	32.00	35.30
16.50	33.00	35.57
17.00	34.00	35.83
17.50	35.00	36.08
18.00	36.00	36.33
18.50	37.00	36.56
19.00	38.00	36.80
19.50	39.00	37.02
20.00	40.00	37.24
20.50	41.00	37.46
21.00	42.00	37.66
21.50	43.00	37.87
22.00	44.00	38.07
22.50	45.00	38.26
23.00	46.00	38.46
23.50	47.00	38.64
24.00	48.00	38.82
24.50	49.00	39.00
25.00	50.00	39.18

Comparison of signal levels in (left to right) microvolts across 75 ohms (car radios), microvolts across 300 ohms (home radios) and dbf (both).

20 Tape I: The Recording Revolution and Basic Choices

Tape has revolutionized recording—twice.

The first of these revolutions affected every music listener. With tape, record producers could go almost anywhere and record almost anything. Tape did as much as the LP record did to broaden the classical repertoire and increase the number of performers who attained fame through recordings. It did even more for rock, much of which could never have been created without the technical tricks that tape made possible. Tape let producers salvage flawed performances, create ensembles of musicians who never met, and devise new sounds. That was one revolution.

Tape's other revolution took place in the home, when the compact, convenient cassette finally attained high fidelity. Suddenly, anyone with enough technical sense to thaw a frozen dinner could make decent recordings—and people did: class notes, baby's first words, music off the air, copies of records. You name it. The cassette also offered new ways to play and enjoy recorded music where it had not been heard before —in the car, on picnics, even when walking or rollerskating: that was Tape Revolution Number Two.

The Shapes of Tape

Tape is just a ribbon of thin, flexible plastic, coated with a film of magnetic particles suspended in a glue called the *binder*. Signals are recorded by varying the patterns in which those particles are magnetized. In playback, the varying magnetic field on the tape is translated back into an electric signal.

Tape comes in several formats. The oldest of these is the *open reel* (figure 20–1)—just a reel with tape wound on it. This format is still used for professional recording by musicians making demo tapes and by amateurs who record live performances. They use open reel because it has very high fidelity and because it can be *edited;* recorded material can be cut or rearranged using simple equipment. Open-reel is still the only format which can be edited easily and cheaply.

Open-reel tapes are good, but they're fairly big (7 inches or 10½ inches in diameter), and before you play or record a tape, you must take one end of it off the reel and thread it through the recorder to the other reel. What people wanted instead was a compact, fumble-free tape format that could be popped into the tape deck like bread into a toaster. They got two such formats: eight-track and cassette.

The *8-track cartridge* format used to be very popular, chiefly because it was offered as a factory-installed playback system on American cars. But it was bulky and its fidelity was fairly low. Today, it's obsolete. No one bothers to improve it anymore, and tapes for it are becoming hard to find. If you have an 8-track player now, you should buy a more up-to-date tape sys-

Fig. 20-1. *An open-reel recorder.* (Courtesy of Revox)

Fig. 20-2. *An audio tape cassette. Note the windows through which the heads can contact the tape.* (Courtesy of TDK)

tem, copy your favorite 8-tracks onto that, and get rid of your 8-track tapes and player.

The *cassette* (figure 20–2) has proved far more successful. It's smaller, gives better sound, and has become the basis of a universal system: you can buy nearly as many recordings on cassette as on LP disc. You can also record your own cassettes. Whether you make or buy your tapes, you can listen to them on players that fit on your shelf, in your car's dashboard, or even in your pocket. Today, when people say "tape," they usually mean "cassette."

Cassette and open-reel are not the only modern tape formats. *Microcassettes* are widely sold for dictation, note-taking, and other purposes where only limited fidelity is required. With *PCM adaptors,* people who want the ultimate in sound-recording quality can record music digitally on ordinary videocassette recorders (VCRs). The new *Beta Hi-Fi* and *VHS Hi-Fi* VCRs can also be used for pure audio recording—without picture—offering better sound than most cassette decks and up to eight hours of recording time per tape. Small *digital audio tape (DAT)* cassettes will be available within a year or two.

Cassette, microcassette, and videocassette all share one useful feature which, surprisingly, many people aren't aware of. You can prevent the recordings you make on any of these tapes from being accidentally erased or recorded over simply by knocking out a small plastic tab on the cassette. Your tape machine will look for this tab when you try recording; if it's gone, the machine will refuse to record. Videocassettes have one such tab; cassettes and microcassettes, which are recorded on two sides, have one for each side. Commercially recorded tapes already have their tabs removed. If you ever want to record over a tape that's been protected in this way, just cover the tab hole with cellophane tape (figure 20–3).

In home stereo systems today, the main tape format is cassette, though some listeners use open-reel as well. Most of what we have to say here concerns cassettes and cassette *decks*—that is, components that play and record cassettes through stereo component systems, as opposed to portable units with built-in amps and speakers.

Defining Features

Tape decks have more operating features and controls than any other stereo components. A handful of these are important enough to define the nature of the deck, the way a car model can be defined as "a four-door sedan with automatic transmission and a V-6 engine." These basic features are the number of tape heads, the presence or absence of auto-reverse, and the types of noise reduction offered. In addition, some cassette decks are *dual-well,* or *dubbing* types, which can hold two cassettes at once, recording from one to the other.

How Many Heads?

The heads are the deck's main contact with the tape. A *playback head* reads the magnetic fields recorded on the tape and converts them into the electrical signal which eventually feeds your amp and speakers. A *recording head* does the opposite: it converts electrical signals into magnetic fields which are then recorded by the tape. During recording, the *erase head* wipes older signals off the tape with a powerful high-frequency signal.

Recording and playback heads are so similar that a single head can be used for both functions alternately, writing signals onto tape when recording and reading them from the tape in playback. Decks with such combination heads are called *two-head* models (the second head is the erase head), and they

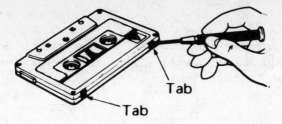

Tab

Tab

Break the tabs off with a screwdriver.

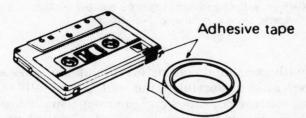

Adhesive tape

Fig. 20-3. *A cassette deck will not record on a tape whose record-protect tab has been knocked out (each side of the tape has its own tab). To re-record a protected tape, cover the tab hole with cellophane tape. (Courtesy of Harman Kardon)*

work quite well. But *three-head* decks, with separate record, play, and erase heads, work even better.

The main reason for this is gap size. A tape head is shaped like the letter *C*, with a coil of wire wrapped around the solid part and the tape moving across the open side—the *gap*—of the C. The wider the *record*-head gap (up to a point), the lower the noise and distortion in recording. But the narrower the *playback*-head gap, the better the high-frequency response. If one head must serve both, conflicting needs, its gap width must be a compromise. If recording and play are handled by separate heads, then each can have the best gap for its job.

There's an added benefit to having three heads: *off-the-tape monitoring.* Because the tape passes over the playback head just after leaving the record head, you can hear the actual recording while it's being made. This way, you can check that everything is working properly. By flicking a switch on the deck, you can compare the quality of the signal going into the

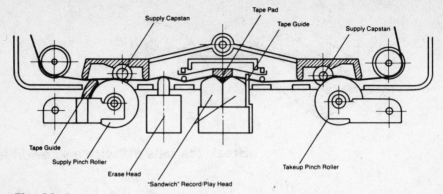

Fig. 20-4. *How the heads and capstans contact the tape in a typical "three-head" cassette deck. (Courtesy of Nakamichi)*

deck with the signal coming off the tape to make sure they're as much alike as possible. That switch is usually marked *monitor,* or *source/rec.* Amps and preamps usually have a similar switch connected to their tape input jacks. With your deck connected to such an amp, you can use either the amp's or the deck's switch to make your comparison; just leave the other switch in monitor or rec position.

Many three-head decks now have automatic monitor switches, which connect themselves to the input (source) signal whenever the tape isn't moving, and to the output signal from the tape during recording and playback. While this is simply a convenience, it's a handy one.

When you look inside some three-head cassette decks, you may see just two heads. Cassettes were originally designed for two-head operation, with only one big opening, through which a record/play head could contact the tape, plus smaller openings, such as the one used for the erase head. Thus, finding space for the third head is a problem (figure 20–4). Some manufacturers deal with this by making either their record or playback heads quite small, to fit one of the smaller openings. Others build the record and play heads into a single, siamese-twin housing that can fit the cassette's big central opening. Both approaches work, but the second approach gives a three-head deck a two-head look.

Auto-Reverse

Stereo cassettes (and stereo quarter-track open-reel tapes) are recorded on four tracks, two going to the left and two going to the right. When you reach one end of the tape, you flip it over to play or record the other two tracks. Auto-reverse decks save you the trouble, either by flipping the tape over for you or by reversing its direction to play the other side. A switch lets you select whether the deck will play one side, play each side once, or play both sides over and over for nonstop music.

There are three basic auto-reverse systems. The simplest uses a transport which can move the tape in both directions, switching between the upper and lower tracks of a four-track tape head as the tape reverses. Another type uses a two-track head which shifts or rotates to position itself for the two reverse tracks. A newer and less common system uses a one-way transport and heads, with a mechanical cassette flipper that turns the cassette around just as you would by hand.

All auto-reverse systems cause problems with *azimuth*, the angle that the head gap makes with the tape. The gap should be at precisely a right angle (90 degrees) to the direction of tape motion. If the azimuth angle is off, the deck can still make good recordings, but unless those recordings are played back on the same deck on which they were made, high-frequency response will suffer drastically. Even mismatching by a fraction of a degree can make the tapes sound "soft," lacking in treble (figure 20–5). With a two-head deck, where the same head both records and plays, azimuth problems may not be noticed as much as with a three-head deck, where the heads can become misaligned relative to each other.

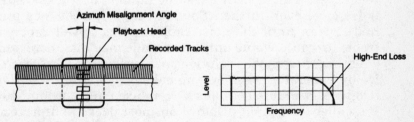

Fig. 20-5. *How tape-head azimuth-angle errors cut high-frequency response.* (Courtesy of Nakamichi)

With cassettes, even if the azimuth is perfect when the tape goes forward, it will be off if the tape's direction of movement is reversed for playing or recording in the opposite direction. At least one tape-deck manufacturer has a system which constantly readjusts the playback head to keep the azimuth correct—which is effective but expensive.

Not all auto-reverse decks will record in both directions. Those that do can record for twice as long without your intervention, but they make it dangerously easy to accidentally record over something you'd intended to keep—unless you remember to knock out the record-protect tab on the back of the cassette.

Two-head reverse-recording decks actually have three heads: one record/play head, plus one erase head for each direction of tape travel. Three-head reverse recording requires either siamese-twin heads with a flip-over system and dual erase heads, or a standard head configuration with a mechanism that flips the whole cassette around, to keep the record and play heads in their proper order.

Noise Reduction

When the cassette first appeared, its small size nearly doomed it as a high-fidelity medium. A 7-inch reel of tape holds anywhere from 1200 feet to 2400 feet of tape, depending on the tape's thickness; a cassette holds only about 280 feet to 570 feet. So, to allow adequate recording time, that tape must move slowly: $1\frac{7}{8}$ inches per second (ips), where open-reel tapes move at $3\frac{3}{4}$ ips to 15 ips. Lowering the tape speed cuts both high-frequency response and signal-to-noise ratio. Making the tape tracks narrower (cassette tapes are $\frac{1}{7}$ inch wide, open-reel tapes $\frac{1}{4}$ inch, with the same number of tracks) raises the noise level even further. Solving the high-frequency problem had to wait until the noise problem was solved, since added treble response would only have made tape hiss more audible.

The first workable solution to a cassette's hiss came from Dolby Laboratories—a system called *Dolby B noise reduction* (Dolby A is a more complex system used in recording studios). It's called just plain "Dolby" on most decks and prerecorded tapes. The Dolby system takes advantage of the fact that hiss is mainly audible when there's not enough high-frequency energy in the music to mask it from our ears. When the signal fed to the recorder lacks sufficient highs to mask tape hiss, the Dolby circuits boost the highs, then cut them down in playback by an equal and opposite amount. This also cuts the hiss. When the signal has enough highs to mask the hiss, the Dolby circuits leave it alone, since boosting already strong highs would lead to distortion on the tape. Dolby B noise reduction improves a tape deck's signal-to-noise ratio by about 10 dB above 5 kHz, the region where hiss is most noticeable. (JVC's ANRS system is similar to, and basically compatible with, Dolby B.)

This 10-dB improvement was enough to make the cassette a truly hi-fi medium. Today no cassette player or recorder with claims to high fidelity can do without Dolby B noise reduction. It is the standard. Virtually all commercially recorded cassettes are made with Dolby B, and all decent cassette machines have it.

But as tapes and heads improved the cassette's high-frequency response, hiss became more audible again, and still better noise-reduction (NR) systems became necessary. Dolby

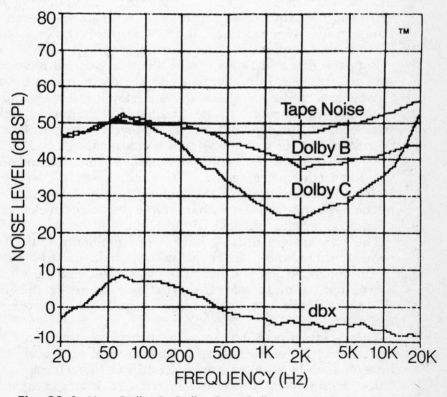

Fig. 20-6. *How Dolby B, Dolby C, and dbx noise-reduction lower tape noise levels.* (Courtesy of dbx)

came up with *Dolby C* NR, which basically does what Dolby B does, but does twice as much of it (yielding 20 dB of noise reduction rather than 10 dB) and reaches down into the middle frequencies, rather than only operating in the treble. And the dbx company came up with dbx II (usually just called *dbx*)—which works rather differently from either Dolby system (figure 20–6).

Like Dolby, dbx boosts weak signals in recording and reduces them by an equal but opposite amount in playback. Unlike Dolby, though, the dbx system also reduces strong signals in recording and boosts them back in playback, and acts on all frequencies rather than just the highs. This process of squeezing and unsqueezing the entire signal, known as *compression* and *expansion* (or *compansion*), enlarges a tape's dynamic range in two ways, as compared with Dolby's one. The action of both systems on weak signals lowers noise, letting you record quieter signals before noise becomes obtrusive; but dbx's action on strong signals also increases the tape's *headroom*—that is, it lets you record louder material without driving your tape into distortion. The result is an increase in overall dynamic range of more than 30 dB. And the better the deck's performance without NR, the more dbx improves it.

Both the dbx and Dolby noise-reduction systems have mild side-effects. Both Dolby B and Dolby C vary their treble cut in playback according to the high-frequency levels they find on the tape. If the recorder wasn't adjusted to match the tape it was recording on, the high-frequency levels in playback won't correspond to those in the signal being recorded, fooling the player into cutting the treble too much or not enough and altering the frequency response. The Dolby systems (especially Dolby C) also exaggerate any high-frequency response errors in the deck they're used with, making overbright decks sound even brighter and dull decks duller.

The dbx system doesn't have those problems; but under some circumstances (such as with signals like percussive piano notes), it lets you hear the noise level shifting up and down, a swishing sound called *breathing*. However, the lower the deck's intrinsic noise (without noise reduction), the less this effect will occur.

These side effects, however, are not the reasons more cassette decks have Dolby C than dbx; several open-reel decks have dbx, and virtually none have Dolby C. In each case, more substantial reasons prevailed: for cassette, it was compatibility; for open-reel, dynamic range.

A mass, universal medium like cassette depends on every

recording being more or less compatible with every player. For a new noise-reduction system, this includes compatibility with earlier players not specifically equipped for it. One reason Dolby B was so successful was that tapes made with it could be played back reasonably well on decks without Dolby. The tapes' high frequencies sounded a bit excessive when played back that way, but turning down the treble control could restore reasonable response. Besides, systems so primitive as to lack treble controls usually were so poor in highs that this extra, unintended boost came as a benefit. Dolby C boosts the highs (and mids) too much to be played with no decoding, but not so much that the same trick won't work reasonably well when playing Dolby C tapes on decks equipped only with Dolby B decoders—which all good modern players have. Tapes made with dbx sound almost unbearably tinny and squashed when played through systems lacking dbx decoders, so these tapes are basically usable only on playback systems which are dbx-equipped. In a pinch, playing dbx tapes through a Dolby C decoder helps with the tinniness, but not with the squashed quality. (Most dbx-equipped decks can also decode dbx-encoded LP records, of which a few dozen have been issued.)

In open-reel tape, compatibility is less of an issue, and compatibility with Dolby is no issue at all. Few, if any, open-reel decks have Dolby. But open-reel decks, both because their fidelity is very high to start with and because their tapes can be edited, are very popular for live recording. And live recording, with its unpredictable sound levels, is just where the dbx system's dynamic-range advantage is most needed. If your tape deck has no dbx circuits (and most don't), you can buy accessory dbx *companders* (compressor/expanders) to use with it.

For two-head decks, a single dbx or Dolby circuit can be used to encode the signal in recording and decode it in playback. For three-head decks, which can record and "play" at the same time, separate encode and decode circuits, one for each head, should be used. Three-head decks with built-in noise reduction have such separate encode and decode circuits (sometimes called "double Dolby" or "double dbx," which is a bit confusing); add-on dbx companders are available in versions for three-head and for two-head use.

Dolby HX and *Dolby HX Pro* are variants of Dolby B which adjust the signals sent to the record head, delaying the onset of distortion when recording strong high frequencies; in other words, extending the headroom. Both HX and HX Pro tapes are fully compatible with Dolby B NR, and quality-conscious tape duplicating companies use them.

Decks with Dolby (or ANRS) noise reduction usually have *multiplex (MPX) filter switches* or *Dolby FM switches* to prevent the 19-kHz pilot tone in stereo FM broadcasts from fooling the Dolby recording circuit into overestimating the signal's audible high-frequency content. Similar switches on some tuners have the same effect; no harm is done in using both the tuner's and the tape deck's filters. On the other hand, do not use the deck's MPX filter when recording non-FM signals rich in natural high frequencies; this can sometimes audibly reduce high-frequency response.

Bear in mind that neither the dbx nor the Dolby noise-reduction systems will affect noise that's already in the signal you're recording. The best they can do is to minimize the amount of noise added in the recording process.

Dual-Well Decks

A surprising number of decks now have two transport mechanisms and two cassette-loading wells. Their original purpose was to allow tape duplication within a single deck. Many dual-well decks save time by copying at double speed, and quite a few can dub in both directions of tape movement, switching automatically at the end of the first side so you don't have to wait around to flip the tapes over.

Some manufacturers have seen additional possibilities in dual-well design. Most decks can be set to play one tape after the other, and some can record an outside source onto two tapes in sequence. This doubles the unattended playback or recording time, as does an auto-reverse deck. If the deck combines both dual wells and auto-reverse, it can play or record for twice as long as a reversing deck, and four times as long as an ordinary, nonreversing, single-well deck.

Open-Reel Features

The features of open-reel decks are much like those found in cassette decks, except that open-reel decks have fewer of them. Conversely, they do have features and specifications rarely found on cassette decks. Four of these specifications (record/play speed, track count, tape width, and reel size) are as much defining qualities as reverse, head count, or noise reduction.

There is one standard cassette speed, 1⅞ ips; all cassette

decks run at this speed, and usually at this speed alone. All open-reel decks offer at least two speeds: 3¾ and 7½ ips for home use, 7½ and 15 ips for serious amateur and professional recording. The higher the speed, the shorter the recording time per tape—but the higher the fidelity. Higher-speed tapes are also easier to edit, since the same amount of signal is spread over a longer stretch of tape.

Most open-reel decks use tape ¼-inch wide, on which they record either two or four tracks. The *four-track,* or *quarter-track,* format, like the cassette's, has two tracks in each direction to conserve tape; after playing one side, you flip the tape over and play the other. The *two-track,* or *half-track* format uses two, wider, tracks to gain a 3-dB improvement in signal-to-noise ratio. Two-track tapes are recorded in only one direction, so they play for only half as long as four-track ones. In serious recording, this reduction in recording time doesn't matter, because the tapes would have to be recorded only in one direction to allow editing. Otherwise, the cuts and splices so carefully placed when editing the material on one side of the tape would wreak random havoc on anything recorded on the other side.

A "four-track" stereo deck only records or plays two tracks at a time. However, four-track machines made for musicians and studios usually record all four tracks in the same direction, allowing complex musical effects to be built up before they're *mixed down* to stereo's two channels. Some of these four-track machines use ½-inch or wider tape; studio decks with eight or more tracks always use wider tapes.

Tape-Deck Performance

As with other components, frequency response in a tape deck should be as wide as possible: for cassette decks, consider 15 Hz to 15,000 Hz a minimum, since 20 Hz to 20,000 Hz is (for a few dollars more) within reach. Remember, too, that frequency-response specs that show tolerance limits (such as ±3 dB) tell you more than specs that don't.

Don't just read the numbers. Read the frequency curves, too, if you can get them. (Manufacturers' literature rarely shows these curves, but good magazine test reports usually do.) Better a deck that's flat to 15 kHz and then drops off than one which goes all the way to 20 kHz but with slopes, dips, or bumps in the curve. Pay attention to response below 50 Hz, where the performance of many decks drops. And compare a deck's frequency response curves, with various noise-reduction circuits and without, for close matching. A mismatch means that the noise-reduction wasn't properly adjusted at the factory.

Signal-to-noise ratios should be as high as possible: at least 55 dB without noise reduction and at least 65 dB with NR (70 dB or more is better). Distortion is rarely listed, but if it is, it should be as low as possible.

Look for wow-and-flutter figures below 0.1 percent (weighted rms), and preferably less than 0.05 percent. (Peak readings for the same amount of flutter will be higher; look for a figure below ±0.15 percent.) Speed consistency, if listed, should be within 1 percent or less; otherwise, tapes made on your deck may sound off-pitch when played on other decks, and vice versa.

About the only tape-deck specifications likely to be new to you are *bias frequency* and *fast-forward/rewind times. Bias* is a high-frequency current mixed with the audio signal in recording to reduce distortion. To ensure that it won't interact with the audio signal, it should be at least five times as high as the highest audio frequency the deck can record—i.e., 100 kHz or more for a deck which can record audio up to 20 kHz. As to fast-winding times, the faster they are, the less time you'll spend waiting for the tape to reach the spot you want to hear. But some decks with very fast speeds don't wind the tape as smoothly as they should, and the resulting wrinkles or edge-wear can affect the signal.

The numbers we've mentioned so far apply to cassette decks. Open-reel decks should do somewhat better, especially in high-frequency response and S/N without noise reduction. If a deck has more than one speed (common on open-reel, rare on cassette) it will sound and measure best at its highest speeds.

You needn't judge performance by numbers alone. There are several ways to check a deck's performance in the store. Bring along a good, commercially recorded cassette (for example, one produced by Mobile Fidelity, In-Sync Labs, or Angel/Capitol/EMI XDR-series tapes, Nakamichi, or any tape made with Dolby HX Pro) of the kind of music that you listen to, and hear how well the deck plays recordings made on other machines.

Then try recording from a wide-range source such as a Compact Disc. If the deck has three heads, you can switch back and forth between the original and the recording for comparison. If it doesn't, you'll have to record a bit, then go back to the beginning of the tape and of the disc and try to restart them in sync with each other. Listen for changes in frequency balance, and for noise and distortion. The ideal is a deck whose recordings sound exactly like the original material—not "better" and certainly not worse.

Another good test, and one which works as well with two-head as with three-head decks, is to record the noise found between stations on FM. Dial to a spot where there are no signals on nearby frequencies, and switch off the tuner's muting and any MPX filters on the deck or tuner. Now record the noise, setting the deck's recording-level control for a reading of about −10 on its level meter. Compare the original noise and its recording to see how much or little the deck alters what it records. Try this with and without noise reduction, but pay more attention to results with NR, since that's the way you'll usually use the deck.

You can also check for headroom by repeating this test at 0 dB on the recording meter. At this higher level, there will usually be a drop-off in high-frequency response when the tape gets all the highs it can handle. The higher the deck's headroom, the less of this effect you'll hear.

Cassette decks usually sound their best with metal (Type IV) tape, next best with Type II (chrome, CrO_2, or chrome-equivalent), and still fairly good with the better Type I (ferric) tapes. Most serious listeners use Type II for most of their recording since it gives a good balance between Type IV's performance and Type I's low price. Open-reel decks using the new EE tapes get better performance at low speeds with that formulation; at high speeds, there's little difference between EE and regular tape.

Besides listening to the deck's performance, listen to the deck itself as it goes through its paces. Does it perform silently or do you hear motor noise? When you start, stop, and rewind, does it perform with a quiet "click" or a solid "kerchunk"? Or does it jingle tinnily? In our experience, the more solid-sounding mechanisms tend to be more solidly built and reliable.

Pay attention to the feel of the controls and to their placement. You spend more time at the controls of a tape deck than any other component; get a deck whose controls are enjoyable to use.

Frills and Fundamentals

You can narrow your tape-deck choices considerably just by deciding whether you want a two-head or a three-head deck (we recommend three), whether or not to get auto-reverse (convenient, but it adds cost and complications which can slightly compromise performance), and which noise-reduction systems to get (we recommend Dolby B plus either Dolby C, dbx, or both). You can then speed your selection even further by narrowing your choice to decks whose specifications reflect the kind of performance you want and are willing to pay for.

But that still leaves a long list of features to consider. Some are fancy but useful variants on such fundamental features as meters and controls to regulate recording level, counters to help you find where you are on a tape, and controls to move and stop the tape. Others are extras, designed to help you make better recordings or just to make recording and playback easier and more fun. All of them (we hope) will be found in the next chapter.

21 Tape II: Features and Fundamentals

Tape decks perform a dual job, recording as well as playing back. Recording is an active task, requiring attention and involvement, at least some of the time. For these reasons, tape decks offer a smorgasbord of features, more than any other kind of audio component.

The choice may seem *too* dazzling until you break the list down into manageable chunks. The main division is between features which help you get better sound and those which simply add convenience. Most of the sound-improvement features deal with recording and most of the conveniences with playback. And some features affect recording and playback equally. Let's begin with those.

The Transport and Tape Fidelity

The transport is the part of the deck which moves the tape. Like a phonograph turntable, it must be able to do this at a precise and steady speed or speeds. But the transport must do more than this. Since you can't just move an arm across the tape's coiled surface to play different portions of it, the transport must be able to shuttle the tape back and forth at high speed. And if the deck has auto-reverse, the transport must be able to move the tape with equal steadiness and precision in either of two, opposite directions.

Naturally, a tape transport is visibly more complex than a turntable. The main parts are the two *spindles* which engage the cassette (or reel) hubs, and a metal *capstan* and a rubber pinch or pressure roller through which the tape must be threaded (figure 21–1).

In playback and recording, the pinch roller presses the tape against the capstan, which turns at a constant speed. Meanwhile, the *take-up spindle* gently winds up the tape as it feeds from the capstan and pinch roller, and the *rewind spindle* releases tape just reluctantly enough so that it will pass snugly over the tape heads.

In the very simplest transports, one motor drives the capstan and both spindles. In better decks, one motor drives the capstan while the spindles are driven by either one common motor or one motor apiece. Three-motor decks offer the smoothest performance, fastest tape winding, and greatest reliability (the complex mechanical linkages to multipurpose motors are more likely to break down then the motors are), but they also cost

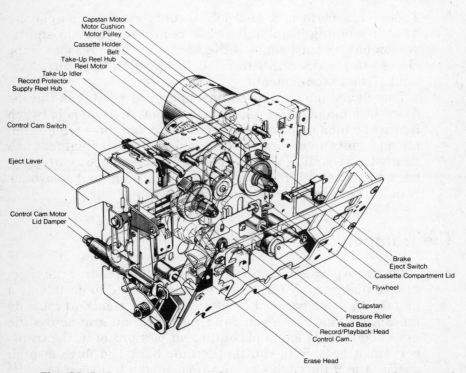

Fig. 21-1. *Tape transports can be very complex mechanisms.* (Courtesy of Nakamichi)

the most. We recommend two motors as the minimum worthy of serious consideration.

A deck can have more than one capstan, too. Auto-reverse decks are especially likely to have *dual capstans,* since it's easier to pull than push tape smoothly across the heads. In some such decks, only one capstan works at a time. In others, though, both capstans work at once, regardless of the tape's direction—and many nonreversing decks use dual capstans this way too. In this type of transport, the two capstans form a *closed loop* which isolates the tape from outside influences (such as irregularities in the cassette shell), allowing only the capstans, pinch rollers, and the smoothness of the heads to influence tape motion. Many of the best transports are made this way.

Like turntables, capstans on multimotor decks are usually driven either directly, from a motor operating at the capstan speed, or by a belt from a faster-turning motor. Both types can produce good performance, but direct-drive is potentially more reliable, especially if the deck has more than one tape speed. *Servo-controlled motors,* whose speed is regulated by electronic circuits instead of by the pulses of the AC power line, can be used with both types of drive. With any type of drive, large flywheels can increase speed stability.

Don't just consider a transport's features. Check it out physically. Do its controls work smoothly? Does it sound and feel solidly built, not tinny? How smoothly does it wind tape? (This is easier to judge on open-reel decks, where the tape is out in the open.) Is it quiet during recording and play? (You want to hear the signal, not the tape or recorder.) Are the tape heads accessible for cleaning with a cotton swab or small, soft brush? (This is more often a problem on cassette than reel decks.) How easy is it to load and unload tapes?

If you're buying an open-reel deck because you want to edit your tapes, check the following points: Are the heads easily accessible, so you can mark the tape for editing? Is there a way to hold the tape reels still while the tape contacts the heads, so that you can "rock" the tape across the heads to find just where to edit? (This usually works best in the "pause" mode, but some decks have special edit modes for this.) Is there a tape-dump switch? (This editing feature, not too common, lets you disconnect the take-up reel motor temporarily, so you can dump undesired sections of tape into the wastebasket as you play them.)

Matching the Deck to the Tape...

Tapes look alike, but the resemblance ends there. Different types of tape differ substantially, and even between tapes of the same type there are significant performance differences—which most tape decks can be adjusted (at least internally) to take best advantage of. Cassette tapes vary most widely, so cassette decks offer the most ways of coping with those variations.

In playback, the only important difference is in frequency *equalization*, the system of boosting high frequencies in recording and cutting them back in playback to produce an overall flat response. As in phonograph recording, this also results in lower noise than you'd find in "flat," unequalized recording.

There are two standard cassette playback equalization curves. One, called the *120-microsecond curve,* is used for *Type I* tapes, the most economical kind, which use ferric oxide (much like precision-ground rust) as their magnetic material. The other, called the *70-microsecond curve,* is used for Type II and Type IV tapes.

The original *Type II* tapes used *chromium dioxide* (CrO_2), commonly called "chrome," as their magnetic material; many now use other materials and are called *chrome-equivalent* tapes, because they offer similar performance and use the same recorder settings. Type II tapes generally offer the best compromise between cost and fidelity.

The magnetic materials in *Type IV* tapes are particles of pure metal rather than metal oxides. Such tapes can be magnetized more intensely than ferric or chrome ones. However, they cost more to make, and older cassette decks (any which lack a *"metal"* control setting) cannot record them properly. Any deck can play them back, however. *Type III* tapes never became popular and have disappeared.

To cope with all of these, most decks have a switch to select the proper equalization for each tape type. On many decks, the switch is automatic, triggered by code notches on the back of the cassette. If it's a manual switch, it may be marked "120/70 μS," "normal/chrome," "normal/metal," or "Type I/Type III-IV." Most tapes are marked to show which equalization they require; those which aren't are almost always Type I and take the 120-μsecond setting.

Playback equalization is something to notice but not to worry about. The only problem with using the wrong setting is a slight change in frequency response. Playing a Type I tape with 70-μsecond equalization will roll off its high frequencies and make it sound dull; using 120-μS equalization to play a 70-μS tape will overemphasize its highs, and make it sound "hotter" and hissier. But the tape itself is unchanged by this and will sound normal as soon as you play it with its proper equalization.

When you make a recording, though, tape matching becomes more critical and more complex. It's more critical because only the right settings will give you the best possible recording, and any errors you make will become part of the recording, lasting until you erase the tape and re-record it. It's more complex because you now have not one but three parameters to worry about. (These are equalization, bias, and tape sensitivity—more on the last two shortly.) Also, the differences between tapes of the same type show up more in recording than in playback.

The simplest decks basically ignore these complexities. There may be a single switch with three positions (one for each tape type), which selects bias and equalization together, or there may be separate switches for bias and "EQ." As long as you select the right bias for recording, and the same equalization for recording and playback of any tape, the results will be pretty good.

For recordings which are great instead of pretty good, you need to set your deck to precisely match the particular tape you're using. (If "pretty good" is good enough for you, skip down to the subhead "Making Recordings Right"; between here and there we cover nuances and niceties, not basics.) Tapes of different brands and varieties require slightly different settings in recording—and even tapes of the same variety may have slight differences, as manufacturers keep making slight improvements in them.

The most important of these characteristics is *bias*. This is a high-frequency current sent to the recording head together with the audio signal, to nudge the tape into accepting signals properly. If there's too little, the recording will be distorted; too much, and the recording will have poor high-frequency response.

A few years back, recorders appeared with bias-control knobs so users could vary bias to apply just the right amount for every tape variety. You could set those knobs by ear, comparing the sound of a sound source and its recording (much easier to do with three-head decks, of course) until the two sounded as much alike as possible. More elaborate models (mostly three-head) had circuits to generate test tones, whose level could be read on a meter to show when bias is correct.

Now, more and more decks have computers which automatically match the deck's bias and other parameters for each tape. Some of these, however, still let you vary bias slightly by pushing buttons when the deck is setting itself. These buttons let you adjust for the type of music. Standard bias is best for classical and folk music, which is strong in middle tones but has comparatively gentle highs. However, it tends to dull the sizzle of treble-heavy rock recordings; slight underbiasing is best for them. Slight overbias might be best for speech recordings, which have little high-frequency energy.

Decks with automatic tape-matching computers also fine-tune equalization and sensitivity, which are otherwise not under your control. While playback equalization is standardized, *recording equalization* is not. The deck should use whatever equalization will make each particular tape yield a recording which will play back with flat frequency response on a deck with standard playback EQ. The automatic system varies the recording EQ to do just that.

Tape-sensitivity adjustments are only necessary because of Dolby noise reduction. Both Dolby B and C vary high-frequency response in playback according to the levels they find on the tape. If a tape has very low sensitivity, it will put out an unusually low signal level in playback, fooling the Dolby circuits into cutting back the highs too far. If the tape's sensitivity is high, it will put out a very strong signal and the Dolby circuits won't cut back the highs enough. The tape-matching computer records a test signal, measuring its playback level, then adjusting the signal level fed to the tape. Once that adjustment is made, a signal just strong enough to register at the Dolby-level mark (a small Dolby logo) on the recording meter will produce a specific level of magnetism on the tape.

Some tape-matching computers are better than others, either because they offer finer gradations of adjustment or make more revealing tests, or both. But almost any of them will give you slightly better recordings than you'll get by using stock settings which match the average tape in any given class, but not the particular tape you're using. Some also have "error" lights, to warn you when you've set the deck for the wrong tape type, or if there's something wrong with the tape.

How much all this means to you depends on how critical you are of your recordings. Nonetheless, a lot of people worry unnecessarily. If you do the worst thing you possibly can—set the deck for one tape type when recording with another—all you'll do is ruin that recording. If you set for the right tape type but don't do a precision match, your recording will be just a bit less good than it would otherwise have been. If you set your deck for the wrong tape type in playback, your high-frequency response will be off until you notice and reset your switches. But nothing you can do in playback can permanently affect the tape, and no control settings you use in recording or playback can physically harm the tape or permanently affect the deck.

. . . And Matching the Tape to the Deck

The most common question tape-deck owners ask is "What's the best tape?" The question they should be asking is "What's the best tape for my deck?" For the tape which performs best on my deck may not be the best one to use on yours—especially if either or both decks lack the elaborate tape-matching facilities we've just been describing.

This is least true of metal tapes, whose bias and equalization requirements are quite similar. But it's definitely the case with Type II tapes; some of these have flat response and others have rising high-frequency response under the same conditions.

Theoretically, a rising high end is an offense against good fidelity. But if your deck has a fall-off in high-frequency response, or over-biases (which also diminishes high frequencies), or if you record a lot of sizzly rock and can't reduce your deck's bias to accommodate it, such tapes will give you better overall fidelity than truly flat ones.

The only way to find out which tapes work best for you is to buy a batch of different ones and test them. Such experimentation is affordable: tapes don't cost much, and you can always use the lower-performing tapes for less critical applications, such as taping off FM (whose high-frequency response is limited to 15 kHz) or copying older records.

The tests are simple. For each tape, first adjust your recorder to match the tape's requirements as best you can, then record some FM interstation noise (or pink noise, if you have a pink-noise generator). Record at −10 dB on your recorder's level meter, then compare the recording to the original noise source. The original and the recording should sound as much alike as possible. If you record much music with strong high frequencies, repeat the test at −5 dB; listen to see which tapes lose the least high-frequency response on this test; most will lose at least some.

Then repeat the tests on music, using the highest-fidelity examples you can find (Compact Discs are ideal) of the kinds of music you expect to tape most often. Record at normal levels —that is, with the meter reading zero or below most of the time, with occasional flicks into the red zone above zero—and use noise reduction. This time, listen not only to frequency response but to distortion and noise (which you can't readily detect on the FM-noise test). You still want the tape which will change the sound the least.

Once you find what tape works best for you, stock up on it. When your stock runs low, buy current samples of whatever's available, and repeat your tests. Tape formulations change as manufacturers improve them, and the one that best matches your machine today may be eclipsed (or improved past compatibility) tomorrow.

Making Recordings Right

Tape has a limited dynamic range. If you record a signal too softly on it, that signal will be obscured by noise. If you record too strong a signal, it will become distorted. So every tape deck has a *recording-level control* to help you keep your signals within the proper range, and a *recording-level meter* to tell you when you have or haven't done so.

In general, on recording-level meters, the level is correct when it registers at or a bit below the meter's zero point most of the time, with occasional flicks into the red zone above zero. If the signal is so low that the meter doesn't flicker, you can be pretty sure it's being buried in the noise; if it spends much time above zero, you can be almost as sure you'll hear distortion when you play it back.

Just how sure you can be of these things depends on the meter. For example, if the tape deck's manufacturer set his meter's zero point low (below the Dolby-level mark), recordings that poke above zero will be less likely to distort, but those well below zero will be closer to the tape deck's noise floor. If the manufacturer sets his zero point high above the Dolby mark, you'll have less *headroom* for strong signals before hitting the distortion point but will have more leeway in avoiding noise. (There is an international standard zero setting, about 2 dB above the Dolby-level mark, but not all manufacturers follow it.)

The design of the meter and meter circuits is important, too. You'll know more about what's happening to your signal with a meter that reads from −40 to +6 dB than with one which merely reads from −20 to +3.

Since metal (Type IV) tape has more headroom than Types I and II, some decks also expand their scales for Type IV, either by extending the scales physically or by showing a different zero point. And since the high-frequency boost in recording equalization limits high-frequency headroom, some tape decks (chiefly those made in Europe) have *equalized meters,* which read the signal after recording equalization rather than before.

Meters also come in slow (average-reading) and fast (peak-reading) varieties; both kinds are easy to use and give you good results in recording, though each takes a bit of getting used to. *Peak-reading* meters are usually a bit easier to understand, especially if they have *peak hold.* This feature lets the meter keep showing a peak for a few seconds after its passage, so you can judge your recording levels without watching the meters like a cat watching a mousehole. *Average-reading* meters (mainly the ones with needles rather than all-electronic displays, and especially the ones labeled "VU") are sometimes supplemented by lights which flash when peaks reach the distortion point.

The older, needle-type meters are a bit hard to read at times, especially from a distance. But their needles can show even very small signal differences, if you look closely enough. This makes them ideal for decks on which you fine-tune bias manually.

The newer, all-electronic displays respond faster and are easier to read from afar. But they show signal differences in a series of small steps rather than on a continuous scale. The more steps per dB, especially in the critical region around the zero point, the more precisely you can read the meter. Don't judge the number of steps by counting the lines on the meter but by recording a steady noise source (such as FM noise) and slowly adjusting the recording level. If those little lines turn on and off three at a time, there are only one-third as many meter steps as the number of lines seemed to indicate.

One last point. Consider how high you'll place your deck when you're recording and make sure the meter will be easy to read from there.

Recording-level controls come in a few varieties, too. The control itself, for instance, may be a conventional knob, a sliding button, or a pair of buttons which control an electronic up/down fader circuit. If you only tape records and radio programs, any of these will do. If you do much live recording, though, avoid push-buttons. You'll get most precise control from the old-fashioned knob and slightly less precision but more speed from the slider.

The most common knob arrangement is to put the left- and right-channel recording controls on one shaft, with a clutch, so you can move them both together or reset one higher or lower than the other if your signal is unbalanced. Many decks, however, have a large, *master level control* plus small, individual-channel level-adjust knobs or a *recording balance control,* both a trifle more convenient than clutched controls.

It's possible to avoid the whole recording-level problem with *automatic level control (ALC)* circuits. These are universal in small portable recorders used for recording speech, but they compress the dynamic range of music too much, cutting its dramatic impact. Some portable recorders used for music recording have *limiters* instead. These leave most music unaffected, but do lower the gain when the signal gets too loud, on the principle that it's better to lose some impact and retain clean sound than to overload the tape into distortion—and lose the impact anyway.

If you intend any live recording, make sure your deck has *microphone jacks*—not all decks do. On many decks, if you plug in only one mike, its mono signal will feed both channels, which is handy when you don't feel like bothering with stereo. Some decks (mainly open-reel models, these days) have separate (*mixing*) recording-level controls for the microphone jacks and for the *line input jacks* which connect your deck to the rest of your stereo system. This lets you do tricks like recording yourself playing with the Philharmonic (or the Stones) and mixing background music or sound effects from records in with your voice. If you're really serious about live recording, you may want to use more than one mike per channel, plugging them into an external mixer. In that case, you can do without mike inputs on your deck.

These are the basic aspects of tape decks—the considerations essential to recording the music well for your future enjoyment.

22 Tape III: All Modern Conveniences

In that great smorgasbord of tape-recorder features we mentioned a while back, we come at last to the dessert. Not a feature mentioned in this chapter is really necessary—but most all are worth having, since they make tape easier and more fun to use.

Find That Tune

People spend more time playing tapes than recording them, so most tape conveniences are mainly for playback, the majority of them to help you find and play the tunes you want.

On records, that's an easy task. You can see where each band starts and ends, and move the arm across directly to the one you want. On tape, you can't see where selections start and stop, and have to wind through yards of intervening tape to reach them. The deck has to help you; and it does.

As simple a feature as a backlit tape well, which lets you see roughly how much tape is left, can help. And even the very simplest decks have *tape counters* to help you gauge how far you've come along the tape. If you remember to set them to zero (a simple button-push usually does that) at the start of each tape side, you'll have a reference against which you can mark where each new selection starts. (What's being counted is the number of times the feed or take-up spindle turns, which means that the amount of tape per hundred counts will vary according to how much tape has already wound onto that spindle.)

On most decks, if you set the counter to zero in the middle of the tape, and press a *memory counter button*, you can rewind or fast-forward to that spot automatically, without watching the counter dial. Some decks can even be set to begin *auto play* once they reach the memorized spot, rather than just stopping there and waiting for you to push the play button. A few can also be set to play up to the zero point, then either stop or rewind the tape so you can play it over. Alternatively, the *auto rewind* feature can play to the end of the tape and rewind to the zero point.

With electronics, the counter can be made to do even more. If nothing else, it will be bigger, brighter, and easier to read from a distance—handy if you want to check whether the tape's moving or not. The only catch is that these counters can't remember where they were when the power went off—even if you left off in midtape, they wake up at "0000" the next time you switch the deck on.

Electronic counters often can measure tape position by elapsed or remaining time as well as by the traditional system of counting turns of the feed or take-up spindle. That's a great improvement; the number of counts per minute of tape varies with the amount of tape that's already built up on the spindle in question.

Some time counters are merely stopwatches, ticking off time while the deck is in play or record mode, but not showing where you are during rewind or fast-forward. True time counters, which operate in all modes, are the best. To translate tape turns into time, these counters must know how much tape was in the cassette to begin with. Most require that you enter the tape length by setting a switch, but some sense it automatically.

Helpful as it is to know where something is on the tape, looking for that tune is still a nuisance. To help you, many decks have *cue and review*, a feature that lets you listen to the tape during fast-forward or rewind. The sound of this is often described as "monkey chatter," but it's usually enough to let you know what part of the tape is going by.

Even fancier are systems which locate selections on the tape for you by sensing the silence between selections, as long as those silences are long enough (four or five seconds, on the average). Alas, these *"auto locator"* systems (each manufacturer calls his by a different name) will also often stop at quiet passages in the music—more of a problem for classical and folk than jazz and rock listeners. It's also more of a problem if the system is *programmable*, whether it can be programmed

Fig. 22-1. *Decks with dual tape wells can be used for copying tapes or to double playing or recording time by using two tapes in sequence. (Courtesy of Onkyo)*

only to skip ahead a given number of bands or to play several selections and skip the rest.

A *scan* feature, like the one on FM tuners, will play the first few seconds of each taped selection, stopping when you signal that you've found one you want to hear. Cleverer decks can do even more, such as automatically skipping long blank sections (usually 40 seconds or so), fast-winding to the tape's end, and, if they can, reversing to play the other side.

Once you've found what you want to hear, the deck may let you hear it over and over. *Repeat* functions can do many things, depending on the deck: replay the whole tape, one song, the complete list of programmed selections, the stretch between either end of the tape and the memory zero point, or between two memorized positions.

To prevent the tape speed from wobbling as the deck takes up take slack at the start of recording or play, some decks have *automatic slack take-up,* which acts as soon as the tape is loaded. And several decks have *pitch controls,* for the same reasons turntables have them—to let you play an instrument along with the recording, and to let you sharpen up the tone and speed the tempo slightly (or do the opposite, of course). These controls do not work in recording, to ensure that you won't accidentally record something at the wrong speed; decks without pitch controls would then be unable to play the tape back correctly.

Recording Aids

Recording, too, has its tape-location aids—but fewer of them, found on fewer models. If you want to add one more selection to a partly recorded tape, *blank search,* on some decks, will find the next long, unrecorded spot and rewind to its beginning. You may also find an *auto skip* feature, which fast-forwards the tape a few inches after you rewind it so that you won't start recording on the tape's unmagnetizable plastic *leader.* If your recording isn't going well, a few decks let you press an *auto return* button to cancel the recording and rewind to the spot where it began, ready to start over.

More common is *punch-in,* which lets you switch from playback to recording without stopping the tape. This is useful if you want to record over part of an earlier recording: just listen for the end of the part you want to keep, and hit "record." Some decks let you do this with a single button, for convenience; others make you hold down the "play" button when you touch the "record" one, to make sure you don't tape over your previous recording by accident. Punch-in is rarely mentioned in spec sheets, but you'll find it on many decks if you try their controls.

It's desirable to have silence between selections, to tell both your ears and auto tape locator systems where each song begins and ends. You can do this by turning the level control down, then fading it back up again. *Recording preset pointers* on some recording-level controls make it easier for you to restore the level you began with. This process becomes easier still with *automatic faders,* which fade the level down to zero at the touch of a button and fade back up to your previous recording level at the touch of a second one. It's best if you can control how fast these fades occur; they usually go slowly if you simply press the button and release it, quickly if you hold the button down.

More abrupt, but far more common, are the *record mute button* (which records silence as long as you hold it down) and the *auto record mute* (which records just enough silence for the auto-locator to find, then puts the deck into "pause" mode).

Incidentally, the difference between a deck's *pause* and *stop* buttons isn't always clear to first-time tape users. Pressing "stop" turns off the tape deck's motors and recording circuits and fully retracts the pinch roller from the capstan. Pressing "pause" stops the tape's motion but pulls the pinch roller only a small distance from the capstan and leaves the capstan turning so the tape can get off to a flying start as soon as you press the pause button again; if you enter "pause" when recording, you'll resume recording as soon as the tape restarts, without having to press "record" a second time.

It's a good idea to have an easily noticed pause control, or a light to signal when it's on. Otherwise, you may waste time wondering why your deck will light up and fast-wind the tape but won't start playing or recording. Even experienced tape users can get caught this way—it's happened to us. On some decks, pressing the start button automatically disengages the pause mode, which prevents such puzzlements.

For taping records, several manufacturers offer a specialized pause system called *automatic cueing*. This synchronizes the deck with one of the same manufacturers' turntables, so that recording will begin the moment the turntable sets its tonearm on the record and will stop the moment the arm is raised. At least one deck has an *auto pause system,* which shifts from record to pause mode if the signal stays quiet for 40 seconds or so. This can prevent much wasted tape.

Miscellaneous Niceties

Electronics is taking over many of the tape deck's mechanical functions. You can feel that effect in the main transport controls, which are more and more often soft-touch pushbuttons instead of the old, mechanical "piano keys." Those controls don't just feel nicer—they do more, letting you jump straight from one function to another without having to press the stop key first. You can, for instance, shuttle back and forth between fast-forward and rewind, or fast-wind and play, to find a precise spot on the tape. The automatic tape-location systems are made simpler and less expensive by electronic (sometimes called *logic, computer,* or *microprocessor*) control.

So is *remote control.* If that's important to you, remember that some manufacturers offer one remote controller for their tape decks and other components (tuners, receivers, amps, even turntables) so you don't need separate controllers for each one. Just be sure that all the components on that control system meet your needs before you let the remote feature sway you.

Timer start switches don't depend on electronic control, but are also more common because of them. These switches let you start and stop the deck by turning its power on and off with an external timer, either so you can wake yourself with music or so you can tape a radio program when you're not around to turn the tape on by yourself. Without timer start, you'd have to leave the deck in play or record mode for hours, with its power off; in most mechanically controlled decks, this would wear flat spots on the pinch roller, which would then cause wow and flutter, and electronic decks would release their pinch rollers as soon as the power went off, to prevent just that.

Control "Feel" and Human Engineering

All these controls—the necessities, the fancied-up necessities, and the pure frills—are there in hopes you'll use them. Before you pay for them, make sure you will. A deck with every automatic feature can do a lot for you, but only if you really study how to operate it. If you find the sight of a button-studded deck rather daunting, then go for a simpler model. It will handle all the important basic tasks and will also cost you less.

But take a second look at the more feature-loaded decks before making your final decision. For one thing, there's an indirect link between complexity and performance: since high-performance decks cost more, the makers tend to load them with extra features to ease the buyer's mind about their cost. There can also be a direct link when some of those extras are such features as automatic tape matching, which can help you get better sound.

And a well-designed deck with a lot of buttons can actually be easier to use than a poorly designed deck with fewer of them. Good designers group controls by related functions and emphasize the most important ones by making them bigger or placing them more prominently.

Sometimes the lesser controls can be tucked out of sight in useful ways. For example, it makes sense to put the tape-type and noise-reduction selector switches in the tape compartment, where they'll only be seen when you're changing tapes, because you're then reminded of those controls precisely when you're likely to be using them. On the other hand, features whose only purpose is to hide controls, such as motorized front panels, strike us as a bit silly—needless complications which improve the look of things but actually make the deck less functional, not more.

We've now covered all the major components of a stereo system. All that's left is to tie them together—the next step, and the next chapter.

23 Putting It All Together

After all the time we've spent on how to select each individual component of a hi-fi system, you may well have braced yourself for a massive tome on how to hook it all together. Well, unbrace. Setting up a hi-fi system is a lot simpler than it looks—basically it's a matter of deciding where things go and plugging them together.

Where to Put It All

When you look for places to put hi-fi equipment in your room, you should consider sound, convenience, and your room's furnishings.

First decide where you'd like to sit when listening. Ideally, the speakers should be placed where that seat will face them and be equidistant from either (figure 23–1). The other components of the system will be easiest to use if they're placed near the listening seat, their controls within reach. While stores often place the components on the wall between the speakers for display, there are no technical reasons to do so at home.

Depending on their design, the speakers should either rest on the floor, on floor stands, or on wall shelves or (for some small speakers) hooks. The other components leave you more choice: you can put them on wall shelves, in special hi-fi cabinets, or atop other pieces of furniture; or you can build them into cabinets not originally designed for hi-fi. Your furniture

Fig. 23-1. *Matching cabinets are available to house audio, video, and other home-electronic equipment. (Courtesy of Custom Woodwork & Design)*

choices should allow for plenty of cooling air to circulate around each component (especially the amplifier), give you access to the controls in front and the wires behind each (open-backed cabinet on casters help), and let you conceal the wires so the installation looks neat. Keep components at least a foot or two away from the heat of radiators and even farther from vibrating devices such as air conditioners.

If you're stacking components in a vertical cabinet or rack, pay attention to the order you stack them in. Most turntables have lift-up lids, which dictate that they be placed on top. Power amplifiers usually go on the bottom of the rack, to lower the center of gravity and so you can leave a few inches above them free of other gear, for ventilation. Of the other components, decide which one's controls you'll use most often and mount it at whatever height is most convenient for you, give the second most convenient position to whichever component you fiddle with second most, and so on.

Speakers can be placed at long distances from amplifiers, but the other components should be close enough to be connected by cables no more than about four feet long. Longer cable runs can affect the sound quality and will almost certainly leave the components too far apart for you to operate them all conveniently. No component should be farther from the amplifier than your arm span, and your tape deck should be at least that close to your other program sources, for your convenience when recording them.

Your stereo system won't be the only furniture in your room, nor will listening be the only thing you use the room for. Bear in mind the location of other furniture (so that none blocks the sound path from the speakers to your ears) and traffic patterns through the room (so that passersby will rarely block the sound and will never need to detour around your components).

These basics aren't the whole story. In audio, they never are. Once you've settled on approximately where your stereo components go, it's time to fine-tune the setup for the best possible sound—putting the speakers where they'll sound the best and putting the turntable where it will be least affected by the speakers.

Placement, Sound, and Room Acoustics

Speakers and rooms vary too much to allow blanket rules for speaker placement; but there are basic guidelines.

We've already mentioned that the speakers need a clear shot at your ears. Low frequencies can work their way around small pieces of furniture, but the high frequencies cannot. If the speakers beam high frequencies tightly, you may also have to aim the speakers so that the highs aim directly at your seat. On the other hand, if the speakers' highs are too energetic, you may choose to aim them just outside the listening area, to tame them.

Bass response can also change dramatically with speaker (and listening-seat) placement. The more room surfaces (walls, floor, and ceiling) are near your speakers, the more bass you'll get. More bass isn't always better bass: a speaker with weak bass may sound better in a corner on the floor, while a speaker with a more robust low end might sound best on a stand in the middle of the room. Shockingly few speakers' instructions even mention these matters, and those which do aren't always correct, so experiment a bit before choosing your speakers' final location. You can get some clues from the showroom where you bought your speakers—a canny dealer will probably have placed them approximately where they'll sound best; use his location as a starting point.

Bass does not always spread evenly around the room. It often sets up *standing waves,* patterns of alternating loud and soft bass. Listen for this by playing either low-bass tones, FM inter-station noise, or pink noise, with your treble turned down and your bass turned up. If you hear changes in bass level at differ-ent spots in the room, you can often even them out somewhat by moving your speakers a foot or so to the side. After you've evened out bass distribution as much as you can, check that the bass level will be correct at your main listening seats. If not, move the seats or speakers.

You want your turntable to be exposed to as little of the speakers' bass as possible, to avoid *acoustic feedback* (spur-ious signals caused by sound vibrations from the speakers shaking the record). Never put the turntable on top of your speakers, and try not to place them along the same wall, espe-cially if both speakers and turntable are wall-mounted. If you can, try to put the turntable in one of the room's bass dead spots. And since midrange frequencies can also be picked up as feedback, try to place the turntable out of the speakers' di-rect sound path, too.

Turntables must contend with footfalls as well as feedback. Most homes have some loose or springy floorboards which will convey footfalls to any turntable resting on them. It's usually easier to move the turntable cabinet than to fix the floor. A turntable on a wall-mounted shelf will usually have less prob-lem with foot-thuds than one on a floor-standing cabinet. Try for a wall without doors, whose slamming can shake the sty-lus, and with no vibrating air conditioners in its windows.

You room's furnishings affect the sound, too. Too many pad-ded or upholstered surfaces make the room sound dead—too few make it echo-y, like a tunnel or a tiled bathroom. A rug on the floor and padded surfaces grouped near the speaker end of the room can often clarify the sound by reducing the amount of sound reflections from around the speaker. Reflections from the back and sides of the room, however, often enrich the sound. Draw drapes give you a way to adjust the room's acous-tics by opening and closing them.

Pulling the speakers out from the wall by two or three feet often seems to clarify the sound, too, even with speakers whose design features (such as unfinished backs) suggest they're de-signed to be placed against the wall. If this is true of your speakers, you may find that the best position, acoustically, does not look right or disturbs the room's traffic patterns. Should that be the case, you can always leave the speakers against the wall for casual listening or when the system is off, and move them to their best-sounding position when you're listening more critically. In that case, try to place some landmarks (such as pictures on the wall or rosettes in the carpet pattern) to help you relocate them next time.

Wiring It Up

A fully wired system looks complex, but it all goes together one wire at a time. Most connections are logical and clearly marked. As a woman we know put it, "Even though it was my first stereo system, wiring it together was easy. The hard part was figuring how to put the cabinet together."

Two kinds of wires are used in most hi-fi systems: unshielded wires for the amplifier to the speaker and shielded cables with *phono plugs* (also called *RCA plugs*) between components. Most components come with shielded cables, about three or four feet long, but you'll need to buy wire for your speakers. All components should be switched off until you finish wiring. Once connections are made, all plugs should be unplugged and replugged, with a gentle twisting motion, once or twice a year, to clean off any airborne contaminants that may have gotten onto them.

Connecting Your Components

The cables that come with your components do their job, but you can get better ones—the question is, how much better ones should you bother getting? Your original cables will be thin, with molded-on plugs. These have several minor problems: Their wires tend to break where they enter the plug, and there's no way to repair them without cutting off the plug and soldering on a new one (a minor job, if you have and can use a soldering iron). Their plug surfaces tend to pick up a thin film of corrosion after anywhere from months to years of service, depending on what's in your atmosphere (the problem is worst at the seashore and in industralized areas). And there is some evidence, by no means conclusive, that such cables can subtly alter the signals they deliver.

For a few dollars, you can pick up cables which have flexible *strain-relief collars* molded onto their plugs. These taper down from the plug's large outer diameter to the wire's smaller one, distributing the stress when the cable is bent. For another few dollars you can purchase cables with gold-plated plugs, which won't corrode. For significantly more money, you can get cables designed to enhance your sound in subtle ways; again, let your ears judge whether or not they are worth it.

Each cable should be just long enough to reach between the two components it connects, including any twists to bypass shelves or other obstacles—plus about 6 inches to 18 inches more, so you can pull out either component from its shelf far enough to get at its rear connections. Longer cables just tend to tangle up, making the space behind your system look like the nest of some electronically minded bird.

Getting the right plug into the right jack is simple: just connect one cable at a time and read the labels on the jacks. For instance, if you have a separate tuner, the cable connected to its output jacks will usually go into an input jack marked "tuner" on your preamp, receiver, or integrated amp. If no input on your amp or preamp has the same name as the component you're connecting, try an "aux" jack. Make sure you connect the stereo channels correctly, right to right and left to left—they're marked on the panels by the jacks, and the cables are color-coded.

Turntables require not only signal connections but also an extra, *ground,* connection to the amp or preamp. Sometimes a small, black wire is molded into the turntable connecting cable, along with the two audio plugs; if it's not, there will either be a separate black or green ground wire, or a grounding terminal on the turntable to which such a wire can be attached. Most amps and preamps have grounding screws to which this wire can be attached; otherwise, you can usually make the needed ground connection by loosening one of the screws on the preamp's or amp's back panel *just enough to get the wire under it.* (Loosening the screw more than that may make something fall off inside the amplifier.)

Tape decks are a little more complex, with two pairs of connections. The amplifier's "tape out" or "rec out" jack should feed the deck's "line in" or, simply, "input" jack, while the deck's output jacks should go to "tape in" or "monitor" jacks on the amp. If you have two tape monitor circuits, make sure that you don't cross-connect a tape deck between the two circuits—to "rec 1 out" and "mon 2 in," for example.

Wiring Speakers

Ordinary lamp cord will work as speaker wire, if it's of sufficiently heavy gauge. The longer the wire between amp and speaker, the heavier the wire should be; for most homes, *16-gauge (#16 AWG)* wire will do, but it never hurts to use still heavier wires, such as 14- or even 12-gauge, if you can afford them and have room. Some hi-fi shops sell "speaker wire" of thinner gauges, such as #18 or even #20. Pass up such cables and, if possible, pass on to another shop.

There are a great many premium-priced speaker wires which claim to deliver superior sound. The improvement, if any, will be subtle; but if you can hear that difference, go ahead and buy. Do, however, check with your dealer as to whether that wire and your amplifier will work well together. Some premium speaker wires have high capacitance, a property which can make some amplifiers misbehave, or even break down. Most combinations are safe, but it never hurts to be sure.

You'll probably run your speaker wires around corners, and perhaps up and down to clear doorways. Figure this in when calculating how long a wire you need. If you conceal your wires beneath your carpets, place them in untrafficked parts of the room, where they won't be stepped on.

Speakers must be wired *in-phase*—that is, so that both pull or push at the same time when the signal is common to both of them. Otherwise, the stereo image will wander and low bass will disappear. Phasing them correctly isn't difficult; just see to it that both speakers are wired alike.

This is easiest to manage if you pay attention to your speaker wires. Every wire pair offers some clue toward telling the two wires apart. The two wires might be of contrasting colors, their insulations might contrast, or each might have a different-colored thread running inside its insulation; one wire's insulation might have a raised rib or other mark. Check your wires to see which kind you have. Check especially carefully with common lamp cord, which usually has a raised rib, the hardest wire identification mark to see.

First lay the wires in place, without connecting them. Connect one end of one wire pair (it doesn't matter which), and note which wire went to which terminal. For example, if you wired the left speaker first, you might note that the ribbed side of that wire went to a red terminal on that speaker. If so, you should go at once to the right speaker, and wire it the same way (ribbed to red). Then you should repeat the process at the other end of the wires: connect one channel any way you please, then connect the other in precisely the same way. For instance, if you ran the ribbed wire to the black amplifier terminal in one channel, you should run ribbed to black at the other.

Most amplifier output and speaker terminals will accept bare wire ends, and some accept special plugs as well. There are three common types of terminal. One consists of red and black plastic blocks with holes which open to admit the wire when you press small levers. The second type is just a pair of screws. Loosen them about ⅛ inch to ¼ inch (don't unscrew them all the way—they may be hard to get back in), wrap the wires around them, then retighten (wrap the wires clockwise, and it's less likely to come off). The third, sometimes called a *five-way binding post,* has a plastic collar which you loosen by hand before either wrapping the wire around the post or sticking it through a small hole (often, alas, set at an awkward angle). You can also use some types of plug with terminals of the first and third types.

Aside from being sure that both channels are wired alike, it seems to make a slight difference which way you wire each channel—that is, whether you wire the speakers' red terminals to the amplifier's black ones or wire red to red. The trouble is, that difference won't be constant for all records. Some may sound best wired one way, while others sound best wired another. This is due to the difference in *absolute phase* between the sound picked up by the microphone and the sound reproduced in your home. A bass drum, for example, first pulls air in, as the drumstick impacts it, then pushes air back out. If the drumbeat you hear starts with a push followed by a pull, its absolute phase is incorrect. However, record producers rarely pay attention to this, so you have no way of knowing whether your system does or does not have correct absolute phase *for that record* unless you listen to it both ways and can hear a difference.

If you want to experiment with this, it pays to use plugs on one end of both speaker wires, so that you can easily reverse the phase of both channels. Just be sure that if you reverse one, you reverse both, so as not to get the two channels out of phase with one another.

24 Beyond the Basics: Adding to Your System

Component hi-fi systems are open-ended. You can add to them at any time, for any purpose—to add a sound source you didn't want to buy originally, to add newly developed sound sources (such as Compact Disc), or to add accessories that enhance the sound of your existing sources. All you have to do is plug them in.

Some amplifiers and receivers already have inputs labeled with the names of such new additions as "CD" or "video." But even if they don't, virtually all signal sources plug into "aux" inputs, while most sound-enhancing accesssories (such as equalizers and delay or ambience systems) plug into external processor loops or tape monitor jacks.

Hooking into Video

It's always seemed a bit ridiculous for owners of good stereo systems to listen to television through the puny amplifiers and scrawny speakers found in most TV sets. But for many years, the TV set's sonic limitations served a purpose: helping to veil the poor quality of the mono sound transmitted with the programs.

In the past few years, that's changed. The stations and networks are paying more attention to their sound—and had been paying attention even before TV broadcasts in stereo began. Videodisc players have long offered stereo sound of extremely high quality, which can be matched by many of the latest videocassette recorders (VCRs)—the Beta Hi-Fi and VHS Hi-Fi models. Some videodisc players now double as CD players (which is logical, since both use laser playback systems), and videodiscs with CD-like digital soundtracks have begun to appear. CDs themselves will soon include graphic information to display on a TV screen, from song lyrics to slow-moving images accompanying the music.

So now it really makes sense to hook your video and audio systems together. The set manufacturers are making the hookup easier, too, providing receivers with audio output jacks to feed into aux or other high-level audio inputs. More and more audio amplifiers and receivers have inputs marked "video" and "CD" instead of "aux 1" and "aux 2," to clarify the idea. Some audio receivers and amps can also switch video signals so that you can select which video signal (off the air, cable, disc, or VCR) feeds your screen at the same time you select which audio signal feeds your speakers.

As far as hooking into your amplifier or receiver is concerned, your video system is just another audio signal source. The difference is that the picture has to be considered, too.

Speaker Considerations

If the sound is to accompany the picture, then both should come from the same direction in your room. The speakers should be fairly close to the screen, too—especially with stereo; you don't want to hear someone at a 45-degree angle to your left when you see him at a 5-degree angle. With large-screen projection sets, a normal stereo speaker spacing of six feet or so works fine, but when those speakers flank a 19-inch screen, they'll have to be spaced closer together to sound natural. If your main speakers are small, and you don't switch between music and video too often, you might simply move the speakers for each use. Otherwise, you might want to have a set of large, widely spaced speakers for stereo music listening and a second set of screen-flanking speakers for video use.

You may also find that putting regular stereo speakers right next to your video screen distorts the colors, or even shapes, on it. This is the result of interference from the speakers' magnetic field. Cheap speakers with weak magnets may not cause the problem, but they won't sound good either. Several manufacturers now make special speakers for video use, with powerful magnets that are shielded to keep their magnetic fields from leaking. While this raises the speaker's cost a bit, some shielding techniques make the speaker more efficient by using magnetism that would otherwise be radiated away.

Stray magnetism is less likely to cause problems with projection screens (figure 24–1), whose picture tubes are buried inside, farther from the speakers than the exposed picture tubes of conventional, direct-view sets.

Sound Enhancers

Even with good video equipment, most of the program material available is not up to hi-fi sound standards. Most older movies (and a fair number of current ones) have monophonic sound, and the older movies have noisy, distorted soundtracks, too. Occasionally, bad duplicating adds noise and distortion even to films and programs which originally had good sound. A number of sound enhancers are available to help with these problems.

Not much can be done about distortion, other than to filter out the higher frequencies where most of that distortion and comparatively little of the program's sound are to be found. Your audio system's scratch filter or the higher-frequency bands of an equalizer (covered later in this chapter) can be used for this. The same techniques will reduce noise a bit,

Fig. 24-1. A large-screen projection system, integrated with an audio system. (Courtesy of Custom Woodwork & Design)

though not as much pas the noise-reduction accessories described later in this chapter.

To make the most of monophonic material, *stereo synthesizer circuits* are also built into many audio/video components. These don't give you the same sense of left-right localization as true stereo, but they do make the sound seem more spacious.

A step beyond that are *quadraphonic decoders,* which perform two functions. They decode the rear-channel information mixed into many movies with stereo soundtracks, and they simulate some rear-channel information from stereo program material (including your audio recordings), much as stereo synthesizers simulate stereo from mono. You may or may not like the synthesized rear information, but you'll certainly appreciate the dramatic impact of surround sound on movies made with that in mind.

Video Buying Tips

If you're buying video equipment with the idea of integrating it with your stereo sound system, there are a few things to keep in mind.

For one thing, make sure that there's a way to feed audio from your TV set's tuner to your sound system. *Component television systems,* with separate tuners and monitor screens, always have such outputs; *monitor receivers* usually do (though some have only inputs, no outputs). But ordinary TV receivers often don't. Look at the back of the set and check for yourself before buying.

When you buy a VCR, make sure it says hi-fi. The Beta Hi-Fi and VHS Hi-Fi sound systems are truly superior. VCRs labeled merely "stereo" or even "Dolby stereo" sound more like AM radios.

Make sure the tuners in your TV set and VCR can receive stereo TV broadcasts *in stereo.* Older models cannot—including even some VCRs which can record stereo from other sources. Some sets or recorders which lack built-in stereo decoders have jacks for external decoders. That's fine, as long as the decoder is available, and as long as the unit and decoder cost less than a unit with built-in decoding. Don't buy such a VCR or TV set now with the idea of adding the decoder in a year or two—add-on decoders may not be available that long.

Stereo TV broadcasting may also bring the return of *TV-sound tuners*—audio tuners designed to pick up only sound from the TV bands. From our experience with their monophonic predecessors, we know that such tuners can be made with excellent fidelity, and that they add the flexibility of listening to (or taping the soundtrack from) one TV program or video source while watching another. But using them to get stereo sound for the show you're watching would eliminate the convenience of tuning sound and picture with one knob.

If you do buy such a tuner, make sure it picks up all the TV bands that interest you—which may include not just the VHF channels 2 through 13, but also the cable channels (typically denoted with letters from A to W or so) and the UHF channels (14 through 83). The same holds true, of course, for audio tuners and receivers which add TV sound to their regular FM and AM bands. With so many channels to cover, spread throughout so much of the radio-frequency spectrum, digital tuning would be a convenience worth looking for. As for specifications, consult chapter 19, on FM tuners.

Audio Enhancers

New signal sources appear only rarely. New signal enhancers appear all the time, as new solutions to old problems (or, sometimes, new problems) come to light.

Enhancers don't generate signals; they process them. Which means the signal must pass through the processor en route from the original source to the amplifier. Not all signals need processing; it's usual to put enhancers outside the main signal path, in a side chain through which the signal can be passed or not, as you prefer.

Some amplifiers and receivers do this with *external processor loops*—output jacks through which the signal branches off, plus inputs with switches for selection of the main or processed signal. If your amplifier lacks these circuits, tape monitor circuits will do as well; most signal processors have duplicate tape monitor jacks and switches, so you won't run out of places to plug tape decks.

One reason processors are usually plugged into external loops is that every extra circuit through which your signal passes can degrade it slightly. The extra noise, distortion, and frequency limitations imposed by one processor or enhancer may not be audible by itself; but several processors working at once can noticeably make the sound worse even as they are enhancing it. It's best to leave all processors switched out of the circuit except when the circumstances that require their use arise.

Equalizers

These are the most popular signal processors. Equalizers are just assemblies of tone controls, each covering a narrow band of frequencies. The most common types are *graphic equalizers,* with five, ten, or thirty-one bands, so-called because their controls form a graph of the frequency curve they're adding to the signal.

As you increase the number of bands, you narrow the range that each one covers, from two octaves apiece in a five-band model to an octave each in a ten-band one, up to one-third octave for each of thirty-one controls. The more and narrower the bands, the more flexible but more complex the control.

Five-band equalizers are best used as you would use your bass and treble controls, to alter tonal balance to your taste. Such equalizers give you more precise control than the two or three bands of normal tone controls, without requiring finicky adjustment. For simpler operation, most five-band equalizers (especially those built into some receivers in place of the usual bass and treble controls) have *ganged* controls, each adjusting both the right and left channels at once.

Third-octave equalizers, at the other extreme, are best used to reduce the effects of frequency problems in a room or a speaker system. They're designed for meticulous adjustment, one channel at a time, usually with the aid of instruments such as *real-time analyzers,* which measure the system's frequency response. Once adjusted, their controls are frequently locked behind a cover to keep idle hands away.

Ten-band equalizers are the most popular, because their bands are narrow enough to allow some correction of system problems, yet there are few enough of them to be manageable, and their cost is not outrageous. Many have real-time analyzers built in (figure 24–2), to help you get them properly adjusted. While ten-band models are neither as convenient as five-band models nor as precise as third-octave ones, they are better than either one at doing the jobs of both. If you intend to use one mainly to alter the sounds of different recordings to your taste, get one with ganged controls; if you want to use it to correct sound problems, separate controls for each channel will be better for you.

The bass ranges usually benefit most from equalization, and some companies make equalizers which affect only the lower frequencies. Bass equalizers may have bands spaced only a half-octave or so apart over the small frequency range they cover. A few full-range equalizers copy this technique, with

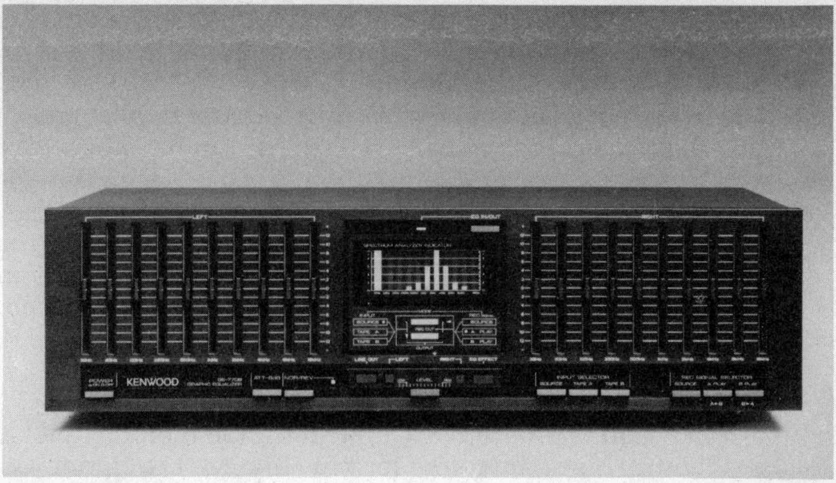

Fig. 24-2. *A ten-band equalizer with a built-in, real-time spectrum analyzer.* (Courtesy of Kenwood)

closely spaced bands at the bass and more widely spaced ones at the upper frequencies.

In addition to the graphic equalizers we've described there are some *parametric models*. These usually have only two to four bands but are very flexible; those bands can be shifted through the frequency spectrum and made wider or narrower, to match the dimensions of the frequency peak or dip they're supposed to correct. *Paragraphic equalizers* are basically graphic types whose multiple bands can be shifted over a small range of frequencies and, sometimes, made slightly wider or narrower.

Equalizers cannot completely eliminate frequency response problems, for two reasons: the room and the speaker color the sound differently; and the room is always altering the sound the speaker produced a few thousandths of a second ago (it takes time for sound to be reflected), rather than the sound the speaker is producing now.

Still, equalizers can help with some problems if they're used intelligently. The first step is to minimize the problems at their source by selecting good speakers, placing them where they sound best in the room, and furnishing the room to minimize its sonic problems, as we discussed in the last chapter. Then use the equalizer, first to flatten down frequency peaks, then to boost out dips in the frequency response. If your equalizer has an analyzer, use it (though you may find that, once response is flat, you prefer to slope the treble portion gently downhill). If you have no analyzer, switch the equalizer in and out after each adjustment to make sure that what you've done actually improves the sound.

Always boost frequency bands moderately if you boost them at all. Adjustments of 3 dB to 6 dB are to be expected, but if you have to go past 9 dB or so, there's usually something wrong with your system, your recording, or your sonic judgment. Be very cautious when boosting the extreme top or bottom of the frequency range; every 3-dB boost doubles the amount of power that your amplifier must deliver and that your speakers must handle. It's all too easy to drive your amplifier to distortion or your woofer and tweeter to destruction by boosting too much.

Most equalizers have duplicate tape-monitor jacks and switching. Many therefore let you equalize the signal you feed to your tape deck when recording, either to permanently improve material while dubbing it or for special effects (such as narrowing a voice's bandwidth till it sounds like a telephone call). If this feature is important to you, make sure your equalizer has it.

Electronic ("active") crossovers

These are a different type of frequency control, one designed to divide frequencies between two or more different amplifiers, each powering different drivers in a speaker system. The most common use is to split off frequencies below 100 Hz or so to feed to a *subwoofer*, a speaker designed to handle only low bass tones. Adding a subwoofer usually extends the system's bass response. It also improves the sound in the midrange and upper bass by freeing the main speaker and amplifier from the stresses that powerful low bass imposes. Some speaker systems can also be *bi-amplified* (with separate amplifiers for woofer and tweeter) or *tri-amplified* (with a third amp added for the midrange), which also requires crossovers.

Active crossovers, unlike most other processors, are installed between the preamp and the amplifiers. Their controls (for the relative level of each band and, sometimes, for the frequency at which the signals cross over between amplifiers) are adjusted once, then left alone. After that, the crossover can be tucked away out of sight.

Ambience systems

These are designed to add spaciousness to the sound in your listening room. Among the most common ones are *delay sys-*

tems, which feed the signal to a second pair of speakers (at the sides or rear of the room) after a delay of a few thousandths of a second, to simulate the delayed sound reflections of large concert halls. The quadraphonic decoders mentioned earlier in this chapter, under "Sound Enhancers," also add ambience, by feeding the rear speakers a phase-shifted version of the main signal.

Not all ambience systems require additional amplifiers or even, in some cases, speakers. The *Hafler system* involves only additional speakers, placed in the back of the room and wired across the two channels of the main amplifier (figure 24–3). The added speakers must be wired through a level control to keep the sound level of the "echoes" well below that of the main signal from the front speakers.

Another type of ambience system injects altered versions of the main signal back into the main (front) amplifier system. The alterations may include phase changes, delay, or frequency alterations designed to simulate the changes that the outer ear imposes on signals arriving from directions other than straight ahead. There is no generic name for these. A somewhat similar device, the Carver *Sonic Hologram,* is designed more to sharpen and solidify stereo imaging than to add ambience (though it does a bit of that, too).

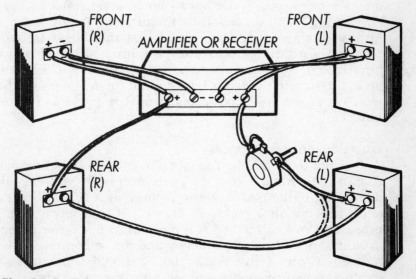

Fig. 24-3. *The Hafler system for connecting rear or side speakers for ambient sound. (Courtesy of Stereo Review)*

Noise-reduction accessories

These are three basic types: impulse-noise reducers, dynamic filters, and encode/decode systems. *Impulse-noise reducers* sense the sharp onset of ticks and pops caused by dirt on records and eliminate them. Some of these devices merely blank out the sound for a few thousandths of a second—long enough to eliminate the pop, but too short to be heard easily. Others fill in the blank with a portion of the sound just preceding the tick, for even more imperceptible action.

Dynamic filters include the *DNR* system and the *autocorrelator* (not currently available as a separate accessory). All work by sensing the treble content of the signal and cutting back on the system's high-frequency response when the signal's treble level falls too low to mask the system's noise. Dynamic filters can be used to reduce hiss and other noise from any source. Encode/decode systems, such as dbx or Dolby, which must be used both in making a recording and in playing it back were covered in chapter 20.

Expanders

These increase a signal's dynamic range, making the loud sounds louder and the soft ones softer for more dramatic effect. There's a side-benefit: making the soft sounds softer also reduces noise a bit. Sometimes there's a side-effect as well: a "breathing" sound caused by fluctuations in the noise level. Multiple-band expanders, which expand bass, treble, and sometimes midrange separately, minimize this problem. Combination compressor-expanders (*companders*) also let you decrease dynamic range for background-music listening. So you won't miss the softer passages even though the loud ones are quiet.

Using multiple processors

This is not too difficult. You can purchase switchers especially designed to handle multiple enhancers. Or you can simply daisy-chain them all together, plugging each into the next one's tape-monitor jacks. Either way, the order in which the processors are connected is important. Since other processors are influenced by the frequency and phase content of the signal, equalizers (which alter both) should come last in the chain. Ambience devices which alter the main signal should usually come after any dynamic filters or impulse-noise reducers. Expanders should come after those noise-reducers but before the equalizers.

Delay systems can go almost anywhere in the chain. Encode/decode systems should be connected directly to the tape decks they're used with, treated as parts of the deck. Electronic crossovers always go between the preamp and amp sections of the system.

Other Add-ons

Headphones

These are the easiest add-on of all: just plug them in (most amps and receivers and tape decks, and many CD players, have jacks for them), switch off your speakers, and put them on your head to listen in privacy. That privacy is a two-way proposition: headphones also keep the music you're listening to from disturbing others in the house (or next door, if you live in an apartment).

Alas, nothing in audio is ever *completely* simple, and there are a few things to watch out for. There are two basic types of headphones: those designed for home use, which have impedances of 8 ohms and ¼-inch plugs (figure 24–4) and the lightweight ones designed for use with Walkman-type portable players (figure 24–5), which have 3.5-mm plugs, and, frequently, impedances of 32 ohms or so. Some lightweight phones are designed specifically for home systems (the large plug is the tip-off), while others are designed for home and portable use (and come with 3.5-mm plugs plus adaptors for quarter-inch jacks).

Headphones for portables are usually of the *open-air* type, which rest lightly on the ears and let sound in around them. Some home headphones are of this type, though often larger, to cover more of the ear. Other headphones for home use, however, are the *surround* type, which encloses the ear. Such phones do a better job of keeping outside noises out and often have better bass response. However, you should never use surround-type phones while walking around or bicycling, lest they block out sounds that might warn you of impending danger.

When buying headphones, judge the sound as you would judge the sound of speakers (and expect much better sound for the same amount of money). But judge comfort, too: the phones should rest easily on your head, and, if they are surround types, they should not press on your ears. Phones with metal bands which press too loosely or tightly on your ears can be bent until they fit you; phones with plastic bands cannot be bent.

Fig. 24-4. *Headphones which surround the ear, like these, can help isolate the listener from noisy surroundings. Note the coiled cord, which stretches as the listener moves away from the stereo system, and the ¼-inch plug for use with home components. (Courtesy of Audio-Technica)*

Fig. 24-5. *Lightweight headphones such as this are designed for use with Walkman-type portables, but plug adapters (often supplied with the phones) allow their use with home audio components as well. (Courtesy of Mura)*

Never put headphones on before your sound system is going and adjusted. Flicking the switch after you've put the phones on could subject your ears to a literally deafening sound blast if you've accidentally left the volume turned up.

Power Switchers
Many system add-ons don't affect the signal but merely help you with the task of switching your components on and off. Perhaps the best-known of these are *timers* (figure 24–6), which turn the system on and off at preset times so you can tape radio programs when you're occupied elsewhere; or you

can wake yourself to music. Another type of timer is the *automatic shut-off*, which turns your system off if there's no signal for several minutes, so you won't accidentally leave it on when you're away or sleeping.

Amplifiers and receivers usually have switched AC convenience outlets to turn other system components on and off when you flick the amp's or the receiver's front-panel switch. Complex systems and powerful amplifiers put more and more of a strain on that switch; *system power controllers* (chiefly made and sold for home-computer use) switch several outlets on and off when the component plugged into one key outlet is switched.

Yet another system convenience lowers the system's volume when the telephone rings, to make sure you hear both the bell and your caller. Some versions also lower the volume if you pick up the phone to make a call yourself. With either type, when you hang up the phone, the volume rises back to normal.

The open-endedness of audio component systems extends into the future. Other signal sources, processors, and convenience gadgets will arise in the years to come. But you've now made the acquaintance of every major kind of audio equipment and most of the minor ones.

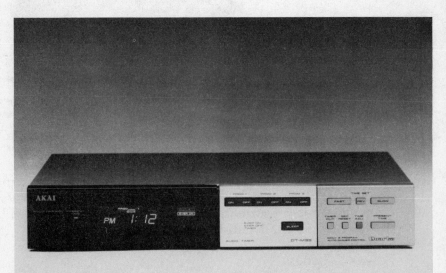

Fig. 24-6. If your tape deck has a "Timer Start" switch, you can turn it on with a timer such as this to record radio programs when you're away or to wake you with music in the morning. (Courtesy of Akai)

25 Music on the Move: Portable and Car Stereo

Until recently, you could take your music with you, but you had to leave good sound at home. No more: today, you can have good—even great—sound in your car, or even in your pocket.

There are three basic types of sound systems for people on the go: car-stereo systems, portable systems (with built-in batteries) that play through speakers, and pocket-sized, "personal" portables (generally called "Walkman-type" portables, after Sony's original), which play only through headphones. In all three categories, the available products range in quality from miserable to excellent.

Most of what you need to know to get the good products has been covered in previous chapters. All that's left is the differences, major and minor, between stationary and movable sound systems.

Portables

Portables introduce new factors, such as size and weight (which are usually unimportant in home systems) and battery life (a problem which never arises with equipment that runs off AC lines). Obviously, the smaller and lighter the system, the easier it is for you to carry. Just be sure that the features and performance you need haven't been left out as excess weight. If you'll be carrying the unit by its handle, make certain the handle feels comfortable and the system's weight is balanced. If you'll carry it in your pocket, make sure the controls won't snag on your clothes, yet will still be accessible to your fingers.

Battery life is a function of battery capacity and the unit's power drain. The more powerful the unit (and the louder you play it), the sooner its batteries will go; the bigger and more numerous the batteries, the longer their life—but the heavier the unit, too.

You can extend battery life by plugging your portable into an AC socket whenever possible. This requires a power supply, to convert the 120-V AC voltage to the lower-voltage DC of your batteries. A built-in power supply ensures that you always have it with you when there's AC available. But always having it with you makes your portable a little heavier. Many portables buzz or hum when used with AC supplies (especially external supplies); check this before purchasing. If a unit which did not buzz originally begins buzzing after a while, check its batteries —worn ones can contribute to this problem.

Rechargeable batteries are cheaper, in the long run, than batteries you throw away when they're used up. But they (and their charger, if there isn't one built into your portable) have a higher initial cost. If you use your portable a lot, you might want an extra set of rechargeables to use while the other one is charging. Most rechargeable batteries are the nickel-cadmium type. If you recharge these before they're fully discharged, they go dead sooner than if you deplete them almost (but not quite) fully before recharging.

As a portable's batteries run down, its performance usually grows worse before it stops working altogether. So a unit which seems defective should have its batteries replaced before you try any other cures. The same is true of portables which perform poorly in the store: ask a salesperson to replace its batteries before you judge it.

If you'll be using your portable while you walk, check how steadily it plays tape when in motion. Also make sure that it performs properly, no matter what angle you hold or rest it in —some players work beautifully when upright, but grow fluttery when operated on their sides, or vice versa.

You'll rarely find much in the way of specifications listed for portable models. This makes listening tests even more important.

Walkman-type portables (figure 25–1) owe their success to the development of compact, lightweight headphones which sound good when powered by amplifiers that deliver only fractions of a watt. Their sound can be astonishingly good, largely

Fig. 25-1. *Pocket portable tape decks and radios let you hear music any-where without disturbing others. (Courtesy of Sony)*

because it's easier to design great headphones for the limited range of human ear sizes than to design speakers which will sound great in all the different listening environments that they must face.

The headphones are therefore responsible for most of the sound quality (or lack of it) in portables of this type. If the headphones that come with a given model are uncomfortable or don't sound right, it may be possible to use better ones: but since impedance and power requirements vary, not all such combinations work. Try before you buy.

Headphone listening is not without its hazards. Phones make it harder to hear outside sounds; so extra caution is needed if you listen while you walk, and listening while riding a bicycle can be extremely dangerous. Phones also make it easier, somehow, to listen at deafening levels without noticing the fact.

Pocket portables have few special features: there isn't room for many. One of the most basic is a second headphone jack, so you can share your music with a friend. (Test, though, to be sure the unit can deliver enough power for loud but clean sound through both pairs of headphones at once.) If you want the best possible sound quality, look for units with noise reduction and tape-equalization ("normal/metal" or "normal/chrome") switches. Several portables have Dolby B noise reduction and many also have Dolby C, which is very important if you plan to make Dolby-C tapes on your home deck and want to play them as you move around.

If you want to listen at the beach or while skiing, consider one of the many portables which are weatherproofed to keep grit and moisture out of the works. Grit can get in when the lid is open, so stay out of the wind and up above the sand when you're flipping or replacing tapes. Auto-reverse is a big help in these situations since it halves the times you'll have the unit open; otherwise, it may not be worth the extra cost, complexity, and weight.

Some portables can record as well as play tapes. This adds weight and bulk but also increases the unit's versatility. The choice is yours.

Portables with speakers vary considerably in size and weight. In general, the bigger the unit, the better its bass. But a unit with well-designed, small speakers can still deliver more bass than one with larger, cruder speakers.

The sound from any speakers depends on their surroundings. A portable's surroundings vary, so try to judge any portable's performance in surroundings similar to those you expect to play it in. For example, you'll hear minimum bass when carrying a portable, more bass when it's resting on a floor or wall shelf, more still if you put it in the corner of a room. You'll hear more treble indoors, where the room walls can reflect it, than you will when listening on grass.

The stereo effect will be limited if the two speakers are close together, as they are in most such portables (figure 25–2). Some models therefore incorporate circuits to widen the stereo image. These vary in effectiveness, so don't choose a portable because it has such a circuit unless it sounds to you as if it does the job. Other models (figure 25–3) have speakers which can be removed for greater stereo separation or remounted for

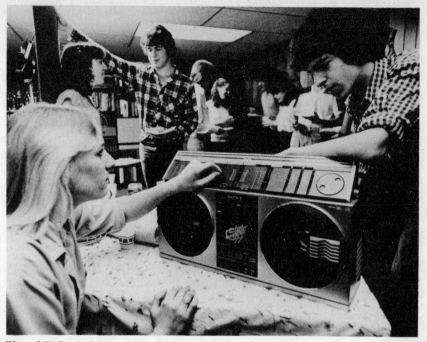

Fig. 25-2. A larger portable, with built-in speakers, lets you share your sounds; but the short distance between its speakers limits the stereo effect to those nearby. (Courtesy of Sony)

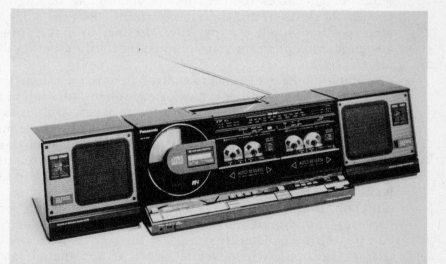

Fig. 25-3. Detachable speakers can be spread apart to broaden the area of stereo effect. This portable also features a CD player (left) and a dual-well cassette deck. (Courtesy of Panasonic)

easier carrying. Outdoors, because of ambient noise, you're likely to sit close to your portable when listening, which also improves the stereo effect.

Car Stereo

Car stereo is a mixture of the familiar and the unfamiliar. As in home stereo equipment, you can get all-in-one systems or build up systems from separate components, and specifications are available to give you some idea of how a system will perform. But the mixture of components is different (for example, the tuner and tape deck are nearly always combined), some of the specs must be read with a critical (even skeptical) eye, and the car's spatial and acoustic limitations make installing a good system much trickier.

Control-panel design (figure 25–4) is far more critical in car than home stereo equipment. The car system has to cram all the controls of a typical home system into a panel smaller than is found on any single home component. At the same time, those controls must be easy for the driver to find and use, both day and night, without having to focus on the stereo instead of the road. To complicate the designer's life still further, no two users quite agree on what controls should be emphasized and what design makes them easiest to use. Before buying a receiver, check its controls, preferably from about the same relative position you'll occupy when driving, to make sure its design is convenient for you—not just for comfort, but for driving safety.

Automation (if it's simple to control) becomes a safety factor in the car. Two common types of car-stereo automation are scan and seek tuning. *Seek* advances to a new station every time you trigger its control, rather than making you tune manually to find where the next station is. *Scan* samples each station for five to ten seconds, then moves on to the next, until you trigger it off when you hear something you'd like to keep listening to. On most sets, scan and seek work only in one direction, from lower to higher station frequencies; on some, however, they work both ways, which is more convenient. *Diversity tuning* constantly compares the signals from two antennas, selecting whichever is better at any instant as its signal source.

Even more automation is common with tapes. There are equivalents of station-seek (called *music search* or any one of so many, similar names that it's impossible to describe the feature without using someone's trademark) and scan (called *scan*), both usually operating bidirectionally. Auto-reverse is common, and systems without it frequently have *auto repeat,* which lets you repeat the same side of the tape over and over. More important are systems which automatically eject the tape when it has been played or when you shut off your car's ignition. This prevents your leaving the tape in place when you park the car and eliminates the possibility of the tape jamming your stereo if it warps in hot sun.

Because a car-stereo system must compress nearly all a home system's functions into such a tiny space, such systems may lack features you'll miss. So make sure that your choice has all the features you need. For example, many systems omit such features as tape-equalization (normal/metal) switching and Dolby noise reduction, which critical listeners will want.

Systems vary in complexity. A typical, simple car sound system will consist of a single, in-dash unit (variously called the *receiver, head end,* or *deck*), combining a tuner, a cassette player, and an amplifier, plus speakers mounted in the car's interior body panels. Common speaker mounting places include the front doors or dashboard and the rear deck.

More complex systems may include an equalizer, a more powerful amplifier (sometimes built into the equalizer), and possibly a crossover and separate amplifier to power a subwoofer. Except for the equalizer, these components are usually installed out of sight. Expensive systems may also include a Compact Disc player, in addition to or instead of the cassette deck. The number and placement of speakers (other than subwoofers) will be about the same as in a simple system, but those speakers will usually be better ones.

The *receiver* must be selected with an eye toward the kind of system in which it will be used. Lower-cost receivers have built-in amplifiers, of fairly low wattage (typically less than five watts per channel), so they can drive the speakers of a simple system directly. The most deluxe receivers generally have no built-in amps at all, on the assumption that they will be used only in expensive, complex systems with amplifiers whose high power makes them too big to be built-in.

Many medium-priced units have both amplifier and preamp outputs, so they can be used at once to drive a pair of speakers, yet still allow the system to be expanded with high-quality separate amps when the money is available. (Few buyers, however, actually do expand their systems once they are installed, because of the difficulty of getting at things in the car.)

Another route to after-the-fact expansion is to add an inex-

Fig. 25-4: A

Fig. 25-4: B

Fig. 25-4: C

Fig. 25-4: D

Fig. 25-4: A, B, C, D. *The old, standard car-stereo design, with knobs at each end and an analog tuning dial in the middle (A), is giving way to knobless designs with digital dials (B). To fit more controls into the small space available, some knobless models hide rarely-used controls behind a flip-down dial (C,D). (Courtesy of Kenwood [A], Pioneer [B], and Jensen [C,D])*

pensive *booster amp* to a unit which has only amplifier-level outputs. The power increase is limited, but still significant. The chief problem is that the booster also amplifies whatever noise and distortion may have been added to the signal by the receiver's amplifier stage. Some amplifiers include both booster-level and preamp-level inputs, so you can use them to expand a simple system now, then reuse them as nuclei of more complex, higher-powered systems, later.

Power is one of those specs we said should be read skeptically. When you see an amplifier power specification given in full (e.g., "20 watts per channel, from 50 Hz to 18,000 Hz, at 0.5 percent distortion"), you can assume that it means almost the same thing it would for a home amp. The "almost" is because car amplifiers are usually rated for the power they can deliver into 4-ohm speakers, rather than the 8-ohm ones used in rating home amps—which is quite legitimate, as most car speakers have 4-ohm impedances.

However, be extra-skeptical when any of these qualifications are omitted from the specs. If no power bandwidth is listed, assume the power rating applies only at 1 kHz, with rather less available at the extreme frequencies. If no distortion figure is specified, assume that the power is measured at an unlistenably high 10 percent distortion. And if the spec does not list power "per channel," assume that the figure given is for the sum of all the channels, not just for a single one. Without all this data, the amplifier fully described in the preceding paragraph could be listed as delivering 60 watts or more!

Tuner sensitivity is another specification to watch out for. Sensitivity figures in dBf mean the same thing in car or home tuners. But sensitivity figures in microvolts are not equivalent: a car tuner with a sensitivity of, say, 2 microvolts at its 75-ohm antenna inputs is equivalent to a home tuner with a sensitivity of 4 microvolts at its 300-ohm antenna input. This is solely due to the different voltages developed across these differing impedances—both are equivalent to the same figure in dBf.

Equalizers are more common in car than in home systems. In theory, they're used to overcome the sonic problems of the car's interior and the limitations of car speakers and speaker placement—tasks the usual five-band, ganged-control equalizer is ill-equipped to handle. In practice, all too many listeners simply set the top and bottom controls full up, so they'll always hear bass and treble, but seldom hear what the music really sounds like.

If your system needs equalization to sound true, then you should probably rework that system, if you can afford it, until equalization is no longer necessary. Equalization can help—as aspirin can help a broken leg. For this use, the *more* controls there are, the more flexibly the system can deal with your system's problems. Real flexibility requires more controls than a driver can cope with; some elaborate equalizers are designed to be set up by professional installers and then hidden away.

If you want to use an equalizer as a tone control, the *fewer* controls the better. One of us has switched from conventional, five-band equalizers to a three-band one in his car, and finds it both as easy and versatile as he could wish.

Electronic crossovers, which divide bass and upper frequencies among different amplifiers, are also far more common in car than in home systems, and are often built into equalizers or amplifiers. The car's space limitations make it difficult to fit speakers that are large enough to deliver good bass into locations where their upper frequencies can be heard. So, to get low bass in a car, it's easiest to relegate low frequencies to subwoofers, which can be tucked conveniently into the trunk or elsewhere. At the same time, because of the difficulty of building high-power amplifiers to run on the car's 12-volt DC power rather than on 120-volt home AC and because of limited space and ventilation for high-powered amplifiers, it makes even more sense than at home to power the subwoofer separately. This allows the use of two moderate-power amps instead of one, more powerful amp.

The higher the crossover frequency, the smaller the main speakers can be, which makes them easier to place. But the lower the crossover, the less you'll notice that the bass is coming from behind you. The presence of a separate subwoofer is least obtrusive when the crossover frequency is below 100 Hz, and in no case should it be above 250 Hz. (Some manufacturers offer components with built-in crossovers at about 2,000 Hz, well into the midrange. A 2-kHz crossover is all right when the tweeter and woofer are close together. But with front tweeters and rear woofers, the musical effect is like having your soup in front of you and your spoon behind.)

Car interiors tend to resonate at about 150 Hz, making the upper bass too prominent. Installers frequently stagger their crossover frequencies in order to leave a dip between the subwoofer and upper-frequency speakers, underemphasizing the frequencies that the car's acoustics will overemphasize.

In complex car systems, the amplifiers and crossover are frequently mounted on an *amp rack* in the trunk or elsewhere. This usually simplifies wiring and service, while giving the owner visible evidence of what he has when he feels like showing off. It can also make the components more visible to any thieves who happen by when the trunk is opened; some installers conceal their amp racks behind removable panels for this reason.

Choosing speakers for a car is far different from choosing them for home use. Most home speakers are built into enclosures when you buy them. Because space is so limited in a car, speakers must usually be built into the body panels so most car speakers are naked drivers, without enclosures of their own (figure 25–5). To conserve space, such speakers are usually *coaxial* types, with the tweeter mounted in front of the woofer. Systems with separately mounted tweeters and woofers, however, sometimes allow more choice of placement, with the woofers mounted where they'll fit and the tweeters where they can face the listeners most directly. The woofer and tweeter should be within a few inches of each other, for natural sound. A speaker whose woofer and tweeter are factory-mounted on a flat plate will ensure that.

The speaker designer cannot know for sure what enclosure volume the back of his flush-mounted speakers will face. Self-enclosed mini-speakers, sometimes mounted on rear decks or slung beneath dashboards, can help with this problem.

Speakers should be placed and aimed so that the passengers

Fig. 25-5. *Front and side views of a flush-mounting, coaxial speaker for cars. The ring shown holds the speaker about one-half inch out from the surface, for installations where there is insufficient depth behind the panel for the speaker's magnet; it also shields the back of the speakers from rain dripping down a door's window channels.* (Courtesy of Sony)

can hear the more directional high frequencies, not so that treble is lost by being aimed at the car's upholstery or the passengers' socks. This is often easier said than done, however. It helps to have both front and rear speakers (most car receivers, and many equalizers, have *fader controls* to balance them), so that sound can reach front and rear passengers at equal levels. Otherwise, the passengers at the end of the car without speakers will only hear clearly when the speakers are loud enough to curdle the ears of passengers at the other end. Rear-deck speakers usually deliver deep bass more easily than front-mounted speakers, because they can be made larger and because they can use the trunk's large volume as an enclosure—another good reason to have them in your car. However, front-mounted speakers usually give a more natural impression, since we usually listen to music in front of us, not behind us.

The best values in car speakers tend to be two-way (woofer/tweeter) or three-way (woofer/midrange/tweeter) systems. Four-way, five-way, and others tend to raise cost more than quality, while single-driver systems tend to have limited, poorly directed frequency response.

Installation is usually best done by professionals. A car is a cramped and awkward place in which to work, the tools required are not found in most home workshops, and it takes a good deal of knowledge to place speakers correctly and to install the electronics so they won't pick up noise from the car's electrical system. This is not to say you can't install your own system, especially if it's a simple one. Many people do. But most do it only once or twice, then leave it to professionals thereafter. (We speak from experience.)

It takes research to find the best installers in your area. Go by their reputation, by the sound quality and craftmanship of the installations they've already done, and by their understanding of your needs. Make sure, too, that you and your installer know exactly what results you want and how they're to be achieved, and that you have a fairly firm estimate of what the installation will cost.

If you plan to buy equipment yourself, take it to an installer. Make sure he'll go along with this: many installers won't touch equipment that they're not familiar with, and quite a few won't install equipment that they didn't sell. For a complex system, it might pay to choose your installer first and work with him to pick a system, rather than picking the system and hunting for someone to install it.

If you're buying a new car, check the sound systems offered by the factory. Since the success of the GM/Delco/Bose system, Lincoln and other car manufacturers have moved toward producing premium sound systems of their own, some of them quite good. If you're considering a factory-installed system, make sure you hear a demonstration first, preferably in the same model and body style as the car you're ordering.

Car stereo prices may seem high at first. But $500 or more for one little box and a couple of speakers seems more reasonable when you itemize that amount as covering an FM/AM tuner, amplifier and cassette deck, speakers, and a custom installation. More elaborate systems, of course, cost more: $1,000 to $2,000 for a system is not unheard of, and we've heard of systems that cost up to $5,000 or so that were worth the money—at least, to those who owned them. As usual, diminishing returns set in, where every cost increase brings less sonic benefit than the preceding one. Some of that cost may go for cosmetics (such as concealed speakers and equipment—neater, and more likely to escape theft), and some may go for alarms and other security measures. In very high-priced systems, a lot of money may go for mindless multiplication of components. The phrase "16 speakers per channel" sounds far more impressive than the resulting system does! Your estimation of a good system depends on your tastes, your income, and the amount of time you spend in your car.

While this discussion by no means exhausts the subject (books have been written on car stereo alone), it covers the basic points. But to say any more would risk exhausting *you*. So now, appropriately enough for a chapter on music in motion, it's time to move on to our final chapter.

26 Getting the Most for Your Hi-Fi Dollar

At the beginning of this book, we mentioned that people who didn't have "trained ears" wondered if hi-fi was worth it. That's a lot like asking if a good meal is worth it, if you don't have trained taste buds. In either case, even the inexperienced can relish some of the difference—and exposure to the best is the most pleasurable training your senses can have.

Behind that reluctance, though, is worry about the cost. It's not unjustified: the good usually costs more than the mediocre, and the best costs even more. You can buy a table-model "stereo," with turntable, tuner, and tape deck built in, for $300 or so. You can get a good stereo system for $800 to $2,000, and a great one for not too much more. If you really worked at it, you could spend over $100,000 for a system (but no one does). But whatever you decide to spend, you'll want the most for your money.

To do that, you first need to know just what equipment to buy—what will fulfill your present and near-future needs without making you pay for features and capabilities you'll never use or appreciate. We hope the previous chapters on how to listen to and evaluate equipment have helped you in this.

Dealing with Dealers

The next step is to buy equipment as economically as possible—which doesn't necessarily mean getting it for the lowest price. In any area, some dealers will charge more for the same equipment than others do; if so, they may offer extra services for that extra cost. It's up to you to decide whether those services are worth it.

Some of those services are obvious as soon as you come in the store. The ideal store would have a wide selection of equipment for you to choose from. That equipment would be divided (usually by price range) among several demonstration rooms, whose size and furnishings gave them similar acoustics to typical home listening rooms, so you could judge performance better. The salespeople would be courteous and knowledgable, able to help you understand and intelligently select the store's offerings.

When you buy, the store might offer financing on equipment too expensive for your credit card, deliver the equipment, and maybe even set it up for you. If something went wrong, they'd help you isolate the trouble, arrange for repair of any faulty units, and perhaps even loan you equipment to tide you over if repairs took a long time. If the manufacturer goes out of business, the store would handle in-warranty repairs at their own cost.

If the equipment worked properly but didn't satisfy you, the store might take your equipment back at full price (within a specified, short period) against equal- or higher-priced components. Speakers might even be loaned out for a few days, so you could tell how they'd sound in your own room.

We're not talking of Utopia: most dealers offer at least some of these services, and a few offer all of them or more. But all this costs a dealer money. Don't expect such treatment from a discounter who sells on price alone—he can't afford it. If you want service, look for a dealer who offers it. But don't expect to pay bottom dollar.

Dealers tend to fall into a hierarchy. At the top of the price and service ladder you'll find specialist shops that handle only audio equipment. The highest-priced (and generally, but not always, best) equipment is found only in such stores, but many of them carry lower-priced equipment, too. Audio chains tend to concentrate on medium-priced equipment, with some low-priced, introductory equipment and a sprinkling of high-end components. Specialist dealers are more likely to take your old equipment in trade and are therefore more likely to have used-audio departments full of other people's trade-in equipment. (More on that later.)

Next in line are stores which carry electronics of all kinds (ham radios, computers, telephones, and so on); they tend to offer less elaborate selections and less intimate showrooms, and their salespeople, though hardly ignorant, may be less knowledgable about stereo. Their prices, however, usually run a bit lower than the specialist's.

Department stores and other mass merchandisers usually offer less knowledge, more limited stock, and few specialized services. But they usually offer other services, of a more general nature, such as convenient credit terms, delivery (but rarely installation), and easy exchange of defective or unsatisfactory merchandise. They're generally in convenient locations, too—all the more so if you already shop there regularly for other things.

Discount houses cater to those who know (or think they know) exactly what they want and want to make no-nonsense deals at the lowest price possible. Their selections may be limited to the most popular items, and their showroom facilities may be practically nonexistent. But part of what they save on such amenities is passed on to you.

With any dealer, it pays to play fair. (But be sure that he is playing fair with you.) Customers, too, should have some ethics. So if you make your buying decisions on the basis of long listening sessions and helpful advice at an audio salon, don't implement those decisions at a discount store that gave you no help whatsoever.

On the other hand, make sure the store is giving you good value for your money. If you're shopping for low price, shop around. Some discounters (especially those which don't put price tags on equipment) may beat the competition's price, but only when you know what that price is; if you don't, you may end up paying more.

If you've never heard of a brand, check to see that it's a national brand, not one made just for that specific store. Such "house brands" may offer good value—but a value that's hard to check out if you can't verify the ostensible price at other stores or in hi-fi equipment directories. House-brand equipment will also have lower trade-in values than name-brand stuff, an important consideration if you plan to trade up in less than five years. And service may be hard to get if you move away from the retailer for whom the brand was made. Nonetheless, if you find a house-brand component that offers good value when compared to others in its price range, give it your full consideration. Some of today's best-known, respected brands began as makers of such private-label audio components.

At the store, be open and aboveboard with salespeople. Don't balk if a salesperson asks you (often indirectly) a series of questions designed to find out just what you want and need. The size and furnishings of your listening room, the price you intend to pay for your equipment, the ways that you will use it—these are not asked from nosiness, but from a desire to help you to get exactly what you want. A good salesperson takes pride in matching the equipment to the customer and knows that the satisfied customer will eventually come back for more.

Don't try to misrepresent your knowledge. Some salespeople may take advantage of your ignorance, if you admit it, but even more will figure that those pretending expertise are fair game. And when salespeople give you good advice, you may miss it if you're pretending to have more knowledge than you possess. If you really do know something, let the salesperson know—it will save time and boring explanations for both of you.

Give more trust to salespeople who admit occasional ignorance or refuse to answer questions until they have more information as to what you mean, than to those who have a snap answer to every question. Be leery, too, of salespeople who denigrate your choices or those who can't admit that they don't stock a given item without telling you it's junk.

On the other hand, don't be afraid to listen to salespeople who have reasons to suggest other equipment than you originally had in mind. The alternatives they offer may simply be equivalents of items that they do not carry, but may sometimes be improvements on your original selections.

Don't give in to pressure. "Better hurry, it's the last one in stock" may be honest advice, but is more likely a ploy to make you decide under pressure. Good audio equipment is a major purchase. Take time to mull things over and be sure you're getting what you want.

Bargains and "Bargains"

There are many more ways to save money on equipment. One is to wait for sales, which many dealers (especially mass merchandisers) run on major holidays such as President's Day in February, Independence Day in July, and Labor Day in September. The selection of sale-priced merchandise is often limited, but if such a sale is coming soon, you may benefit by waiting.

If you're buying several components, or even a whole system at once, you may get a better price by buying all of them at one place than by shopping for the best individual prices. Many dealers are willing to take a smaller percentage of profit to make a bigger sale.

The dealer may also suggest *pre-packaged systems*, from a single manufacturer or of the dealer's own devising. If such a system fulfills your requirements, consider it carefully. Be aware that the speakers in such systems may be little-known or house brands, unknowns whose prices can be inflated to make the package seem a better deal.

Discontinued models are often sold at lower, *close-out* prices. Rarely is this because that model suffered quality problems (though it may be, if the model was discontinued after less than one year). New models frequently supersede the old, for many reasons: the manufacturer may want to introduce new features or match those his competitors have introduced since his original model. If his costs go up, he may bring out a new model to justify a higher price more in keeping with those costs. Or he may be discontinuing a model that failed to achieve popularity for reasons unrelated to its quality—for instance, the lack of some "hot" feature (which you may not need). But because dealers and manufacturers must sell off the old model to make room for the new, closeouts are often bargains. To decide, compare closeouts against more current models normally selling at the discontinued item's new, lower price.

However, do beware of items which are discontinued because their manufacturers have gone out of business. Getting service and parts for them may be difficult.

Used equipment usually sells for even less than closeouts. It should. As the purchaser, you take a risk of inheriting the prior owner's known or unknown problems. That risk is highest with mechanically complex items, such as tape decks and some turntables, is lower with electronic items such as amplifiers and tuners, and is practically nonexistent with loudspeakers— with loudspeakers, what you hear is what you get. If you're worried, buy from a reputable dealer rather than from private parties. Dealers charge a bit more, but they offer guarantees, which usually last for about ninety days.

The more expensive and better-built the equipment, and the fewer new models that have arrived since it was made, the less its price will drop on the used market. Still, you can often find superb equipment, used, that you could never afford if it was new. And much of it is in top-flight condition. Many affluent and enthusiastic audio hobbyists trade in equipment frequently, in pursuit of unattainable perfection. Their loss can be your gain.

Kits that you can put together are rarely the bargains, today, that they once were. With most, the benefit of building your own is the fun of doing it and the pride of knowing (and telling) that you did. You can damage a kit by not following instructions properly, but most kit makers will repair any such damage for a reasonable, prestated fee.

Selling your old gear to raise money for the new is a sensible way to keep costs down. Dealers who take trade-ins will usually offer less than you could get in a private sale. But to sell equipment privately, you may have to wait for buyers, and perhaps even pay to advertise for them.

Buy for the long term. It's better to spend a bit more, now, for something you'll be happy with for quite a while than to temporize with something cheap and unsatisfactory that you'll soon pay to replace. Good equipment is hard to supersede, and progress isn't quite as fast as the ads imply. It usually takes about five years for technology to advance far enough to really justify trading in your old components for more modern ones. With occasional maintenance, many components can give satisfactory performance even longer.

Appendix I:
When Things
Go Wrong

Good equipment rarely breaks down. But rarely isn't never.

If something does go wrong, you can quickly learn how to track down logically any troubles that your system may develop. As often as not, the problem will turn out to be something simple enough to cure without calling a repairman. And when professional repair is needed, you can save some of the cost of a service call by figuring out which component is at fault and bringing it to the shop.

You probably don't need to know all this *right now*. But when the need arises, follow these trouble-shooting techniques.

Good News! It's Dead!

The most frightening problem, to most people, is when things fail to work at all . . . which happens to be the problem that's usually easiest to fix.

If *nothing* works—no lights light, and no wheels spin—the odds are that whatever seems dead is actually just not getting power. So check first for things so obvious they may seem dumb. Is everything plugged in? (Follow the wires and see.) Is the outlet they're plugged into live? (Plug a light into that *very* outlet and see if it works.) Is that outlet controlled by a switch that's turned off?

Is a fuse or circuit-breaker blown? If so, fix it. Should the fuse or breaker blow again, unplug your audio equipment and replace the fuse, to see if it's your stereo or something else that's blowing it.

If nothing else is blowing that fuse, shut off as many other things on that same circuit as you can find, then try plugging your audio components back in and turning them on, one at a time. If the fuse blows after one particular component goes on, that unit probably needs service. If the fuse is unperturbed by your entire system, the trouble may have been simply that the combination of your system and the other lights and appliances on that circuit exceeded the fuse's capacity. (This is especially likely in summer.) Don't replace an oft-blowing fuse with a larger one. Accept its limitations and try to shift some of your load to a different circuit, with a different fuse.

When one component is dead, double-check that it's plugged into a live outlet and that it's properly switched on. Then see if there's a *fuse post* on the back of the component, near the powercord. If there is, push in the post's cap and twist it a bit to the left, until it pops out into your hand. The fuse will be a glass tube with metal ends. If the glass shows an unbroken wire or thin bar of metal, then the fuse is probably okay, and the component isn't. If the wire is broken, or the glass looks smoky or stained, the fuse probably needs replacement.

The fuse's value and type may be written on your component's rear panel, in the component's instruction manual, or both. It will certainly be engraved into the metal end-caps of the fuse (though not too readably). Look for the fuse's value, in amperes (e.g., "5A," for "5 amperes"), and for the words "slo-blo" or "fast-blo" (most fuses are neither, and therefore say nothing of the kind). You may also see notes on the size, such as "3AG" or "AGC." When in doubt, take the fuse with you to an electronics store when you buy a replacement. Buy at least two replacement fuses. If turning your component back on blows the first replacement, save the other and take the component in for repair.

Silence and Other Funny Noises

The first step in curing such a problem is to make sure it's not caused by misadjusted controls. For example, if everything lights up but there's no sound (or only a faint hum or buzz), first check that the volume control is turned up to its usual level (if you've turned it higher than that, turn it back down to normal), then check that you haven't pushed some switch which can cut off the sound, such as "tape monitor" or "speakers off."

The next step is to trace the problem to its source, a simple matter of deduction and elimination. It's usually easiest to zero in on the component or cable that's causing the problem by eliminating from consideration all cables and components that can't be involved.

To do this, first draw a mental (or real) road map of your system, like the one we saw in the frontispiece. In the first section of the system, the signals branch in from many sources to your system's main control section (in the preamp, integrated amp, or receiver). Then, in the second section, all signals flow through the amplifier and split off to the right and left speakers.

Obviously, problems which affect sound from *all* sources can't be caused by any *one* of them. So flick your signal-selector switch. If the problem persists on more than one source, then it's probably not in that source but in the amplifier or speakers, which are common to all sources. If the problem exists on only one source, then either that source or the amplifier stages leading up to the selector switch are at fault. Problems that occur beyond that point would affect all signal sources. And problems affecting both stereo channels probably don't involve your speakers, each of which is connected to only one channel.

If the problem only affects one channel, trouble-shooting becomes easy; you can use your stereo system's unaffected channel as a test instrument. Let's say, for example, that the problem is a nasty buzz in the left channel, which you only hear when listening to the tuner. Obviously, it's either in the tuner, the amplifier, or the cables and plugs connecting the two. (Never forget cables and connections. They're the most common source of problems, and the cheapest and easiest to fix.)

Let's call the tuner's left and right outputs T_L and T_R, the amplifier's left and right inputs A_L and A_R, and the cables connecting them C_L and C_R, and let's mark the noise with an asterisk. So initially, our system looks like this:

T_L – – –> C_L – – –> A_L* (left channel)
T_R – – –> C_R – – –> A_R (right channel)

To trouble-shoot this usually takes three steps, at most.

1) Turn the amplifier to another input and check to see that both cables are firmly plugged in to both the tuner and the amplifier. Twist the plugs of the tuner cables about a half-turn, then twist them back, being careful to twist the cable with the plug. Then turn the amplifier back to its tuner input. If the problem has disappeared, it was probably caused by loose or dirty connections. (If it disappears but then comes back, it's probably a loose connection in cable C_L.)

2) Turn the amplifier to another input, and switch the cables around at one end, so the system now looks like this. (We've used double lines to show which connections have changed since the last diagram.)

$$T_L - - - > C_L = = = > A_R{}^*$$
$$T_R - - - > C_R = = = > A_L$$

Then turn back to the tuner input. Note that the amplifier's right channel is now receiving the left signal, and vice versa. If the buzz stayed in the left channel, then the amplifier's left channel (the only part of the system still feeding the same speaker as it always was) would have to be at fault.

But that's not the case here. Our buzz has now switched channels, so either the tuner or the cable must be at fault. So:

3) Switch the cable's other end around, and you get this:

$$T_R = = = > C_L - - - > A_R$$
$$T_L = = = > C_R - - - > A_L{}^*$$

If the noise had stayed in the amplifier's right channel, then the cable C_L would have been at fault. Instead, the noise switched back to the amplifier's left channel as soon as the tuner's left channel did. So the tuner must be at fault. (Note that, in all three diagrams, the noise is in the same channel as tuner section T_L, is never in the same channel as T_R, and can appear in either amplifier channel and through either cable.)

Nine times out of ten, however, it will be the cable that's at fault—and a good thing, too, as that's the one part of the system anyone can fix. Just buy a new one.

There's a reason for our constant cautions to turn to a different input before plugging or unplugging cables. Plugging into a live signal input can generate a big blast of noise—annoying, at the very least, and possibly injurious to your amplifier or speakers. If you're plugging into a power amp, which has no input-selector switch, turn the amp off for a few seconds before plugging in, then turn the amp back on again. If you're changing speaker leads around, the amplifier should also be turned off, lest stray filaments of speaker wire create partial short-circuits across the amplifier's output terminals. (If that does happen, most amplifiers will just shut off or distort, but a few will be damaged.)

Component-Specific Problems

Some problems can only be caused by specific components in your system. Other problems automatically absolve some components. Here, component by component, are examples:

Speakers

Speakers can go dead, can go partially dead (for instance, losing all treble if a tweeter blows, or losing all bass if a woofer does), and can distort a signal, adding rattles or scrapes to it, especially when it's loud. But speakers can't generate signals of their own. So if you hear a noise when there's no signal, the speaker is not at fault.

And because each speaker usually handles just one stereo channel, problems occurring in both channels at once are usually not the speaker's fault. If both speakers develop similar faults at once they do need fixing, but their problems were probably caused by something else, such as a defective amplifier. (Two dead tweeters, for instance, probably mean an overdose of treble fed them by other components in the system.)

Phono problems

It's when you're playing records that you're most likely to hear funny noises or odd qualities in the sound. These usually have very prosaic causes. Fuzzy sound, for instance, usually means the stylus isn't tracking properly, most often because of dirt.

Check the record first. (For best results, clean every record side just before playing it—keep your record cleaner handy, to encourage this.) If it's clean, look at the stylus under a good light. If you see fuzz there, clean it off, preferably with a commercial stylus cleaner (figure AI-1). Always wipe your stylus from the back of the cartridge toward the front, and do it very gently. Wiping it with your finger leaves slight oil deposits, which make the stylus fuzz up more quickly, next time—and risks bending or breaking the stylus.

If the stylus is clean, check to see that you have sufficient tracking force. That doesn't just mean checking that your arm's tracking-force dial is set correctly; wind that dial down to zero to make sure the arm is still neutrally balanced, then reset the tracking force. Check the antiskating dial, too, especially if one channel sounds fuzzier than the other.

If none of these measures help, check the stylus itself. If the stylus skates across the grooves, check it (with a magnifying glass, if necessary) to make sure it hasn't broken off and that the tiny diamond hasn't popped out of the stylus cantilever. (Also check that your arm lift isn't partway up, keeping the stylus from settling fully into the grooves.) Otherwise, take it to a dealer who has a good microscope, and have him examine it for wear. Should either test show that you need a new stylus,

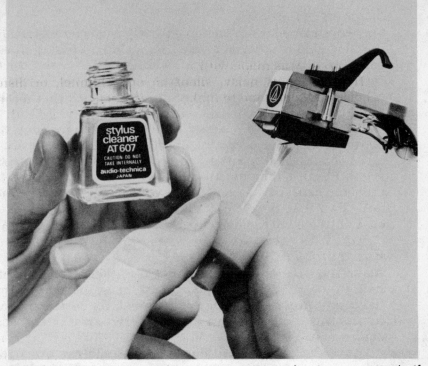

Apx. I-1. *Cleaning your stylus is as important as cleaning your records, if not more so.* (Courtesy of Audio-Technica)

buy one forthwith. *Never play records with a worn stylus or one you even suspect is worn.* Worn styli can do irreparable damage to your records.

To cure turntable speed problems, first check the pitch control. Consult your turntable manual if that doesn't get speed back to normal or if the speed sounds wavery (wow and flutter). You may need to lubricate the motor or replace the belt.

Boomy sound is usually due to the turntable's picking up bass from the speakers. To check this, play a recorded passage twice, once with the speakers on and once with them turned off (or with the amplifier's volume control turned down), taping both halves of the test. If only the tape made with the speakers on is boomy, try moving the turntable, moving the speakers, putting the turntable on a wall shelf, or suspending it on isolation feet or an isolation platform.

Hum or buzzing noises usually mean that the ground wire from your tonearm to your amplifier's rear-panel ground terminal has come loose or broken.

Tape-deck problems

If playback sounds a bit odd, check to see that you're playing back with the same equalization and noise-reduction settings as the tape was made with.

If playback is noisy, silent on one channel, or distorted, check a second tape to make sure it's not just that recording. Check the tape deck's controls (if the problem's on both channels) to make sure that you haven't either turned its output level down all the way or turned it up so high that it's overloading the amplifier input that it's feeding. If the problem is in one channel, go through the three-step test mentioned earlier in this appendix.

If your own recordings sound distorted or hissy, and other tapes do not, then you're probably using the wrong recording level. Set levels so that the meter is visibly moving most of the time but rarely goes into the red and never very far or for very long. If you have trouble getting enough level on one channel when you record, go through the three-step check, this time with the cables that bring signals from your amplifier to your tape deck.

If the problems actually are in your deck, determine whether its record or playback section is at fault. With your amplifier's tape-monitor switch on, record something, switching at the tape deck between the incoming and playback signal. On three-head decks, this simply involves flicking the deck's "source/tape" switch; on two-head decks, you have to listen in "source" as you record, then stop the tape and rewind about a minute's worth to check the playback. If the problem seems to be in playback only, double-check by playing a tape made on another deck, or made on yours before the trouble started; trouble-free playback would indicate that it is your deck's recording section that's at fault.

Wow and flutter indicate that the deck needs service. While turntable belts are frequently accessible for you to change, tape-deck belts aren't.

Tuner problems

When reception problems appear, the antenna is usually at fault. Make sure it's still securely connected, and still aimed in the right direction. Gradually deteriorating reception may signify an aging tuner. But if you live in the city, it might also signify that a big building has gone up between you and the transmitter. (If others in your neighborhood have the same problem, on the same stations, that's usually the case.)

Dealing with Service Shops

Good service shops are hard to find. To understand and cure problem components, a repairer must know almost as much as an engineer—in which case a better-paid career as an engineer may prove irresistible. Ask both your dealer and your component's manufacturer for recommendations, but take both with a grain of salt. If the component is still under warranty, you'll have to send it to one of the manufacturer's authorized repair shops. If it isn't, the authorized shop is usually still a good bet, since the people there will have most of the right parts and will know your component instead of having to figure it out from scratch.

Word-of-mouth is some help in finding a good service shop. But because most equipment is reliable, and different shops specialize in different brands, few people have had many occasions to use any given shop. As a result, you may hear from the one person in twenty-five who got a bad repair from a good shop or a good repair from a bad one. The manufacturer or importer generally does the best repair job (though, alas, not always); but you usually must ship your component off to him, which is a nuisance and risks its getting damaged when it's shipped back to you.

Unless your component is still under warranty, you'll probably have to pay for an estimate. Don't scream. In order to make that estimate, the service shop must figure out what's wrong, which is usually at least half the work. Some shops give binding estimates; of those shops that don't, the price may turn out slightly higher (and occasionally even lower) than the estimate.

Describe your problem in as much detail as possible, telling under what circumstances it does and does not occur. Write it out beforehand (typed, if your handwriting's not crystal clear), since the person at the repair shop's desk may lose some details trying to take it down as you talk. The more the repairer knows, the sooner he can find the trouble, and the less you'll have to pay.

Intermittent problems are a plague, to user and servicer alike. The problem may obstinately refuse to occur when you bring the component to the shop, or may occur only until the repairer has replaced some part that isn't really causing it. Either way, the repairer can't be sure whether it's really fixed or not—and the problem is likely to start up again as soon as you get the component home. You and the repairer must bear with each other, each trusting the other's diligence in dealing with the problem. The more you can tell—even seemingly irrelevant things ("It only occurs when the air-conditioner starts up, unless the component has been running for two hours or more"), the sooner the trouble will be cured.

Unless the problem causes blats of noise which sound as though they might damage your speakers, you're probably best off leaving intermittent problems be, for a while, in hope that they'll become permanent, and therefore easier to fix.

Good service shops give warranties on their work. If your original problem recurs within the warranty period, they'll fix it for free. If new problems develop as soon as you get your component back from the shop, they should fix that, too, on the assumption that the shop probably caused it. New problems that develop later in the warranty period probably are not the shop's fault, and most shops will charge to fix them.

Appendix II: Making Tape Recordings

Making good tape recordings is far easier today than ever before, especially when you're recording from a source like radio or one of your records, where studio engineers have done most of the work for you. We can cover most of what you need to know about that in a few paragraphs.

For recording live performances directly, though, those paragraphs are just a beginning. So, in fact, is the somewhat longer section on that subject that ends this appendix. Entire books have been written on the subject, and recording schools give courses on it. Here, more than anywhere else, high fidelity becomes an art, one which, like all arts, takes a little effort to pick up and much to master.

The Basics: Setup and Adjustments

Once a tape deck is connected to its signal source (such as your audio system or some microphones), a few adjustments are usually all you need to get started. Some of these adjustments should be made before recording begins. First, check that the *bias* and *equalization* (EQ) are set to match the tape you're using. All cassette decks have manual or automatic switches to set bias and EQ for the tape type in use (normal Type I, chrome Type II, or metal Type IV); some also have manual or automatic controls for adjusting them to the exact tape formulation.

Next, check that you have selected the right *noise-reduction* system for your intended use. You should usually use the most potent noise-reduction system that will be compatible with all the players for which the tape is intended. For example, if your home deck has Dolby B and C NR, and you intended to play the tapes on that deck and on a car system which was also equipped with Dolby B and C, you should probably record with Dolby C. But if you also intended the tapes for use in a portable which had only Dolby B, you should use Dolby B noise-reduction for that recording. (If your portable did not have any noise reduction, you might still prefer to record with Dolby B, since the resulting tapes would sound more or less okay when played without NR, as long as the treble was turned down a bit in playback.)

When recording FM stereo broadcasts with either Dolby system, use your deck's *Dolby FM* or *Multiplex (MPX) Filter* switch, to make sure that the Dolby system's calibration won't be upset if your tuner or receiver lets any of the 19-kHz stereo pilot tone leak into its output signal. Otherwise, the high-frequency balance of the recording may be off. That switch can sometimes also help when recording from noisy sources, such as AM radio or old records, by cutting off some of the high-frequency noise. When recording from other sources, though, leave the switch off, to avoid filtering off high frequencies in the music.

The next and final adjustment is *recording level*. Try to preview your source, to find its loudest section. Do this by putting your tape deck into record-standby or record-pause mode, then adjusting its input level so that the meters usually register some movement when there is sound to record (ensuring that the signal won't be buried in tape hiss), but only occasionally flicks into the red zone (so the signal won't be distorted). How far and how often you can safely record into the red depends on the tape type and your deck's metering system; check your recorder's manual.

If you're using a digital recorder or a PCM digital adapter with a video recorder, this becomes especially important. With conventional analog recorders, distortion will rise when you let your signal go over the limit, but only in proportion to the signal level. Slight overloads aren't too noticeable, and you have to overload severely before you really crunch the sound. With digital, a miss is as bad as a mile—go one bit over the limit and the sound becomes as bad as gravel going through a meat-grinder. So you should make digital recordings well below your system's specified level limits; the noise in digital recording is low enough that you need not fear burying your signal in noise.

Previewing your source is easier to do with some sources than with others. Phonograph records are easy to preview: the sound is usually loudest where the record grooves look coarsest, and quietest where the grooves fit together like fine, silky threads. Play the loud passages a few times while you set levels. If you're dubbing from a tape, you can skip around the tape in search of loud passages, which takes a little longer.

Radio broadcasts have a more limited dynamic range, which makes the level easier to set. This is especially true in FM, where peak levels don't vary much; loud passages in different pieces of music, or on different stations, will have similar levels. And some tuners have built-in record-calibration tones that you can set your recording level to.

Live performers can sometimes be persuaded to perform a loud passage or two, if you're taping a rehearsal or if they're performing specifically for your recording. Otherwise, you'll have to set levels based on your prior experience, hope for the best, and fine-tune the levels as you go.

Fine-tuning record levels, though frequently needed when recording live, should seldom be needed otherwise. However, live sound levels can vary enormously, and other sources may turn out a bit louder or softer than your previewing suggested. In either case, you'll have to readjust recording level as you tape. Do it wrong, and you can ruin your recording; do it right, and no one will ever notice.

The wrong way is to jerk the level control down when the music goes into the red, then jerk it back up when the meter stops moving. Either way, the sound level jumps unnaturally —usually when it's not supposed to change, or when the damage you're trying to prevent has already been done.

The slick and unobtrusive way is to make your level changes slowly, mildly, and while the music's level is changing in the opposite direction. For example, if the music is getting louder, threatening to reach the distortion level when the volume crests, you should turn the recording level down as the music's level rises. You don't want to stop the crescendo, since that's part of the music, but to slow down its rate of rise. Done properly, this just barely prevents distortion at the peak, yet leaves the listeners with a feeling of the music's original dynamics. Similarly, when the music's level threatens to drop down to the level of tape hiss, you should raise the recording level gently and slowly as the music's level declines.

In either case, change level as little and as slowly as you possibly can. Familiarity with the music helps; if you can, you might even follow a score of the music as you're taping it to see where trouble spots may loom ahead.

Recording Live

For live recordings, all you really need to add is microphones, and the knowledge of where to put them.

Selecting microphones is the easiest part. First find out whether your recorder has microphone inputs (many don't, these days), the size of plug those input jacks take, and the *impedance* the microphone should have. (Consult your recorder's manual for the latter.)

Microphone impedances range from about 50 ohms to several thousand ohms; most tape decks now require microphone impedances of a few hundred ohms. The microphone need not have exactly the recommended impedance but should not be too far off. Don't confuse recommended microphone impedance with the *input impedance* of the deck's mike inputs—it's common for an input to have much higher impedance than the source which will feed it.

The lower the microphone's impedance, the longer its cable can be before you start losing high frequencies or picking up hum and other noises. This is especially important when you're recording performances put on before an audience, where the recorder (and, often, the mikes) must be out of sight. Professionals use *balanced-line* microphone connections, a three-wire system which reduces noise pickup even further. The standard jack for this is the Cannon XLR, or one of the many equivalents made by other companies (figure Apx. II–1). To adapt home recorders to this system, you'll need either a matching transformer or a *mixer* with unbalanced microphone inputs. A mixer will also let you use more than two microphones at once, or mix microphones with other sources (such as background-music or sound-effects records).

Microphones also differ in the ways they generate their signals. Inexpensive microphones are usually *dynamic* or *moving-coil* types. They work like loudspeakers in reverse, with sound moving a diaphragm which moves a voice coil in a magnetic field, generating the signal. Dynamics are rugged and require no batteries. They can also sound very, very good, especially the more expensive models.

Condenser microphones are a bit more complex, sometimes a bit less rugged, and require batteries. But their sound can be exceptionally crisp and clean. This is true of even amateur models, but low-priced condenser microphones sometimes have less dynamic range than dynamics—very loud sounds can make them distort sooner than dynamics will.

Ribbon microphones are the most delicate of all, and their

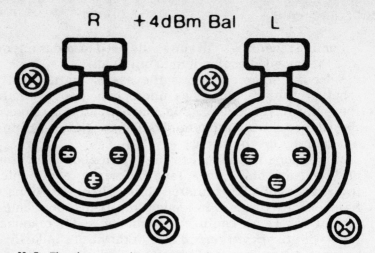

R   +4dBm Bal   L

Apx. II-1. *The three-conductor XLR jack is most common on professional or semi-pro recording equipment.* (Courtesy of Nakamichi)

high-frequency response is often limited. But their response is very smooth and sweet.

Where you put a microphone depends on what you're recording and on the mike's *directional pattern. Omni-directional microphones* (figure Apx. II–2) pick up sound almost equally well from all directions (their high-frequency pickup toward the rear is slightly diminished). These microphones tend to have the flattest frequency response. To avoid picking up too much sound reflection or audience noise, omnis are usually used fairly close to the performer.

Cardioid microphones (figure Apx. II–3) pick up very strongly from the front, rather less from the sides, and not much from the rear. This makes them ideal when you can't place the microphones near the performers, or when you want to screen out room echo or audience noise. *Bidirectional,* or *figure-eight,* microphones have narrower pickup patterns which point equally to front and rear, with almost no pickup to the sides. They are ideal where the sounds to be suppressed are to the sides, or where the desired sounds lie in two, opposite directions. Most figure-eights are ribbon microphones, and vice versa.

Stereo microphone setups usually work best with two microphones which are as identical as possible. Try to get a good blend between the left and right performers, but with some

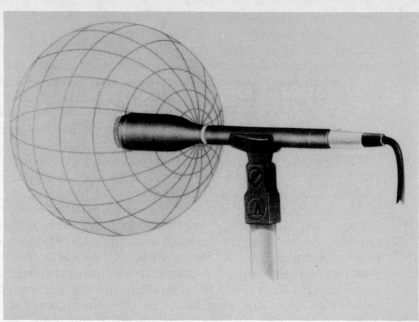

Apx. II-2. *Omnidirectional microphones are equally sensitive to sound from all directions. (Courtesy of Audio-Technica)*

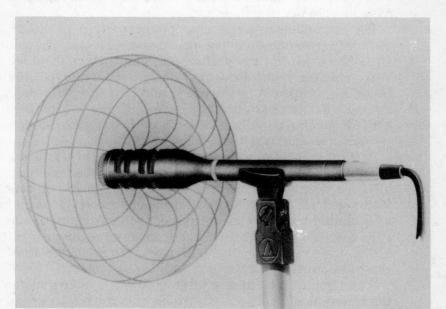

Apx. II-3. *A cardioid microphone is most sensitive to sounds from dead ahead, fairly dead to sounds arriving from the rear. (Courtesy of Audio-Technica)*

separation, too. The ideal is a setup which lets you hear just where each performer is, lets you hear at least some of the spatial qualities of the room that you're recording in (how much you want depends on the room's own sound), picks up all instruments just as the ear would hear them, and blends them together into a smooth whole. There are some contradictions, here: all these qualities are desirable, but the more you have of some, the less you'll have of others. Just be aware of all these qualities, and pick the mix that sounds best to you.

When you're recording in the same room as the performers, you'll have to monitor the signal with surround-type headphones both to keep the headphone sound from leaking back to the mikes and to help you tell which sounds are coming through the microphones without confusing them with those coming direct from the performers. To judge stereo effects, however, you'll have to listen through loudspeakers (unless you intend your tape for binaural listening, through headphones only). While you're setting up and the performers are rehearsing, stop and play back the tape through speakers as often as possible, to check the stereo. If you can, play the speakers in a different room than the one you are recording in; otherwise, the room's acoustic faults will be exaggerated because you're hearing them twice.

The commonest stereo microphone pattern is the *spaced pair,* with two microphones spaced several feet apart, pointing straight forward at the performers. The spacing distance will vary with the room acoustics, the microphone type, the distance from mikes to performers, and how the performers are disposed before the microphones. You'll have to experiment: a six-foot spacing usually makes a good first approximation, but try narrower and wider spacings, too.

With directional microphones, you can also use a *crossed pair,* disposing the two microphones very close together (usually, one right atop the other), with their patterns pointing in a V (for cardioids) or an X (for figure-eight mikes). This makes a very simple setup, usually with good stereo effects. If some of your listeners will be hearing your tapes monophonically (over radio, for example), this will work much better than the crossed-pair.

When you're recording a large group, it usually pays to put the microphones fairly high, which cuts the difference in distance from the microphone to the nearest and farthest performers. Tall microphone stands are available for this. You can also suspend the microphones on wires (don't use the mike's signal cables for this, lest you weaken their connections). Suspending microphones also works well if microphones on floor stands are picking up footsteps and similar noises.

Microphone Features

If you'll be using your microphones out of doors, make sure they have effectve *windscreens,* so you won't get a constant roar (or, worse, puffy gusts) of wind noise. Windscreens also cut the amount of breath pickup when recording very close to singers. With some singers, you may also need *pop filters* to soften the impact of percussively popped P-sounds (the old Peter Piper problem). If the singer will be handling the microphone, make sure its innards are insulated from its outer shell, so you don't pick up handling noise.

Cardioid microphones often suffer from *proximity effect*— they emphasize bass from very nearby sources. You may like the resonant quality this adds to voices when they speak or sing right into the mike. But the effect is an unnatural one, and many cardioids have *filters* to roll off the bass when this becomes a problem. The same filters can be used to roll off bass room noises.

Many microphones have *on-off switches*—a problem if they accidentally get switched off while you're recording. Tape those switches up before recording. If you don't need it, disable it. Some microphones even come with removable plates to block their switches, a neater solution than tape.

The main things to remember in making good recordings are to practice, so your skills become second naure, and to always prepare and check everything beforehand. There's nothing more frustrating than to discover, just when it's too late, that you left your tapes home, or your microphone cable has a loose connection, or your mike stand isn't tall enough. But just getting the signal from the input onto the tape properly is a breeze, with today's tapes and tape decks.

Index